Essays on Irish Syntax II

Essays on Irish Syntax II

Hideki Maki and Dónall P. Ó Baoill

KAITAKUSHA

Kaitakusha Co., Ltd.
5-2, Mukogaoka 1-chome
Bunkyo-ku, Tokyo 113-0023
Japan

Essays on Irish Syntax II

Published in Japan
by Kaitakusha Co., Ltd., Tokyo

First published 2017

Printed and bound in Japan
by ARM Corporation

Cover design by Shihoko Nakamura

Preface

Hideki Maki and Dónall P. Ó Baoill

Gifu University and *Queen's University Belfast* (Prof. Emeritus)

This is a second volume which continues the work in *Essays on Irish Syntax* published in 2011, containing articles on a variety of syntactic phenomena in Modern Irish, especially, the Ulster variety of Irish, published or presented elsewhere. The main purpose of this volume remains the same as that of the first volume: to collect what we have discovered about Irish syntax into one document, so that linguistically significant phenomena from one of the endangered languages in the world can be easily accessed by future generations.

We still have to admit that Irish is on the verge of extinction. According to a 2011 Census, the result of which is not fundamentally different from that of the 2006 Census reported in the first volume, the number of residents aged three years and over in the Republic of Ireland is 4,370,631, and 1,774,437 people (41.4%) of these report themselves as speakers of Irish. The number of people speaking Irish reflects the fact that Irish is a compulsory subject from elementary to high school in Ireland. Out of the 1,774,437 persons who indicated that they could speak Irish, 519,181 (29.3%) speak it on a daily basis within the education system while a further 38,480 (2.2%) persons speak it on a daily basis outside the education system. Therefore, the combined number of the persons who speak it on a daily basis is 558,661 (31.5%).

However, the majority of people whose predominant language is Irish, live in the Gaeltacht areas. Gaeltacht refers to any of the regions recognized by the government in which the Irish language is the predominant language of use, that is, the vernacular spoken at home and the neighborhood. The number of people in all the Gaeltacht regions of Ireland is 96,628, as of the 2011 census. Out of the 96,628 persons, 66,238 (68.5%) aged three and over speak Irish, and of these, 38,139 (57.6%) speak Irish on a daily basis. Therefore, the number of people aged three and over whose predominant language (the first language) is Irish, and who speak it on a daily basis is only 0.9%. This figure alone indicates the endangered status of the Irish language.

Furthermore, there are three main dialects: Munster, Connacht and Ulster. Munster Irish is mainly spoken in the southern part of Ireland, in counties Waterford (1,271), Cork (2,951), and Kerry (6,185), where the numbers in parentheses indicate the number of people aged three and above whose predominant language is Irish, and who speak it on a daily basis, as of the 2011 census. Connacht Irish is mainly spoken in the western part of Ireland, in Galway City (7,123) and in counties Galway (23,855) and Mayo (6,667). Finally, Ulster Irish is mainly spoken in the northern part of Ireland, e.g., Donegal (17,132).

Therefore, it has been a matter of great urgency to collect linguistic data from native speakers of Irish, and record it in a way accessible to the future generations who might be engaged in linguistic inquiry, one of the significant ways to learn about the nature of human beings. We hope that this book will play a role as a useful reference to linguistically intriguing syntactic phenomena in this verb-initial language.

This book contains 12 articles, dealing with anaphora, case, movement, conditions on movement, properties of the subject position, and scope interactions in Irish. They are arranged in chronological order in line with our investigation of various topics in Irish syntax. The data in each article present linguistically interesting and rather surprising phenomena, so one can start with any one of the articles in which one has a particular interest. It will soon become clear that the articles raise more issues than they solve, which indicates that this book will be a useful reference for interested readers.

The organization of this book is as follows. Chapter 1 investigates the distribution of the reflexive anaphor *sé FÉIN/é FÉIN* 'he self/him self' in Irish, and shows that it is identified as an intensive pronoun in the sense of Baker (1995), which is reinterpreted as an intensive anaphor in this chapter. It is also pointed out that there is a crucial difference between British English and Irish with respect to the properties of intensive anaphors: there is no Case restriction on intensive anaphors in Irish, in contrast to British English.

Chapter 2 examines the Highest Subject Restriction (HSR) effect in Irish, and shows that the HSR does not hold in certain syntactic configurations in Irish. It is suggested that the cancellation of the HSR be attributed to the addition of an extra phrase to the structure in Irish, and Chomsky's (1991) Condition on Chain Uniformity.

Chapter 3 clarifies properties related to the *ceart* 'correct' construction in Irish, and addresses a mystery arising from its structure. It is shown that the newly found data on this construction suggest that the Chain Conditions override the Case Filter in Irish. That is, when the sentence is subject to both the Chain Conditions and the Case Filter, the latter may be violated unless it violates the former.

Chapter 4 investigates the distribution of genitive case in Irish, and points out the generalization that no phrase with a particular morphological case can be adjoined to C'. It is then argued that a morphological case mismatch in a given A'-chain does not affect the full interpretation of the chain at LF.

Chapter 5 examines scope ambiguity in wh/quantifier interactions in Irish, in comparison with those in English and Japanese, and points out some differences between wh/quantifier interactions in Irish and those in English and Japanese. It is claimed that these differences are attributed to the fact that the subject position in Irish is within VP, and Irish has resumptive pronouns for wh-phrases, unlike English or Japanese.

Chapter 6 looks at chain properties of the manner adverbial wh-phrase *cad é an dóigh* 'what it the way = how' in Irish, and argues (i) that an adjunct wh-phrase only creates variables/traces at LF, (ii) that adjunct wh-phrases fall into two categories in Irish: the *how*-type and the *why*-type, (iii) that non-genuine argument operators (*how*, *why*, and the comparative operator) do not simply constitute a uniform category in Irish, and (iv) that Irish has two types of [+Q] COMPs.

Chapter 7 investigates properties of the wh-construction in Irish that involves wh-movement and wh-in-situ, and claims (i) that Irish has two types of [+Q] COMPs, one with a [strong] feature, and another with a [weak] feature, (ii) that adjunct wh-phrases in Irish are categorized into two groups: the manner class and the reason class, and the manner class wh-phrases pattern together with argument wh-phrases, and (iii) that the differences in the A'-chain patterns suggest that there are actually three types of wh-phrases in Irish: argument, manner and reason wh-phrases.

Chapter 8 looks at properties of the cleft construction in Irish, and shows (i) that CPs and APs can be clefted in Irish, unlike English or Japanese, and (ii) that while NP clefting allows six chain patterns with one embedded clause, clefting of the other categories only allows two chain patterns, just like the comparative construction in Irish.

Chapter 9 examines properties of Irish embedded topicalization, and argues (i) that lowering of COMP to INFL does not take place in Irish, (ii) that the Highest Subject Restriction does not apply to resumptive pronouns involved in Irish embedded topicalization, (iii) that the head positions in charge of embedded topicalization are parameterized among languages, (iv) that the difference in the head positions in charge of embedded topicalization lies in the relationship between the COMP and the INFL, and (v) that the ban against adjunction to adjuncts only disallows adjunction to adjuncts by way of internal merge.

Chapter 10 investigates various phenomena related to clausal arguments in Irish, and claims (i) that Irish grammar should contain a language-particular condition on A'-resumption chains, (ii) that the subject position is not a properly governed position in Irish, (iii) that human language allows a bare IP to function as a subject, and (iv) that the chain pattern (aL, that, RP) turns out to be real in movement constructions with one embedded clause in Irish.

Chapter 11 addresses two puzzles arising from syntactic phenomena involving the subject position in Irish, and argues (i) that Irish allows argument wh-phrases to stay in the base-generated positions throughout the derivation, (ii) that HNPS is triggered by agreement with v, not T, in Irish and English, and (iii) that the Irish ECM is different from the English ECM, and in this sense, Irish is an ECM-less language.

Finally, Chapter 12 examines wh-extraction from the complement clause of the factive predicate *is trua le* 'to regret' in Irish, and argues (i) that the complementizer *go/gur* 'that' in Irish optionally has an operator, contrary to McCloskey's (2002) claim, (ii) that Irish allows an invisible COMP, which can host an operator, (iii) that the invisible COMP subcategorized by the factive predicate *is trua le* 'to regret' is a nominalizer, and makes the infinitival complement a barrier for movement, and (iv) that Irish has two types of [+Q] COMPs, one that attracts a wh-phrase in overt syntax, and another that does not.

Original Publication Details

Chapter 1: reprinted with revisions from Dónall P. Ó Baoill and Hideki Maki (2010) "*Sé Féin* 'He Self' in Modern Ulster Irish," *Handbook of the 141st Meeting of the Linguistic Society of Japan*, 16–21.

Chapter 2: reprinted with revisions from Dónall P. Ó Baoill and Hideki Maki (2012) "On the Highest Subject Restriction in Modern Irish," *English Linguistics* 29, 357–368, by permission of the English Linguistic Society of Japan.

Chapter 3: reprinted with revisions from Hideki Maki and Dónall P. Ó Baoill (2012a) "A Mystery with the *Ceart* 'Correct' Construction in Modern Ulster Irish," *Handbook of the 144th Meeting of the Linguistic Society of Japan*, 50–55.

Chapter 4: reprinted with revisions from Hideki Maki and Dónall P. Ó Baoill (2012b) "The Genitive Case in Modern Ulster Irish," *Handbook of the 145th Meeting of the Linguistic Society of Japan*, 262–267.

Chapter 5: reprinted with revisions from Hideki Maki and Dónall P. Ó Baoill (2013) "Scope Ambiguity in WH/Quantifier Interactions in Modern Irish," *Ambiguity: Multifaceted Structures in Syntax, Morphology and Phonology*, ed. by Anna Bondaruk and Anna Malicka-Kleparska, 215–237, Wydawnictwo KUL, Lublin, Poland, by permission of the editors of the book.

Chapter 6: reprinted with revisions from Dónall P. Ó Baoill and Hideki Maki (2013) "*Cad é an Dóigh* 'How' in Irish," *Handbook of the 147th Meeting of the Linguistic Society of Japan*, 524–529.

Chapter 7: reprinted with revisions from Dónall P. Ó Baoill and Hideki Maki (2014a) "Irish [+Q] COMPs," *JELS* 31 (Papers from the 31st Conference of the English Linguistic Society of Japan), 123–129, by permission of the English Linguistic Society of Japan.

Chapter 8: reprinted with revisions from Hideki Maki and Dónall P. Ó Baoill (2014a) "The Cleft Construction in Irish," *JELS* 31 (Papers from the Sixth International Spring Forum of the English Linguistic Society of Japan), 338–344, by permission of the English Linguistic Society of Japan.

Chapter 9: reprinted with revisions from Hideki Maki and Dónall P. Ó Baoill (2014b) "Embedded Topicalization in Irish," *English Linguistics* 31, 130–148, by permission of the English Linguistic Society of Japan.

Chapter 10: reprinted with revisions from Hideki Maki and Dónall P. Ó Baoill (2014c) "Clausal Arguments in Irish," *English Linguistics* 31, 545–562, by permission of the English Linguistic Society of Japan.

Chapter 11: reprinted with revisions from Dónall P. Ó Baoill and Hideki Maki (2015) "Puzzles with the Subject Position in Irish," *English Linguistics* 32, 102–113, by permission of the English Linguistic Society of Japan.

Chapter 12: reprinted with revisions from Dónall P. Ó Baoill and Hideki Maki

(2014b) "Extraction from the Complement Clause of the Factive Predicate *Is Trua Le* 'To Regret' in Irish," *Handbook of the 149th Meeting of the Linguistic Society of Japan*, 290–295.

Acknowledgments

We would like to thank anonymous reviewers of *English Linguistics*, Jun Abe, Panos Athanasopoulos, Lina Bao, Anna Bondaruk, Ronald Craig, Jessica Dunton, Ling-Yun Fan, Tomohiro Fujii, Kazuma Fujimaki, Koji Fujita, Gilles Guerrin, Naomi Harada, Megumi Hasebe, Kiyota Hashimoto, Hironobu Kasai, Kwang-Sup Kim, Keiichiro Kobayashi, Masatoshi Koizumi, Makoto Kondo, Sachiko Kudara, Michael LoPresti, Luisa Martí, Roger Martin, Kazumi Matsuoka, Yoichi Miyamoto, Takashi Munakata, Chie Nakamura, Fumikazu Niinuma, Yoshitaka Nishikawa, Máire Ó Baoill, Masao Ochi, Kenji Oda, Yoshiki Ogawa, Reiko Okabe, Yohei Oseki, Satoshi Oku, Mitsuya Sasaki, Naoto Sato, Michael Sevier, Junko Shimoyama, Koji Sugisaki, Shigeko Sugiura, Yuji Takano, Hisao Tokizaki, Hiroyuki Ura and Alexandra von Fragstein for their helpful comments on earlier versions of the papers in this volume. We are also grateful to the audience at the meetings where the papers were presented for their insightful suggestions.

Our thanks also go to the following native speakers from the eastern borders of Gweedore Parish in North West Donegal with whom the examples have been checked: Donnchadh Mac Fhionnaile, Seán Mac Giolla Chóill, Bríd Bean Mhic Íomhair, Anna Ní Bhaoill, Máire Nic Giolla Chóill, Pádraig Ó Briain, Pádraig Ó Dúgáin (Éamann), Bríd Bean Uí Ghallchóir and Méabha Bean Uí Phíopalaigh.

We would also like to express our gratitude to the English Linguistic Society of Japan, and Anna Bondaruk and Anna Malicka-Kleparska for kindly allowing us to reprint the papers in this volume.

Finally, we thank Masaru Kawata of Kaitakusha for providing us with the opportunity to publish this book.

Research by the first author was supported in part by JSPS KAKENHI Grant Numbers 15720089, 18520303, 21520397, 235083, 25370428 and 17HP5074 to Gifu University.

Abbreviations

1	first person	NP	noun phrase
2	second person	O/OBJ	object
3	third person	Op	operator
A	argument (position)	PAST	past tense
A′	non-argument (position)	PBC	Proper Binding Condition
ACC	accusative case	PIC	Phase-Impenetrability
ADN	adnominal form		Condition
AGR	agreement	PL	plural
AGRP	agreement phrase	PP	preposition phrase
AP	adjective phrase	PP3	third person possessive
ASP	aspect		pronoun
C/COMP	complementizer	PRES	present tense
CED	Condition on Extraction	PROG	progressive
	Domain	Q	question
COND	conditional	RP	resumptive pronoun
COP	copula	S/SBJ	subject
CP	complementizer phrase	SG	singular
DAT	dative	SPEC	specifier
DP	determiner phrase	t	trace
DOBJ	direct object	T	tense
e	phonetically empty element	TOP	topic
ECM	Exceptional Case Marking	TP	tense phrase
ECP	Empty Category Principle	VN	verbal noun
EX	exclamation	v	*verb*
−FIN	non-finite	V	verb
FUT	future tense	vP	*verb* phrase
GEN	genitive case	VP	verb phrase
HNPS	Heavy NP Shift	X^0	head or zero level category
HSR	Highest Subject Restriction	XP	phrase level category
I/INFL	inflection		
ICE	Internal Constituent Effect		
IMPS	impersonal		
IOBJ	indirect object		
IP	inflection phrase		
LF	Logical Form		
MCL	Minimize Chain Links		
MLC	Minimal Link Condition		
N	noun		
NEG	negation		
NOM	nominative case		

Table of Contents

Chapter 1

Sé Féin/É Féin 'He Self/Him Self' in Modern Ulster Irish[*]

Dónall P. Ó Baoill and Hideki Maki

Queen's University Belfast (Prof. Emeritus) and *Gifu University*

Keywords: *contrastive, discourse, intensive, prominent, reflexive anaphor*

1. Introduction

Zribi-Hertz (1989) and Reinhart and Reuland (1991, 1993), among others, point out that anaphors such as *themselves* in English are locally free in certain contexts, and are not regulated by Condition A of Binding Theory proposed by Chomsky (1981). Building on Ferro (1993), Baker (1995) claims that locally free anaphors in British English[1] are non-nominative intensified pronouns. Therefore, they are not regulated by Condition A of Binding Theory.

However, the question arises as to why locally free anaphors in British English are restricted to intensified pronouns with *non-nominative* Case. In this paper, we examine whether the condition on Case with respect to locally

[*] This is a drastically revised version of the paper presented at the 136th Meeting of the Linguistic Society of Japan held at Gakushuin University on June 21, 2008. We would like to thank the audience at the meeting, as well as the following people: Jun Abe, Ronald Craig, Jessica Dunton, Naomi Harada, Roger Martin, Chie Nakamura, Fumikazu Niinuma, Michael Sevier and two anonymous *EL* reviewers for their helpful comments. Our thanks also go to the following native speakers from the eastern borders of Gweedore Parish in North West Donegal with whom the examples have been checked: Donnchadh Mac Fhionnaile, Seán Mac Giolla Chóill, Bríd Bean Mhic Íomhair, Anna Ní Bhaoill, Máire Nic Giolla Chóill, Pádraig Ó Briain, Pádraig Ó Dúgáin (Éamann), Bríd Bean Uí Ghallchóir and Méabha Bean Uí Phíopalaigh. All errors are our own. Research by the second author was supported in part by Japan Society for the Promotion of Science Grant #s 18520303 and 21520397 to Gifu University.

[1] Baker (1995) uses the term *British English* in order to distinguish it from American English based on the fact that locally free anaphors were particularly abundant in the writings of Jane Austen, and the discussion in his paper mainly relied on examples from her two novels *Sense and Sensibility* and *Pride and Prejudice*.

free anaphors is imposed by Universal Grammar (UG), or whether such a condition is language-specific, namely, specific to British English, by investigating the distribution of the reflexive anaphor *sé féin/é féin* 'he self/him self' in modern Ulster Irish (Irish, hereafter). In this paper, we will show that *sé féin/é féin* 'he self/him self,' with a heavy stress on *féin*, exhibits the properties of locally free anaphors mainly based on the examples reported in Ó Baoill (1995), which will provide an answer to the Case issue pointed out above.

The organization of this paper is as follows. Section 2 reviews Baker's (1995) analysis of locally free anaphors in British English, as background to subsequent sections. Section 3 presents anaphor data in Irish. Section 4 discusses what the findings might suggest. Finally, Section 5 concludes this paper.

2. Background: English

Baker (1995: 63) claims that locally free reflexives in British English are best analyzed as intensified non-nominative pronouns, which are subject to two conditions that regulate English intensive NPs in general. The two conditions are shown in (1).

(1) a. *Contrastiveness Condition*
Intensive NPs are appropriate only in contexts in which emphasis or contrast is desired. (Baker (1995: 77))

b. *Condition on Relative Discourse Prominence*
Intensive NPs can only be used to mark a character in a sentence or discourse who is relatively more prominent or central than other characters. (Baker (1995: 80))

Examples of locally non-free reflexives, namely, locally bound reflexives, are shown in (2)–(4), and examples of locally free reflexives are shown in (5) and (6).

(2) a. John believes that [$_S$ Martha$_1$ will defend herself$_1$].
b. John urged Martha$_1$ [$_S$ PRO$_1$ to defend herself$_1$].
c. John appreciates [$_{NP}$ Martha$_1$'s faith in herself$_1$].
(Baker (1995: 63) with slight editing)

(3) a. *John$_1$ believes that [$_S$ Martha will defend himself$_1$].
b. *John$_1$ urged Martha$_2$ [$_S$ PRO$_2$ to defend himself$_1$].
c. *John$_1$ appreciates [$_{NP}$ Martha$_2$'s faith in himself$_1$].

(Baker (1995: 64) with slight editing)

(4) a. *John believes that [$_S$ Martha$_1$'s friend will defend herself$_1$].
  b. *John believes that [$_S$ the car Martha$_1$ bought will disappoint herself$_1$].
  c. *John appreciates [$_{NP}$ Martha$_1$'s father's faith in herself$_1$].

(Baker (1995: 64) with slight editing)

(5) a. Tom$_1$ believed that [the paper had been written by Ann and himself$_1$].   (Ross (1970: 226) with slight editing)
  b. John$_1$ thinks that [Mary is taller than himself$_1$].

(Zribi-Hertz (1989: 698) with slight editing)
  c. John$_1$ complained that [the teacher gave extra help to everyone but himself$_1$].   (Keenan (1988: 2) with slight editing)

(6) a. If Cassandra$_1$ has filled my bed with fleas, I am sure they must bite herself$_1$.
  [Austen L, 94]   (Baker (1995: 68)) with slight editing)
  b. His$_1$ imprudence had made her miserable for a while; but it seemed to have deprived himself$_1$ of all chance of ever being otherwise.
  [Austen SS, 157-8]   (Baker (1995: 67)) with slight editing)

The grammaticality of the examples in (2)–(4) is expected under Chomsky's (1981) Conditon A of Binding Theory shown in (7), but the grammaticality of the examples in (5) and (6) is not.

(7)   Condition A of Binding Theory
   An anaphor is bound in its governing category.

(Chomsky (1981: 188))

The notions "bound" and "governing category" in (7) are defined in (8) and (9), respectively.

(8) α is bound by β if and only if (i) α and β are co-indexed, and (ii) β c-commands α.   (Chomsky (1981: 184) with slight editing)

(9) α is a governing category for β if and only if α is the minimal category containing β and a governor of β, where α = NP or S.

(Chomsky (1981: 188))

In each example in (2), the anaphor *herself* is bound in its governing category S. In each example in (3), the anaphor *himself* is not bound in its governing category, namely, S for (3a, b) and NP for (3c). In each example in (4), the anaphor *herself* is not bound, as it is not c-commanded by its antecedent. Thus, the grammaticality of all these examples is correctly predicted by Condition A of Binding Theory. However, the grammaticality of the examples in (5) and (6) is not expected under the condition, as the anaphor *himself/herself* is not bound in its governing category, yet each example in (5) and (6) is grammatical. In each example of (5), the anaphor is c-commanded by its antecedent, but is not bound in its governing category, namely, the embedded clause. In each of (6a, b), the anaphor is not c-commanded by its antecedent to begin with, and in (6b), the anaphor and its antecedent belong to two independent clauses.

Based on previous studies on locally free anaphors such as Ferro (1993), Baker (1995) proposes that locally free anaphors in English are intensifiers, and their distribution is regulated not by a version of Condition A of Binding Theory, but by the two conditions in (1). Baker (1995) further claims that locally free anaphors are non-nominative pronouns which are simultaneously contrastive and prominent, and that they are realized as *themselves* in British English and as *them*, which is represented as THEM in Baker's (1995) system, in American English, as shown in (10) and (11), respectively.

(10)   Contrast and Intensification in British English

−Contrastive	+Contrastive	+Contrastive
	−Prominent	+Prominent
the students	the STUDENTS	the students themselves
they	THEY	they themselves
them	THEM	themselves (*them themselves)

(Baker (1995: 80) with slight editing)

(11)   Contrast and Intensification in American English

−Contrastive	+Contrastive	+Contrastive
	−Prominent	+Prominent
the students	the STUDENTS	the students themselves
they	THEY	they themselves
them	THEM	THEM (*themselves, *them themselves)

(Baker (1995: 80) with slight editing)

In brief, locally free anaphors such as *themselves* in British English may function as pronouns which are simultaneously contrastive and prominent. Therefore, they are not regulated by Condition A of Binding Theory. Note that the corresponding elements in American English are not morphologically represented as anaphors but as pronouns. Therefore, they are not regulated by Condition A of Binding Theory either.

A note is in order here. Baker (1995) deals with locally free anaphors, but does not discuss local anaphors which are simultaneously contrastive and prominent. It seems that given a proper context, local anaphors such as *himself* may be simultaneously contrastive and prominent, as shown in (12).

(12)   John$_1$ is an excellent football player in the team. So, he$_1$ often praises himself$_1$.

Since *himself* in (12) is not a locally free anaphor, it is not an intensive pronoun in Baker's (1995) system. However, one might wonder how language faculty interprets a given anaphor in sentences such as (6a) as a locally free or locally bound anaphor within the clause where it is generated. It is actually impossible to determine whether it is a locally free anaphor or not until it gets its antecedent in the higher clause or in the discourse. This means that we know in advance that the given anaphor is locally free or not in examples such as (6a), which seems to involve a "look-ahead" problem. Therefore, it seems necessary to define anaphors, not locally free anaphors, which are intensive, namely, simultaneously contrastive and prominent. We know that it is inappropriate to state that intensive anaphors are pronominals, which would incorrectly exclude (13a), just like (13b), as a violation of Condition B of Binding Theory shown in (14).

(13) a.   John$_1$ praised himself$_1$. (where *himself* is assumed to be identified as an intensive anaphor.)
    b.   *John$_1$ praised him$_1$.

(14)   Condition B of Binding Theory
    A pronominal is free in its governing category.

(Chomsky (1981: 188))

In (14), "free" means "not bound." Taking the examples in (13) into account, we define intensive anaphors in British English as those in (15).

(15)   Intensive (= simultaneously contrastive and prominent) anaphors in British English are
    (i)   either anaphors or pronominals, and
    (ii)   non-nominative.

Note that (15i) suggests that intensive anaphors are subject to either Condition A or Condition B of Binding Theory, not both. To see if (15) actually works, let us consider (6a) and (13a), reproduced as (16) and (17), respectively, where the anaphors are interpreted as intensive anaphors.

(16)   If Cassandra$_1$ has filled my bed with fleas, I am sure they must bite herself$_1$.
        [Austen L, 94]   (Baker (1995: 68)) with slight editing) (=(6a))

(17)   John$_1$ praised himself$_1$. (where *himself* is identified as an intensive anaphor.)   (=(13a))

In (16), the anaphor is not locally bound by its antecedent. However, it is an intensive anaphor, so that it may function as a pronoun. As a pronoun, it is free in its local domain. Therefore, (16) is correctly predicted to be grammatical by Condition B of Binding Theory. On the other hand, in (17), the anaphor is locally bound by its antecedent. Therefore, (17) is correctly predicted to be grammatical by Condition A of Binding Theory. Thus, (15) seems to properly work. In the following discussion, we assume (15) for the sake of discussion.

The question arises, however, as to why locally free anaphors in British English are restricted to pronouns with *non-nominative* Case, as the fact that locally free anaphors in British English are non-nominative pronouns which are simultaneously contrastive and prominent does not follow from the two conditions in (1) or any other condition. To be specific, why are examples such as (18) ungrammatical in British English, where the anaphor *himself* is in the nominative subject position, and assumed to be a pronoun simultaneously contrastive and prominent?

(18)   *John$_1$ thinks that [himself$_1$ is taller than Mary].

One might argue that in (18), *himself* is in the position of nominative Case, and has the form of accusative Case, which would result in a Case conflict. However, this situation can be circumvented in (19), where the anaphor is *itself*, which can be nominative, yet the sentence is ungrammatical.

(19)   *[The robot]$_1$ thinks that [itself$_1$ is taller than Mary].

Therefore, the question that needs to be addressed is whether the condition on Case with respect to locally free anaphors is imposed by UG, or whether such a condition is language-specific, namely, specific to British English, and there exists a natural language that is free from such a condition on Case.

3. Irish Data

Having outlined the particular background, let us now examine Irish examples. (20) represents the pronoun system in Irish, and (21) shows the *féin* 'self' forms in Irish.[2]

(20)   The Pronoun System in Irish

person	1		2		3			
gender					male	female	male	female
Case	NOM	ACC	NOM	ACC	NOM		ACC	
SG	*mé*	*mé*	*tú*	*tú/thú*	*sé*	*sí*	*é*	*í*
PL	*muid*	*muid*	*sibh*	*sibh*	*siad*	*siad*	*iad*	*iad*

(21)   The *Féin* 'Self' Forms in Irish

person	1		2		3			
gender					male	female	male	female
Case	NOM	ACC	NOM	ACC	NOM		ACC	
SG	*mé féin*	*mé féin*	*tú féin*	*tú féin/thú féin*	*sé féin*	*sí féin*	*é féin*	*í féin*
PL	*muid féin*	*muid féin*	*sibh féin*	*sibh féin*	*siad féin*	*siad féin*	*iad féin*	*iad féin*

Note that unlike English, Irish allows both nominative and accusative *self* forms such as *sé féin* 'he self' and *é féin* 'him self.' Below, we will show several properties of *sé féin/é féin* 'he self/him self,' with a heavy stress on *féin*.

Firstly, (22a, b) show that the anaphors *é féin* 'him self' and *í féin* 'her self' are allowed when they have their antecedents in the same clauses, while (23a, b) show that the pronouns *é* 'him' and *í* 'her' cannot be correferential with their antecedents in the same clauses.

---

[2] The abbreviations used in this paper are as follows: ACC= accusative, COP = copula, FUT = future, GEN = genitive, NOM = nominative, PL = plural, SG = singular and VN = verbal noun.

(22) a.   Mhol   Seán₁   é   féin₁.
          praised   John   him   self
          'John praised himself.'

    b.   Mhol   Máire₁   í   féin₁.
          praised   Mary   her   self
          'Mary praised herself.'

(23) a.   *Mhol   Seán₁   é₁.
          praised   John   him
          'John praised him.'

    b.   *Mhol   Máire₁   í₁.
          praised   Mary   her
          'Mary praised her.'

When the heavy stress is placed on *féin* 'self' with *é* 'him'/*í* 'her' unstressed, the sentences in (22) have a focus interpretation, as shown in (24a, b).

(24) a.   Mhol   Seán₁   é   FÉIN₁.
          praised   John   him   self
          'John praised himself (and no one else).'

    b.   Mhol   Máire₁   í   FÉIN₁.
          praised   Mary   her   self
          'Mary praised herself (and no one else).'

In the following, we call *féin* 'self' without a heavy stress on the unmarked *féin* 'self,' represented as *féin*, and the one with a heavy stress on the focused *féin* 'self,' represented as *FÉIN*.

Secondly, (25) shows that *féin* 'self' alone does not function as an anaphor, whether it is unmarked or focused.

(25)   *Mhol   Seán₁   féin₁/FÉIN₁.
        praised   John   self/self
        'John praised himself.'

Thirdly, (26a–d) show that *é FÉIN* 'him self' and *í FÉIN* 'her self' are allowed even when they have their antecedents in the higher clauses, just like locally free anaphors in English, as shown in (5a–c), reproduced as (27a–c).

(26) a.   Síleann   Seán₁   gur   mhol   Máire   é   FÉIN₁/*féin₁.
          think   John   that praised Mary   him   self/self
          'John thinks that Mary praised him (and no one else).'

b. Síleann Máire₁ gur mhol   Seán í   FÉIN₁/*féin₁.
    think   Mary   that praised John her self/self
    'Mary thinks that John praised her (and no one else).'

c. Síleann Seán₁ gur dhúirt Róisín   gur mhol   Máire é
    think   John that said   Rosheen that praised Mary him
    FÉIN₁/*féin₁.
    self/self
    'John thinks that Rosheen said that Mary praised him (and no
    one else).'

d. Síleann Máire₁ gur dhúirt Pádraig gur mhol   Seán í
    think   Mary   that said   Patrick that praised John her
    FÉIN₁/*féin₁.
    self/self
    'Mary thinks that Patrick said that John praised her (and no one
    else).'

(27) a. Tom₁ believed that [the paper had been written by Ann and him-
         self₁].   (Ross (1970: 226) with slight editing)
     b. John₁ thinks that [Mary is taller than himself₁].
                              (Zribi-Hertz (1989: 698) with slight editing)
     c. John₁ complained that [the teacher gave extra help to everyone
         but himself₁].   (Keenan (1988: 2) with slight editing)
                                                        (=(5a–c))

Fourthly, (28a, b) show that *sé FÉIN* 'he self' and *sí FÉIN* 'she self,'
unlike *sé féin* 'he self' and *sí féin* 'she self,' are allowed in the subject position of the embedded clauses, unlike locally free anaphors in English, as
shown in (18) and (19), reproduced as (29a, b).

(28) a. Síleann Seán₁ go mbuafaidh sé FÉIN₁/*féin₁.
         think   John that win.FUT   he self/self
         'John thinks that he (and no one else) will win.'
     b. Síleann Máire₁ go mbuafaidh sí FÉIN₁/*féin₁.
         think   Mary   that win.FUT   she self/self
         'Mary thinks that she (and no one else) will win.'

(29) a. *John₁ thinks that [himself₁ is taller than Mary].   (=(18))
     b. *[The robot]₁ thinks that [itself₁ is taller than Mary]. (=(19))

Fifthly, *é FÉIN* 'him self' and *í FÉIN* 'her self' do not show subject
orientation, as shown in (30a, b), just like anaphors in English, as shown in

(31).

> (30) a. Dúirt Máire le Dónall₁ gur fuath le   Róisín   é
>   said   Mary   to Donald that hate   with Rosheen him
>   FÉIN₁/*féin₁.
>   self/self
>   'Mary said to Donald that Rosheen hates him (and no one else).'
>
>   b.   Labhair an dochtúir le   Máire₁ fúithi   FÉIN₁/féin₁.
>   spoke   the doctor   with   Mary   about.her self/self
>   'The doctor spoke with Mary about her (and no one else).'

> (31) [John₁ thinks [that Bill₂ told Mike₃ about himself*₁/₂/₃]].
>   (Katada (1991 (1)) with slight editing)

Sixthly, (32) shows that *é FÉIN* 'him self,' not *é féin* 'him self,' may be correferential with its antecedent in a non-c-commanding position, just like locally free anaphors in English, as shown in (6a), reproduced as (33).

> (32) Is   fuath le   máthair Sheáin₁   é   FÉIN₁/*féin₁.
>   COP   hate   with   mother   John.GEN him   self/self
>   Lit. 'John's mother hates him (and no one else).'

> (33) If Cassandra₁ has filled my bed with fleas, I am sure they must
>   bite herself₁.
>   [Austen L, 94]   (Baker (1995: 68)) with slight editing) (=(6a))

Seventhly, *sé FÉIN* 'he self,' not *sé féin* 'he self,' is allowed in syntactic islands. (34) shows that it may appear in an interrogative clause.

> (34) Níl   a   fhios   ag Seán₁ cén uair a   gheobhas sé
>   NEG   in.his knowledge   at John   when   aL get.FUT   he
>   FÉIN₁/*féin₁ ardú   ceíme.
>   self/self   promotion   degree.GEN
>   'John does not know when he (and no one else) will get promoted.'

Likewise, *é FÉIN* 'him self,' not *é féin* 'him self,' is allowed in an interrogative clause, as shown in (35).

> (35) Is   cuinhin le   Seán₁ nuair a   bhuail Máire é
>   COP   memory   with   John   when   aL hit   Mary   him
>   FÉIN₁/*féin₁.
>   self/self
>   'John remembers when Mary hit him (and no one else).'

(36) shows that *sé FÉIN* 'he self,' not *sé féin* 'he self,' is allowed in an adjunct clause headed by *má* 'if.'

(36) Glacfaidh Seán₁ a leithscéal má tá sé FÉIN₁/*féin₁
accept.FUT John his excuse if is he self/self
contráilte.
wrong
'John will say sorry if he (and no one else) is wrong.'

Likewise, *é FÉIN* 'him self,' not *é féin* 'him self,' is allowed in an adjunct clause headed by *má* 'if,' as shown in (37).

(37) Tosóidh Seán a chaoineadh, má lochtaíonn Máire é
begin.FUT John to cry.VN if criticize Mary him
FÉIN₁/*féin₁.
self/self
'John will begin to cry, if Mary criticizes him (and no one else).'

(38) shows that *sé FÉIN* 'he self,' not *sé féin* 'he self,' is allowed in the complement clause to a noun.

(38) Admhóidh Seán₁ an ráfla go bhfuil sé FÉIN₁/*féin₁
admit.FUT John the rumor that is he self/self
contráilte.
wrong
'John will admit the rumor that he (and no one else) is wrong.'

Likewise, *é FÉIN* 'him self,' not *é féin* 'him self,' is allowed in the complement clause to a noun, as shown in (39).

(39) Admhóidh Seán₁ an ráfla gur lochtaigh Maire é
Admit.FUT John the rumor that criticized Mary him
FÉIN₁/*féin₁.
self/self
'John will admit the rumor that Mary criticized him (and no one else).'

Eightly, and finally, (40) shows that *é FÉIN* 'him self,' not *é féin* 'him self,' does not need an antecedent in the same independent clause, just like locally free anaphors in English, as shown in (6b), reproduced as (41).

(40) Mhol Máire₂ é FÉIN₁/*féin₁.
praised Mary him self/self
'Mary praised him (and no one else).'

(41)   His₁ imprudence had made her miserable for a while; but it seemed
to have deprived himself₁ of all chance of ever being otherwise. [Austen SS, 157-8]

(Baker (1995: 67)) with slight editing) (=(6b))

To summarize, the Irish anaphor *sé FÉIN/é FÉIN* 'he self/him self' has
the properties in (42).

(42)   The Properties of *Sé FÉIN/É FÉIN* 'He Self/Him Self'
a.   It can have its antecedent within the same clause.
b.   *Féin/FÉIN* 'self' alone does not function as an anaphor.
c.   It can have its antecedent in a higher clause.
d.   It can occupy the subject position of the embedded clause.
e.   It does not show subject orientation.
f.   It may have its antecedent in a non-c-commanding position.
g.   It can be in syntactic islands such as interrogative clauses, adjunct clauses and complement clauses to nouns.
h.   It does not need an antecedent in the same independent clause.

4.   Discussion

The Irish data in the above section indicates that *sé féin/é féin* 'he self/
him self' with a heavy stress on *féin*, that is, *sé FÉIN/é FÉIN* 'he self/him
self,' shows a long-distance relation with its antecedent, and it does not need
to have an antecedent in the same clause. Thus, *sé FÉIN/é FÉIN* 'he self/
him self' is not a local anaphor, and seems to behave like locally free anaphors such as *himself* in British English. In the following discussion, we
will examine the exact nature of *sé FÉIN/é FÉIN* 'he self/him self,' putting
aside *sé féin/é féin* 'he self/him self,' whose distribution seems to be regulated by Condition A of Binding Theory, and will reach the conclusion that it
is a locally free anaphor.

As shown above, *sé FÉIN/é FÉIN* 'he self/him self,' shows a long-distance relation with its antecedent, and does not need to have an antecedent
in the same clause. Furthermore, it can have the connotation of being contrastive and prominent. Therefore, let us hypothesize that it is an intensive
pronoun in the sense of Baker (1995), which we reinterpret as an intensive
anaphor in (15), reproduced as (43).

(43)   Intensive (= simultaneously contrastive and prominent) anaphors in British English are
  (i)   either anaphors or prornominals, and
  (ii)   non-nominative.   (=(15))

We know that (43) does not directly hold in Irish, since the nominative form of the intensive anaphor *sé FÉIN* 'he self' is possible in the language. Therefore, we hypothesize that (44) holds in Irish, and examine if it correctly captures the distribution of intensive anaphors in the language.

(44)   Intensive (= simultaneously contrastive and prominent) anaphors in Irish are either anaphors or pronominals.

Note that (44) suggests that intensive anaphors in Irish are subject to either Condition A or Condition B of Binding Theory, not both.

  Firstly, the property in (42a) that the intensive anaphor *é FÉIN* 'him self' can have its antecedent within the same clause, is correctly predicted by hypothesis (44). Consider (24a) again, reproduced as (45).

(45)   Mhol   Seán$_1$ é   FÉIN$_1$.
       praised John   him   self
       'John praised himself (and no one else).'   (=(24a))

In (45), *é FÉIN* 'him self' is bound by the antecedent *Seán* 'John.' However, this does not contradict the hypothesis, as it functions as an anaphor, and does not need to be a pronominal in this case, so that it does not violate either Condition A or Condition B of Binding Theory.

  Secondly, the property in (42b) that *FÉIN* 'self' alone does not function as an anaphor, does not contradict the hypothesis, as *é FÉIN* 'him self' as a whole functions as an intensive anaphor, and part of it cannot be an anaphor.

  Thirdly, the property in (42c) that the intensive anaphor *é FÉIN* 'him self' can have its antecedent in a higher clause, is correctly predicted by hypothesis (44). Consider (26a) and (26c) again, reproduced as (46) and (47), respectively, with slight editing.

(46)   Síleann Seán$_1$ gur mhol   Máire é   FÉIN$_1$.
       think   John   that praised Mary   him   self
       'John thinks that Mary praised him (and no one else).'

                                        (=(26a) with slight editing)

(47) Síleann Seán₁ gur dhúirt Róisín   gur mhol   Máire é   FÉIN₁.
      think   John   that said Rosheen that praised Mary him self
      'John thinks that Rosheen said that Mary praised him (and no one
      else).'   (=(26c) with slight editing)

In (46), the intensive anaphor *é FÉIN* 'him self' is separated from its antecedent *Seán* 'John' by one clause boundary, and in (47), by two clause
boundaries, yet the sentences are grammatical. This is expected, since it
functions as a pronominal, and does not need to be an anaphor in this case,
so that it does not violate either Condition A or Condition B of Binding
Theory.

    Fourthly, the property in (42d) that the intensive anaphor *sé FÉIN* 'he
self' can occupy the subject position of the embedded clause, is also correctly expected by the hypothesis. Consider (28a), reproduced as (48) with
slight editing.

(48) Síleann Seán₁ go   mbuafaidh sé FÉIN₁.
      think   John   that win.FUT   he self
      'John thinks that he (and no one else) will win.'
                                                  (=(28a) with slight editing)

In (48), the nominative intensive anaphor *sé FÉIN* 'he self' is separated
from its antecedent *Seán* 'John' by one clause boundary, yet the sentence
is grammatical. This is expected, since it functions as a pronominal, and
does not need to be an anaphor in this case, so that it does not violate either
Condition A or Condition B of Binding Theory. Note here that there is no
Case restriction on intensive anaphors in Irish by definition.

    Fifthly, the property in (42e) that the intensive anaphor *é FÉIN* 'him
self' does not show subject orientation, does not contradict the hypothesis. Consider (30a) again, reproduced as (49).

(49) Dúirt Máire le Dónall₁ gur fuath le   Róisín é   FÉIN₁.
      said Mary to Donald that hate with Rosheen him self
      'Mary said to Donald that Rosheen hates him (and no one else).'
                                                                (=(30a))

In (49), the intensive anaphor *é FÉIN* 'him self' can refer to its antecedent
Dónall 'Donald,' which is not a subject, across a clause boundary, yet the
sentence is grammatical. This is again expected, since it functions as a pronominal, and does not need to be an anaphor in this case, so that it does not
violate either Condition A or Condition B of Binding Theory.

Sixthly, the property in (42f) that the intensive anaphor *é FÉIN* 'him self' may have its antecedent in a non-c-commanding position, does not contradict the hypothesis. Consider (32) again, reproduced as (50).

(50) Is   fuath le   máthair Sheáin₁ é   FÉIN₁/*féin₁.
      COP hate with mother John.GEN him self/self
      Lit. 'John's mother hates him (and no one else).'   (=(32))

In (50), the intensive anaphor *é FÉIN* 'him self' can refer to its antecedent *Sheáin* 'John.GEN,' which does not c-command it, yet the sentence is grammatical. This is again expected, since it functions as a pronominal, and does not need to be an anaphor in this case, so that it does not violate either Condition A or Condition B of Binding Theory.

Seventhly, the property in (42g) that the intensive anaphor *é FÉIN* 'him self' can be separated from its antecedent by syntactic islands such as interrogative clauses, adjunct clauses and complement clauses to nouns, is also correctly predicted by the hypothesis. Consider (37), for instance, reproduced as (51).

(51) Tosóidh   Seán a   chaoineadh, má lochtaíonn Máire é
      begin.FUT John to   cry.VN   if criticize   Mary him
      FÉIN₁/*féin₁.
      self/self
      'John will begin to cry, if Mary criticizes him (and no one else).'
                                                               (=(37))

In (51), the intensive anaphor *é FÉIN* 'him self' is separated from its antecedent *Seán* 'John' by an adjunct island, yet the sentence is grammatical. This is expected, since it functions as a pronominal, and does not need to be an anaphor in this case, so that it does not violate either Condition A or Condition B of Binding Theory.

Eighthly, and finally, the property in (42h) that the intensive anaphor *é FÉIN* 'him self' does not need an antecedent in the same independent clause, does not contradict the hypothesis. Consider (40) again, reproduced as (52).

(52) Mhol   Máire₂ é   FÉIN₁/*féin₁.
      praised Mary him self/self
      'Mary praised him (and no one else).'   (=(40))

(52) contains no explicit antecedent for *é FÉIN* 'him self' in the sentence, yet the sentence is grammatical. However, the anaphor *é FÉIN* 'him self' in (52) actually refers to some male person who is contrastive and prominent in

the dialogue such as (53).

(53) Bhí Seán₁ an-chineálta, mar sin   mhol   Máire é   FÉIN₁.
      was John   very kind   therefore praised Mary him self
      'John was very kind. Therefore, Mary praised him (and no one
      else).'

Therefore, the anaphor *é FÉIN* 'him self' in Irish can acquire its antecedent in the given discourse, whether or not it is explicitly represented as an
NP within the same sentence. Thus, the grammaticality of (52) and (53) is
expected, since the intensive anaphor *é FÉIN* 'him self' functions as a pronominal, and does not need to be an anaphor in these cases, so that it does
not violate either Condition A or Condition B of Binding Theory.

Thus, hypothesis (44) correctly predicts the grammaticality of all the examples in Irish examined above. It then provides an answer to the question
posed at the beginning of this paper, which is summarized in (54).

(54) Locally free anaphors in British English are restricted to intensive
      anaphors with *non-nominative* Case. Is the condition on Case im-
      posed by UG or is it language-specific, namely, specific to British
      English?

The answer is clear. That is, the condition on Case with respect to locally
free anaphors in British English is not imposed by UG, but it is specific to
this language. The examples that support this are (46) and (48) from Irish,
reproduced as (55) and (56).

(55) Síleann Seán₁ gur mhol   Máire é   FÉIN₁.
      think   John that praised Mary him self
      'John thinks that Mary praised him (and no one else).'   (=(46))

(56) Síleann Seán₁ go mbuafaidh sé FÉIN₁.
      think   John that win.FUT   he self
      'John thinks that he (and no one else) will win.'   (=(48))

(55) contains the accusative form of the intensive anaphor *é FÉIN* 'him self,'
and (56) the nominative form of the intensive anaphor *sé FÉIN* 'he self.'
This indicates that there is no Case restriction on intensive anaphors in Irish,
unlike British English, which indicates that intensive anaphors are in principle allowed to appear in any position, including the subject position, by UG.

There is another piece of evidence for this claim from Early Modern
English. Baker (1995: 74) states that in Early Modern English, one fre-

quently encounters examples of locally free reflexives functioning as nominative intensives. The examples in (57) and (58) are from King James Bible.

(57)   And Azariah, the chief priest, and all the priests, looked upon him, and behold, he was leprous in his forehead, and they thrust him out from thence; yea, *himself* hasted also to go out, because the Lord had smitten him. [II Chronicles 26:20]

(Baker (1995: 74) with slight editing)

(58)   But there was a certain man, called Simon, which beforetime in the same city used sorcery, and bewitched the people of Samaria, giving out that *himself* was some great one. [Acts 8:9]

(Baker (1995: 74) with slight editing)

These examples clearly indicate that intensive anaphors are in principle allowed to appear in any position, including the subject position, by UG.

The two Jane Austin novels from which Baker (1995) cites relevant examples contain absolutely no examples of this kind. This suggests then that the grammar of British English has undergone a slight change in the Case system in the transition from Early Modern English to Modern English, and the grammar at the present stage does not allow nominative intensives by some language-specific condition on Case. We tentatively assume that this condition is closely related to the morphology of the *self* forms in English, in which there is no morphologically nominative anaphor, and that the Case system in this language does not allow morphologically non-nominative forms of nominals in the subject position, so that *himself/herself/themselves/ myself/ourselves/yourself/yourselves* are not allowed in the subject position in Modern English.

If this assumption is correct, what does the ungrammaticality of (29b), reproduced as (59), suggest?

(59)   *[The robot]$_1$ thinks that [itself$_1$ is taller than Mary].   (=(19), (29b))

In the above discussion, it was suggested that morphologically, *itself* can be either accusative or nominative, unlike *himself*, which is obviously morphologically accusative, so that it should be able to appear in the subject position, as well as in the object position, if it is interpreted as an intensive anaphor. The fact that (59) is ungrammatical suggests that in Modern English, *itself* is not morphologically ambiguous any more, and it is unambiguously accusative, so that it cannot appear in the subject position.

5. Conclusion

This paper investigated the distribution of the reflexive anaphor *sé FÉIN/é FÉIN* 'he self/him self' in Irish, and showed that it is identified as an intensive pronoun in the sense of Baker (1995), which was reinterpreted as an intensive anaphor in this paper. Furthermore, it was pointed out that there is a crucial difference between British English and Irish with respect to the properties of intensive anaphors, as summarized in (43) and (44), reproduced as (60) and (61), respectively.

(60)   Intensive (= simultaneously contrastive and prominent) anaphors in British English are
      (i)   either anaphors or pronominals, and
      (ii) non-nominative.   (=(15), (43))

(61)   Intensive (= simultaneously contrastive and prominent) anaphors in Irish are either anaphors or pronominals.   (=(44))

To be precise, there is no Case restriction on intensive anaphors in Irish, unlike British English. Based on this, we argued that intensive anaphors are in principle allowed to appear in any position, including the subject position, by UG. This was also supported by data from Early Middle English, which allows nominative intensive anaphors.

The fact that Early Middle English allowed nominative intensive anaphors, led to the argument that the grammar of British English has undergone a slight change in the Case system in the transition from Early Modern English to Modern English, and the grammar at the present stage does not allow nominative intensives by a language-specific morphological condition on anaphors. It was further argued that given such a condition, in Modern English, *itself* is not morphologically ambiguous any more, and it is unambiguously accusative, so that it cannot appear in the subject position.

Chapter 2

On the Highest Subject Restriction in Modern Irish[*]

Dónall P. Ó Baoill and Hideki Maki

Queen's University Belfast (Prof. Emeritus) and *Gifu University*

Keywords: *chain uniformity, highest subject restriction, Irish, movement, resumption*

1. Introduction

This paper examines the Highest Subject Restriction (HSR) effect in Modern Ulster Irish (Irish, hereafter), and shows that the HSR does not hold in certain syntactic configurations in Irish, which has not heretofore been reported in the literature. We suggest that the cancellation of the HSR be attributed to the addition of an extra phrase to the structure in Irish, and Chomsky's (1991) Condition on Chain Uniformity.

The organization of this paper is as follows. Section 2 reviews properties of complementizers in Irish as background to subsequent sections. Section 3 provides the HSR examples discussed in the literature. Section 4 points out problems associated with the HSR by presenting the data showing that the HSR does not hold in certain syntactic configurations. Section 5 elucidates the mechanism behind cancellation of the HSR in Irish. Finally, Section 6 concludes this paper.

---

* This is a drastically revised version of the paper presented at the 143rd Meeting of the Linguistic Society of Japan held at Osaka University on November 26, 2011. We would like to thank the audience of the meeting, Jessica Dunton, Kazuma Fujimaki, Kiyota Hashimoto, Makoto Kondo, Fumikazu Niinuma, Kenji Oda, Reiko Okabe, Yohei Oseki, Junko Shimoyama, Yuji Takano and two anonymous *EL* referees for their helpful comments on an earlier version of this paper. Our thanks also go to the following native speakers from the eastern borders of Gweedore Parish in North West Donegal with whom the examples have been checked: Donnchadh Mac Fhionnaile, Seán Mac Giolla Chóill, Bríd Bean Mhic Íomhair, Anna Ní Bhaoill, Máire Nic Giolla Chóill, Pádraig Ó Briain, Pádraig Ó Dúgáin (Éamann), Bríd Bean Uí Ghallchóir and Méabha Bean Uí Phíopalaigh. All errors are our own. Research by the second author was supported in part by Japan Society for the Promotion of Science Grant # 21520397 to Gifu University.

2. Background

Let us start by briefly summarizing properties of complementizers in Irish. Irish has three types of complementizers: the [−Q] marker, the direct relative marker, and the indirect relative marker. The properties of the three COMPs are summarized in (1).

(1)   Complementizers in Irish[1]

	types of COMPs	non-past form	past form	symbol
a.	the [−Q] marker	*go*	*go/gur*	that
b.	the direct relative marker	*a*	*a*	aL
c.	the indirect relative marker	*a*	*a/ar*	aN

Let us illustrate the properties of the COMPs by relevant examples. (2) is a declarative sentence, and the embedded clause is headed by the [−Q] COMP *gur* 'that.' On the other hand, when the sentence involves *wh*-interrogative clause formation, as in (3), the embedded COMP must change to the direct relative marker *aL*, and at the same time, another COMP *aL* must be inserted right after the *wh*-phrase.

(2)   Creideann Seán gur cheannaigh Máire an carr.
       believe   John that bought   Mary the car
       'John believes that Mary bought the car.'

(3)   Cad é a chreideann tú   a   cheannaigh Seán *t*?
       what aL believe   you aL bought   John
       'What do you believe that John bought?'   (movement) (aL, aL, *t*)

There is another way to form a *wh*-interrogative clause. Observe the example in (4).

(4)   Cad é a gcreideann tú   gur cheannaigh Seán *é/*t*?
       what aN believe   you that bought   John it
       'What do you believe that John bought?'

---

[1] The complementizer forms used with irregular verbs in the past tense in Irish, namely, the [−Q] marker and indirect relative marker *aN* do not follow the regular usage found with all other verbs. Hence, the regular complementizer forms *gur* 'that' and the indirect relative form *ar* are replaced by *go* 'that' and *a* 'aN,' respectively when used with the following irregular verbs: *bí* 'to be' >> *go/a raibh*; *déan* 'to do' >> *go/a ndearna*; *faigh* 'to get' >> *go/a bhfuair*; *tabhair* 'to give' >> *go/a dtug*; *tar* 'to come' >> *go/a dtáinig* and *téigh* 'to go' >> *go/a ndeachaigh*.

(resumption) (aN, that, RP)

In (4), the topmost COMP of the *wh*-interrogative clause is an indirect relative marker *a*, the COMP of the embedded clause is a [−Q] COMP, and the embedded clause contains a resumptive pronoun (RP) *é* 'it' instead of a gap. Note that (4) becomes ungrammatical, if the resumptive pronoun is replaced by a trace, which suggests that *aN* must bind a resumptive pronoun.

McCloskey (2002) provides an account of the distribution of the COMPs by proposing (5).[2, 3]

---

[2] The first reviewer points out that Rizzi (1990) claims that the adjunct *wh*-phrase *why* in English is base-generated in CP SPEC, while Shlonsky and Soare (2011) claim that it is moved to CP SPEC, and raises the question as to what property the Irish counterpart has. McCloskey (2002) argues that the adjunct *wh*-phrase *cén fáth* 'why' in Irish is inserted at the SPEC of the clause where it takes scope, and is overtly moved to the SPEC of the [+Q] COMP, as shown in (i), where *cén fáth* 'why' only modifies the embedded clause.

(i) Cén   fáth   *a* dúirt Pól a   raibh Seán ann?
     what.the reason aL said Paul aN was John there
     'Why did Paul say that John was there?'   (McCloskey's (69))

McCloskey (1985) provides the other type of data in which the embedded COMP is realized as *go* 'that.PAST,' as shown in (ii), where *an fáth* 'the reason' only modifies the higehr clause.

(ii) Sin an fáth   ar dhúirt sé *go*   ndearna sé é.
      that the reason aN said   he that.PAST did   he it
      'This is the reason why he said he did it.'   (McCloskey's (112a))

The examples in (i) and (ii) thus suggest that the adjunct *wh*-phrase *cén fáth* 'why' in Irish can be base-generated in the SPEC of [+Q] COMP, and can move to such a position when base-generated otherwise.

[3] The first reviewer points out that Pesetsky (1987) claims that a D-linked *wh*-phrase binds the corresponding pronoun, while a non-D-lined *wh*-phrase does not, and raises the question as to whether this distinction holds in Irish. Interestingly enough, it does not hold in Irish. Thus, the examples in (3) and (4) in the text are still grammatical with *cad é sa diabhal* 'what in the devil (= what the hell)' in place of *cad é* 'what,' as shown in (i) and (ii).

(i) Cad é sa   diabhal a chreideann tú   a   cheannaigh Seán *t*?
     what in.the devil   aL believe   you aL   bought   John
     'What the hell do you believe that John bought?'   (movement) (aL, aL, *t*)

(ii) Cad é sa   diabhal a gcreideann tú   gur cheannaigh Seán *é*/**t*?
      what in.the devil   aN believe   you that bought   John it
      'What the hell do you believe that John bought?'   (resumption) (aN, that, RP)

We leave the issue as to why this is so in Irish open for future research.

(5) a.   C whose specifier is filled by Move is realized as *aL*.

    b.   C whose specifier is filled by Merge is realized as *aN*.

    c.   C whose specifier is not filled is realized as *go/gur*.

McCloskey assumes that the SPEC of *aL* contains a null operator/null pronoun (henceforth, null operator) as a result of movement, that in the SPEC of *aN*, there is a base-generated operator, and that in the SPEC of *go/gur*, there is no operator. If this is correct, the structure of the *wh*-interrogative clause construction in Irish looks like a cleft sentence, as shown in (6).

(6)   (it is) WH$_1$ [$_{CP}$ Op$_1$ aL/aN [$_{IP}$...t_1/RP$_1$...]]

Note as well that in the relative clause construction, a COMP is inserted right after the head noun, as shown in (7).

(7) a.   an   carr   a   chreideann   tú   a   cheannaigh Seán   *t*
        the   car   aL   believe   you   aL bought   John
        'the car you believe that John bought'   (movement) (aL, aL, *t*)

    b.   an   carr   a   gcreideann   tú   gur   cheannaigh Seán   *é/*t*
        the   car   aN   believe   you   that bought   John   it
        'the car you believe that John bought'   (resumption) (aN, that, RP)

(6) is thus generalized to (8).

(8)   (it is) NP$_1$/WH$_1$ [$_{CP}$ Op$_1$ aL/aN [$_{IP}$...t_1/RP$_1$...]]

3.   The Highest Subject Restriction (HSR) in Irish: The (Apparent) Facts

McCloskey (1979, 1990) argues for the Highest Subject Restriction (HSR) on the distribution of resumptive pronouns based on languages such as Irish, Hebrew, and Palestinian Arabic, which is roughly stated in (9).

(9)   *The Highest Subject Restriction (HSR)*
    In languages which have a fully grammaticized resumptive strategy, the only position from which resumptive pronouns are excluded is the highest subject position within the relative clause.

                                (McCloskey (2002: 201) with slight editing)

See Hayon (1973) and Borer (1984), among others, for Hebrew data, and Shlonsky (1992), among others, for Palestinian Arabic data.

The HSR applies to resumptive pronouns in both relative clauses and *wh*-interrogative clauses in Irish. The relevant examples are shown below.

The examples in (10)–(13) involve object extraction/resumption, and they are all grammatical.

(10) a. an leabhar₁ a léigh Seán *t*₁
         the book   aL read John
         'the book that John read'   (movement)

    b. an leabhar₁ ar léigh Seán **é**₁
         the book   aN read John it
         'the book that John read'   (resumption)

(11) a. Cad é₁ a léigh Seán *t*₁?
         what   aL read John
         'What did John read?'   (movement)

    b. Cad é₁ ar léigh Seán **é**₁?
         what   aN read John it
         'What did John read?'   (resumption)

(12) a. an leabhar₁ a chreideann tú a cheannaigh Seán *t*₁
         the book   aL believe   you aL bought   John
         'the book you believe that John bought?' (movement) (aL, aL, *t*)

    b. an leabhar₁ a gcreideann tú gur cheannaigh Seán **é**₁
         the book   aN believe   you that bought   John it
         'the book you believe that John bought?'
                                                 (resumption) (aN, that, RP)

(13) a. Cad é₁ a chreideann tú a cheannaigh Seán *t*₁?
         what   aL believe   you aL bought   John
         'What do you believe that John bought?' (movement) (aL, aL, *t*)

    b. Cad é₁ a gcreideann tú gur cheannaigh Seán **é**₁?
         what   aN believe   you that bought   John it
         'What do you believe that John bought?'
                                                 (resumption) (aN, that, RP)

However, according to McCloskey (1979, 1990), the relative clause construction does not allow the resumption strategy for the highest subject, while it allows the movement strategy for it, as shown in (14) and (15). In (14b), the resumptive pronoun is in the highest subject position.

(14) a.   an   fear$_1$ a bhí t_1 breoite
           the man aL was   ill
           'the man who was ill'   (movement)

       b. *an fear$_1$ a raibh **sé**$_1$ breoite
           the man aN was   he ill
           'the man who was ill'   (resumption)

(15) a.   an   fear$_1$ a shíl   mé a bhí t_1 breoite
           the man aL thought I   aL was   ill
           'the man who I thought (he) was ill'   (movement)

       b. an   fear$_1$ ar shíl   mé go raibh **sé**$_1$ breoite
           the man aN thought I   that was   he ill
           'the man who I thought (he) was ill'   (resumption)

The same pattern is observed with the *wh*-interrogative construction, as shown in (16) and (17). In (16b), the resumptive pronoun is in the highest subject position.

(16) a.   Cé$_1$ a léigh t_1 an leabhar seo?
           who aL read   the book   this
           'Who read this book?'   (movement)

       b. *Cé$_1$ ar léigh **sé**$_1$ an leabhar seo?
           who aN read he the book   this
           'Who read this book?'   (resumption)

(17) a.   Cé$_1$ a shíl   tú a bhí t_1 breoite?
           who aL thought you aL was   ill
           'Who did you think that (he) was ill?'   (movement) (aL, aL, *t*)

       b. Cé$_1$ ar shíl   tú go raibh **sé**$_1$ breoite?
           who aN thought you that was   he ill
           'Who did you think that (he) was ill?' (resumption) (aN, go, RP)

McCloskey (1990) also points out that there are cases where the resumptive pronoun which is not apparently in the highest subject position is excluded, based on examples such as (18). (Note that we disagree about the judgment of (18), which we claim to be grammatical, as discussed in the next section.)

(18)   *an fear ar shíl   mé a raibh **sé** breoite
          the man aN thought I   aN was   he ill
          'the man who I thought (he) was ill'   (resumption) (aN, aN, RP)
                                  (McCloskey (1990: 219), our bold on **sé**)

This is because in (18), the second COMP *a* 'aN' has a base-generated null operator in its SPEC, so that the resumptive pronoun in the subject position *sé* 'he' counts as the highest subject, as it is locally bound by the operator, as (19) shows.

(19)   the man$_1$ [$_{CP}$ Op$_1$ aN [$_{IP}$...[$_{CP}$ **Op**$_1$ aN [$_{IP}$...RP$_1$...]]]]

Thus, the above examples all show that the HSR is one of the salient properties of Irish, according to McCloskey.

4.   Problems of the HSR

Our careful examination of the HSR effect in Irish shows that contrary to what McCloskey (1979, 1990) argues, (A) the examples with the HSR effect become grammatical with an extra phrase attached to them to make them sound real and factual, and (B) some of the examples of the HSR, which are considered ungrammatical, are actually grammatical, as they are.

Let us start with Case (A). The examples in (14b) and (16b), which have a simple structure, are ungrammatical, according to McCloskey (1979, 1990). However, the same structure is perfectly grammatical with an additional phrase, as shown in (20). The examples in the rest of the paper are all taken from our own fieldwork unless notified otherwise.

(20)   Tá   an   fear$_1$ a   raibh   **sé**$_1$ breoite más   fíor   anseo anois.
        is   the   man   aN   was   he   ill   if+COP true   here   now
        'The man who was ill supposedly is here now.'

(21) shows the same point with a *wh*-interrogative sentence.

(21)   Cé$_1$ ar   léigh   **sé**$_1$ an   leabhar seo   más   fíor   di?
        who   aN   read   he   the   book   this   if+COP true   to.her
        'Who read this book, according to her/what she says?'

A simple sentence with an intransitive verb is ungrammatical in the HSR structure, as shown in (22). However, (22) becomes grammatical with an additional phrase, as shown in (23).

(22)   *Cé$_1$ ar   imigh   **sé**$_1$?
        who   aN   left   he
        'Who left?'

(23)   Cé₁   ar imigh **sé₁** go hádhúil/is léir/is dócha/inné
      who aN left   he   fortunately/evidently/probably/yesterday
      /trí lá ó shin/in am/le Máire?
      /three days ago/in time/with Mary
      'Who left fortunately/evidently/probably/yesterday/three days ago/on
      time/with Mary?'

According to Cinque (1999), the first three adverbs in (23) *go hádhúil* 'fortunately'/*is léir* 'evidently'/*is dócha* 'probably' are high adverbs, and in the projections of Mood evaluative, Mood evidential, and Mood epistemic, respectively. Therefore, (23) shows that an adverb, whether it is high enough or not, may cancel the HSR. See Endo (2007: 5) for a precise summary of the adverb hierarchy proposed in Cinque (1999).

A simple sentence with a transitive verb is also ungrammatical in the HSR structure, as shown in (24). This indicates that a subcategorized object cannot cancel the HSR. However, again, (24) becomes grammatical with an additional phrase, as shown in (25).

(24)   *Cé₁   a   bhfaca **sé₁** an bhean?
       who aN saw   he the woman
       'Who saw the woman?'

(25)   Cé₁   a   bhfaca **sé₁** an bhean trí lá ó shin?
       who aN saw   he the woman three days ago
       'Who saw the woman three days ago?'

Finally, the examples in (26) and (27) show that the HSR is cancelled not only by an adverb, but also by a coordinate clause.

(26)   *Cé₁   a   raibh **sé₁** breoite?
       who aN was   he ill
       'Who was ill?'

(27)   Cé₁   a   raibh **sé₁** breoite agus ag fáil   bháis?
       who aN was   he ill   and   at getting death
       'Who was ill and dying?'

Let us now return to Case (B). The example in (18), which McCloskey (1990) judges ungrammatical because *sé* 'he' is locally bound by the null operator in the SPEC of *aN*, is actually perfectly grammatical as it is. The examples in (28a, b), whose basic structure is identical to that of (18), are also grammatical.

(28) a.   an   fear$_1$ ar   dhúirt Seán a   dtáinig **sé**$_1$
          the man aN said   John aN came   he
          'the man who John said came'   (aN, aN, RP)

      b.   an   fear$_1$ a   dúirt   Seán a   dtáinig **sé**$_1$
          the man aL said   John aN came   he
          'the man who John said came'   (aL, aN, RP)

The examples in (29a, b) illustrate the same point with the *wh*-interrogative construction.

(29) a.   Cé$_1$ ar   shíl   tú   ar   léigh **sé**$_1$ an leabhar seo?
          who aN thought you aN read he   the book   this
          'Who did you think read this book?'   (aN, aN, RP)

      b.   Cé$_1$ a   shíl   tú   ar   léigh **sé**$_1$ an leabhar seo?
          who aL thought you aN read he   the book   this
          'Who did you think read this book?'   (aL, aN, RP)

The above examples clearly show that contrary to what McCloskey (1979, 1990) claims, (A) the examples with the HSR effect become grammatical with an extra phrase attached to them to make them sound real and factual, and (B) some of the examples of the HSR which are considered ungrammatical are actually grammatical, as they are.

5.   Elucidation of the Mechanism of Cancellation of the HSR

The data in the above section suggest that there are two ways to cancel the HSR in Irish: (A) adding an extra phrase to the HSR structure, and (B) a base-generated operator (resumption operator) in the non-initial position of the chain. In this section, we will consider what these actually indicate.

Let us start with Case (B). If McCloskey (2002) is correct, the relevant structure in Case (B) is the one in (30), where *Op* in bold is a base-generated operator binding the highest subject resumptive pronoun.

(30)   *the man$_1$/who$_1$ [$_{CP}$ Op$_1$ aN [$_{IP}$ ... [$_{CP}$ **Op**$_1$ aN [$_{IP}$ ...RP$_1$...]]]]

McCloskey (1990) claims that the operator in bold binds the highest subject resumptive pronoun, which leads to the ungrammaticality of the structure in (30).

However, if Chomsky's (1991) Condition on Chain Uniformity, part of which is shown in (31), is correct, the base-generated operator in bold should not exist in that position at LF.

(31) *Condition on Chain Uniformity*
      What counts as a proper element at the LF level is a chain in (i):
      (i) $(\alpha_1, ..., \alpha_n)$
           (ii) is a permitted LF object:
      (ii) Operator-variable constructions, each a chain (α_1, α_2), where
           the operator α_1 is in an A'-position and the variable α_2 is in an
           A-position.   (Chomsky (1991: 440))

In (30), the highest Op and the resumptive pronoun should constitute an
operator-variable chain at LF, so that the intermediate operator should not be
able to exist at LF by (31ii). Then, at LF, (30) looks like (32).

(32)   the man$_1$/who$_1$ [$_{CP}$ Op$_1$ aN [$_{IP}$ ... [$_{CP}$ aN [$_{IP}$ ...RP$_1$...]]]]

Then, in (32), the subject resumptive pronoun is not the highest subject
bound by the operator in the structure. Therefore, the HSR effect is cancelled in Case (B), as long as Chomsky (1991) is correct.

      Let us then turn to Case (A). In configurations with a highest subject,
the HSR is not cancelled in the structures in (33a, b), but is in the structures
in (33c, d).

(33) a. *NP$_1$/WH$_1$ [$_{CP}$ Op$_1$ aN [$_{IP}$ [$_{vP}$ sé$_1$]]]
     b. *NP$_1$/WH$_1$ [$_{CP}$ Op$_1$ aN [$_{IP}$ [$_{vP}$ sé$_1$ NP$_{OBJ}$]]]
     c. NP$_1$/WH$_1$ [$_{CP}$ Op$_1$ aN [$_{IP}$ [$_{vP}$ sé$_1$...ADV]]]
     d. NP$_1$/WH$_1$ [$_{CP}$ Op$_1$ aN [$_{IP}$ [$_{vP}$ sé$_1$ [VP...] & [VP...]]]]

For the sake of discussion, we assume that the subject and the object stay
within vP in Irish, following Maki and Ó Baoill (2011: Ch. 1), which does
not affect the main argument in the following discussion.

      (33a) indicates that without an additional phrase, the HSR is not can-
celled. (33b, c) show that the additional phrase that saves the highest
subject is not an argument subcategorized by the verb, but an adverb, irrespective of whether it is a high adverb or not. Finally, (33d) indicates
that as well as adverbs, a coordinate clause can save the highest subject.
Therefore, the generalization behind Case (A) is something like (34).

(34)   The highest subject is saved by an adverb or a coordinate structure.

At first sight, (34) does not seem to be a true generalization behind Case
(A), and the question arises as to what properties an adverb and a coordinate
structure share. In the following discussion, we will revise (34), following
Higginbotham's (1985) idea that adjuncts involve coordination.

Following Davidsonian event semantics, Higginbotham (1985) claims that the example in (35) is given the semantic representation in (36).

(35)   John walks slowly.

(36) $\exists e$ [Walk (John, e) & Slow (e)]

(36) indicates that there is an event such that it is a walking by John and it is slow (for walking by John). If this is true, the structure with an adverb in (33c) has a coordinate structure in its semantic representation, just like the structure with a coordinate clause in (33d). Then, (34) is further generalized to (37), and one may say that the HSR is cancelled by the addition of a co-ordinate clause to the HSR structure.

(37)   The highest subject is saved by a coordinate structure.

On the other hand, the structures in (33a, b) do not have such a structure. Therefore, the highest subject is not saved in these configurations.

Of course, the issue still remains as to why the addition of a coordinate clause to the HSR structure can save the highest subject. We will leave this difficult and important issue for future research.

6.   Conclusion

In this paper, we examined the HSR effect in Irish, and showed that the HSR is cancelled when (A) an extra phrase is added to the HSR structure, or (B) a base-generated operator (resumption operator) is in the non-initial position of the chain. We then suggested that Case (A) was due to the addition of a coordinate clause to the HSR structure in Irish, and argued that Case (B) was a consequence of Chomsky's (1991) Condition on Chain Uniformity. If this analysis is correct, deletion of unnecessary objects does take place at LF, which provides a piece of evidence for Chomsky's (1991) essential idea about chains.

Chapter 3

A Mystery with the *Ceart* 'Correct' Construction in Modern Ulster Irish[*]

Hideki Maki and Dónall P. Ó Baoill

Gifu University and *Queen's University Belfast* (Prof. Emeritus)

In this paper, we examine properties related to the *ceart* 'correct' construction in Irish, and address a mystery arising from them. We will show that the newly found data on this construction suggest that the Chain Conditions override the Case Filter in Irish. That is, when the sentence is subject to both the Chain Conditions and the Case Filter, the latter may be violated unless it violates the former. If this is correct, it suggests that part of the UG principles may be ignored under well-defined conditions.

Keywords: *Case Filter,* ceart *'correct,'* Chain Conditions, *movement, resumption*

1. Introduction

This paper addresses the mystery arising from the *ceart* 'correct' construction in modern Ulster Irish (Irish, hereafter), and investigates what the properties behind the mystery suggest for the theory of (Irish) syntax. The construction we deal with in this paper is represented by the example in (1). (1) is a modal construction meaning 'ought to,' and the subject is preceded by the preposition *do* 'to.'

---

* This is a revised version of the paper presented at the 144th Meeting of the Linguistic Society of Japan held at Tokyo University of Foreign Studies on June 16, 2012. We would like to thank the audience of the meeting, Anna Bondaruk, Jessica Dunton, Tomohiro Fujii, Hironobu Kasai, Yoichi Miyamoto, Fumikazu Niinuma, Mitsuya Sasaki, Koji Sugisaki, Yuji Takano, Hiroyuki Ura and two anonymous *EL* referees for their helpful comments on an earlier version of this paper. Our thanks also go to the following native speakers from the eastern borders of Gweedore Parish in North West Donegal with whom the examples have been checked: Donnchadh Mac Fhionnaile, Seán Mac Giolla Chóill, Bríd Bean Mhic Íomhair, Anna Ní Bhaoill, Máire Nic Giolla Chóill, Pádraig Ó Briain, Pádraig Ó Dúgáin (Éamann), Bríd Bean Uí Ghallchóir and Méabha Bean Uí Phíopalaigh. All errors are our own. Research by the first author was supported in part by Japan Society for the Promotion of Science Grant # 21520397 to Gifu University.

(1) Ba   cheart do Sheán/dó   teach a cheannach.
     COP.COND correct to John/to.him house to buy
     'John/He ought to buy a house.'

The mystery arises when the subject undergoes wh-movement, as shown in (2), where the preposition has disappeared, yet the sentence is perfectly grammatical.

(2) Cé a   ba   cheart *t* teach a   cheannach?
     who aL COP.COND correct   house to buy
     'Who ought to buy a house?'

We will first provide a series of examples with the *ceart* 'correct' construction, and then consider what they might suggest for the theory of (Irish) syntax.

The organization of this paper is as follows. Section 2 reviews properties of the wh-interrogative construction in Irish as background to subsequent sections. Section 3 provides relevant examples with the *ceart* 'correct' construction. Based on the properties of the *ceart* 'correct' construction in Irish, Section 4 discusses what they suggest for the theory of (Irish) syntax. To be specific, we will be claiming that the Chain Conditions override the Case Filter in Irish. At the end of this section, we explore an alternative approach to the mystery on the basis of Kayne's (1984) insightful work on Case assignment on wh-phrases, and show that it does not apply to the present mystery. Finally, Section 5 concludes this paper.

2. Background

Let us start by briefly summarizing properties of the wh-interrogative construction in Irish. (See McCloskey (1979, 1990) and Maki and Ó Baoill (2011), among others, for discussion of operator constructions in Irish.) Irish has three types of complementizers: the [−Q] marker, the direct relative marker, and the indirect relative marker. The properties of the three COMPs are summarized in (3).

(3)   Complementizers in Irish[1]

	types of COMPs	non-past form	past form	symbol
a.	the [−Q] marker	*go*	*go/gur*	that
b.	the direct relative marker	*a*	*a*	aL
c.	the indirect relative marker	*a*	*a/ar*	aN

Let us illustrate the properties of the COMPs by relevant examples. (4) is a declarative sentence, and the embedded clause is headed by the [−Q] COMP *gur* 'that.' On the other hand, when the sentence involves wh-interrogative clause formation, as in (5), the embedded COMP must change to the direct relative marker *aL*, and at the same time, another COMP *aL* must be inserted right after the wh-phrase. In this paper, for expository purposes only, we represent A′-chains using the symbols *aL/aN* rather than the wh-phrase itself, as in (aL, *t*) or (aN, RP), where *RP* stands for a resumptive pronoun.

(4)   Creideann Seán gur   cheannaigh Máire an   carr.
       believe   John that bought   Mary   the car
       'John believes that Mary bought the car.'

(5)   Cad é a   chreideann tú   a   cheannaigh Seán *t*?
       what   aL believe   you aL bought   John
       'What do you believe that John bought?'   (movement) (aL, aL, *t*)

There is another way to form a wh-interrogative clause. Observe the example in (6).

(6)   Cad é a   gcreideann tú   gur   cheannaigh Seán é/*t*?
       what   aN believe   you that bought   John   it
       'What do you believe that John bought?'   (resumption) (aN, go, RP)

In (6), the topmost COMP of the wh-interrogative clause is an indirect relative marker *a*, the COMP of the embedded clause is a [−Q] COMP, and the embedded clause contains a resumptive pronoun *é* 'it' instead of a gap. Note that (6) is ungrammatical, if the resumptive pronoun is replaced

---

[1] The complementizer forms used with irregular verbs in the past tense in Irish, namely, the [−Q] marker and indirect relative marker *aN* do not follow the regular usage found with all other verbs. Hence, the regular complementizer forms *gur* 'that' and the indirect relative form *ar* are replaced by *go* 'that' and *a* 'aN,' respectively when used with the following irregular verbs: *bí* 'to be' >> *go/a raibh*; *déan* 'to do' >> *go/a ndearna*; *faigh* 'to get' >> *go/a bhfuair*; *tabhair* 'to give' >> *go/a dtug*; *tar* 'to come' >> *go/a dtáinig* and *téigh* 'to go' >> *go/a ndeachaigh*.

by a trace, which suggests that *aN* must bind a resumptive pronoun.

McCloskey (2002) provides an account of the distribution of the COMPs by proposing (7).

(7) a.   C whose specifier is filled by Move is realized as *aL*.
　 b.   C whose specifier is filled by Merge is realized as *aN*.
　 c.   C whose specifier is not filled is realized as *go/gur*.

McCloskey assumes that the SPEC of *aL* contains a null operator/null pronoun (henceforth, null operator) as a result of movement, that in the SPEC of *aN*, there is a base-generated operator, and that in the SPEC of *go/gur*, there is no operator. If this is correct, the structure of the wh-interrogative clause construction in Irish looks like a cleft sentence, as shown in (8).

(8)   (it is) WH_1 [$_{Op}$ Op_1 aL/aN [$_{IP}$...t_1/RP_1...]] (where *RP* stands for resumptive pronoun)

We will assume this in this paper.

Having established the particular background, we will observe properties of the *ceart* 'correct' construction in Irish in the next section.

3.　Data

First, the *ceart* construction may have other predicates in the position of *ceart*, which must have a modal meaning, as shown in (9).

(9) a.   Ba　　　　chóir　do Sheán/dó　teach a cheannach.
　　　COP.COND proper　to John/to.him　house to buy
　　　'John/He ought to buy a house.'
　 b.   Ba　　　　dheas　do Sheán/dó　teach a cheannach.
　　　COP.COND nice　to John/to.him　house to buy
　　　'John/He would have been better off buying a house.'

Second, the subject may undergo A-movement, leaving a resumptive pronoun, as shown in (10).

(10)　Ba　　　　cheart　do Sheán/dó　*é*　teach a cheannach.
　　　COP.COND correct　to John/to.him　*him*　house to buy
　　　'John/He ought to buy a house.'

See McCloskey and Sells (1988) for discussion of A-movement in Irish.

Third, the subject must be preceded by the preposition *do* 'to,' without which the sentence becomes ungrammatical, as shown in (11).

(11)   *Ba   cheart   Seán/é   teach   a   cheannach.
        COP.COND   correct   John/him   house   to   buy
        'John/He ought to buy a house.'

Fourth, as shown in (12) and (13), along with (2), reproduced as (14), when the subject undergoes wh-movement, the preposition must disappear.

(12)   *Cé   a   ba   cheart   do *t* teach   a   cheannach?
        who   aL   COP.COND   correct   to   house   to   buy
        'Who ought to buy a house?'

(13)   *Cé   a   ba   cheart   dó   *t* teach   a   cheannach?
        who   aL   COP.COND   correct   to.him   house   to   buy
        'Who ought to buy a house?'

(14)   Cé   a   ba   cheart   *t* teach   a   cheannach?
        who   aL   COP.COND   correct   house   to   buy
        'Who ought to buy a house?'   (=(2))

Fifth, before it undergoes wh-movement, the subject cannot undergo A-movement, leaving a resumptive pronoun, as shown in (15).

(15)   *Cé   a   ba   cheart   *t* é   teach   a   cheannach?
        who   aL   COP.COND   correct   him   house   to   buy
        'Who ought to buy a house?'

Sixth, when a wh-question containing the subject is created using an alternative A′-chain formation technique in Irish, that is, by the resumptive pronoun strategy without movement, the preposition may appear, as shown in (16) and (17).

(16)   Cé   ar   cheart   *é*   teach   a   cheannach?
        who   aN+COP.COND   correct   *him*   house   to   buy
        'Who ought to buy a house?'

(17)   Cé   ar   cheart   *dó*   teach   a   cheannach?
        who   aN+COP.COND   correct   *to.him*   house   to   buy
        'Who ought to buy a house?'

Seventh, when the resumptive pronoun strategy is used, the subject may undergo A-movement, leaving a resumptive pronoun, as shown in (18).

(18)   Cé   ar   cheart   dó   *é*   teach   a   cheannach?
        who   aN+COP.COND   correct   to.him   him   house   to   buy
        'Who ought to buy a house?'

Eighth, and finally, the PP cannot be wh-moved, as shown in (19).

(19)   *Do cé   a   ba   cheart   *t*   teach   a   cheannach?[2]
        to   whom   aL   COP.COND   correct   house   to   buy
        'Who ought to buy a house?'

4. Discussion

Let us now consider what the above data suggest. First, the subject in the *ceart* 'correct' construction in Irish must be Case-marked. This is supported by the contrast between the example in (1), reproduced as (20), and the example in (11), reproduced as (21).

(20)   Ba   cheart   do Sheán/dó   teach   a   cheannach.
        COP.COND   correct   to   John/to.him   house   to   buy
        'John/He ought to buy a house.'   (=(1))

(21)   *Ba   cheart   Seán/é   teach   a   cheannach.
        COP.COND   correct   John/him   house   to   buy
        'John/He ought to buy a house.'   (=(11))

The contrast between (20) and (21) shows that the subject is Case-marked by the preposition *do* 'to.'

Note here that in (12), reproduced as (22), the subject trace ought to be Case-marked, but the sentence is ungrammatical.

(22)   *Cé   a   ba   cheart   do   *t*   teach   a   cheannach?
        who   aL   COP.COND   correct   to   house   to   buy
        'Who ought to buy a house?'   (=(12))

This is due to the fact that Irish disallows preposition stranding in general, as shown by the contrast between (23) and (24).

---

[2] The example in (19) is grammatical when it has the interpretation in (i).

    (i)   For whom should a house be bought?

The example in (19) with the interpretation in (i) is characterized as a case of the impersonal passive construction, which is irrelevant for the present discussion.

(23)   Cé   a   ndeachaigh Seán chuig an   scannán leis?
       who aN went   John to   the   movie   with.him
       'Who did John go to the movie with?'

(24)   *Cé   a   chuaigh Seán chuig an   scannán le   *t*?
       who aL went   John to   the   movie   with
       'Who did John go to the movie with?'

In (23), the matrix COMP is *aN*, which needs to bind a resumptive pronoun in the sentence. Since (23) has a resumptive pronoun, it is correctly
predicted to be grammatical. On the other hand, in (24), the matrix COMP
is *aL*, which necessarily involves movement of an operator in the sentence.
The fact that (24) is ungrammatical indicates that preposition stranding is
disallowed in Irish.

   Second, based on the fact that the subject in the *ceart* 'correct' construction in Irish must be Case-marked, we claim that the contrast between
(20), reproduced as (25) on the one hand, and (14), reproduced as (26), on
the other suggests that the chain conditions on the operator constructions in
Irish, which will be revealed presently, override the Case Filter (Chomsky
(1981)) shown in (27), which prohibits Case-less overt NPs (or Case-less
chains (Chomsky (1986a)).

(25)   Ba   cheart do Sheán/dó   teach a   cheannach.
       COP.COND correct to John/to.him house to buy
       'John/He ought to buy a house.'   (=(1), (20))

(26)   Cé   a   ba   cheart *t* teach a   cheannach?
       who aL COP.COND correct   house to buy
       'Who ought to buy a house?'   (=(2), (14))

(27)   Case Filter
       *NP, where NP has a phonetic matrix but no Case.
                                                 (Chomsky (1981: 175))

In Irish, when wh-movement takes place, the COMP is realized as *aL*, which
(or the wh-phrase in its SPEC) must bind a variable without phonetic content. On the other hand, when the wh-construction does not use the movement strategy, the COMP is realized as *aN*, which (or the wh-phrase in its
SPEC) must bind a resumptive pronoun, as shown in (28a, b).

(28) a. Cad é a   cheannaigh Seán *t*/*é.
         what aL   bought   John it
         'What did John buy?'
     b. Cad é ar   cheannaigh Seán é/**t*.
         what aN   bought   John it
         'What did John buy?'

Based on this fact, we propose the Chain Conditions on the Operator Constructions in Irish, as shown in (29).

(29) Chain Conditions on the Operator Constructions in Irish
      a. A trace must be bound by *aL*.
      b. A resumptive pronoun must be bound by *aN*.

(29b) excludes (28a) with a resumptive pronoun, while (29a) excludes (28b) without a resumptive pronoun.

Given the Chain Conditions in (29), the trace in (26), reproduced as (30), must be bound by *aL*, not *aN*.

(30) Cé a   ba   cheart *t* teach a   cheannach?
      who aL   COP.COND correct   house to buy
      'Who ought to buy a house?'   (=(2), (14), (26))

If this is true, then, the subject trace is Case-less in (30), and runs foul of the Case Filter, which would incorrectly predict that (30) is totally ungrammatical, along with (21), reproduced as (31).

(31) *Ba   cheart Seán/é   teach a   cheannach.
      COP.COND correct John/him house to buy
      'John/He ought to buy a house.'   (=(11), (21))

The fact that (30) is perfect, however, strongly suggests that the Chain Conditions override the Case Filter in (27) in Irish. That is, when the sentence is subject to both the Chain Conditions and the Case Filter, the latter may be violated unless it violates the former. If this is true, it makes an interesting claim regarding the function of Universal Grammar, that part of the UG principles (such as the Case Filter) may be ignored under well-defined conditions.

With this claim, let us then consider the example in (32). (Note that (32) is minimally different from (13), where the trace left by wh-movement is put after *dó* 'to him.')

(32) *Cé   a   ba   cheart dó   teach a   cheannach?
      who aL COP.COND correct to.him house to buy
      'Who ought to buy a house?'

(32) contains a prepositional pronoun, in which a pronoun and a preposition
make a unit, and *dó* 'to.him' functions as a resumptive pronoun for the wh-
phrase in CP SPEC. (32) does not violate the Case Filter, but violates the
Chain Condition in (29b), since the matrix COMP is *aL*, not *aN*. Therefore,
(32) is correctly excluded. This fact indicates that the Chain Conditions
override the Case Filter, not vice versa.

Third, the ungrammaticality of (15), reproduced as (33), is accounted
for independently of the Chain Conditions.

(33) *Cé   a   ba   cheart *t* é   teach a   cheannach?
      who aL COP.COND correct   him house to buy
      'Who ought to buy a house?'   (=(15))

In (33), A-movement takes place from *é* 'him' to *t*, and then wh-movement
takes place from *t* to *cé* 'who.' The A'-chain (cé, *t*) is well-formed, as it
does not run foul of the Chain Conditions. However, the A-chain (*t*, é) is
not. This is because an A-chain must involve movement to a Case position,
as shown by the contrast between (10), reproduced as (34), and (35).

(34) Ba   cheart do Sheán/dó   *é*   teach a   cheannach.
      COP.COND correct to John/to.him *him* house to buy
      'John/He ought to buy a house.'   (=(10))

(35) *Ba   cheart Seán/é   *é*   teach a   cheannach.
      COP.COND correct John/him him house to buy
      'John/He ought to buy a house.'

In (34), the head of the A-chain is in a Case position, as it is assigned Case
by the preposition *do* 'to.' Therefore, the A-chain in (34) does not run foul
of the Case Filter. On the other hand, in (35), the head of the A-chain is
not a position assigned Case. Therefore, the A-chain in (35) runs foul of the
Case Filter, and is correctly ruled out. If this is correct, the ungrammaticality of (33) is due to the fact that the A-movement involved targets the position which is not assigned Case, so that the A-chain violates the Case Filter.

Note here that the example in (33) is still ungrammatical without the
trace, as shown in (36).

(36) *Cé   a   ba   cheart é   teach a cheannach?
      who aL COP.COND correct him house to buy
      'Who ought to buy a house?'

The ungrammaticality of (36) is straightforwardly expected under the Chain Conditions, because the resumptive pronoun is not bound by *aN*.

Fourth, the Chain Conditions also explain the grammaticality of (16), reproduced as (37), where the resumptive pronoun is Case-less.

(37) Cé   ar   cheart *é*   teach a cheannach?
      who aN+COP.COND correct *him* house to buy
      'Who ought to buy a house?'   (=(16))

The Case Filter in (27) would incorrectly rule out the example in (37), since the resumptive pronoun *é* 'him' has no Case. However, (37) is perfect. The reason is as follows. In (37), the wh-chain (aN, *é*) is created, which is permitted by the Chain Condition in (29b), although the resumptive pronoun is Case-less. However, given the above discussion, the Chain Conditions override the Case Filter, so that in (37), the resumptive pronoun need not be Case-marked. Therefore, (37) is correctly predicted to be grammatical.

Note here that the grammaticality of (17), reproduced as (38), shows that the resumptive pronoun can be Case-marked.

(38) Cé   ar   cheart *dó*   teach a cheannach?
      who aN+COP.COND correct *to.him* house to buy
      'Who ought to buy a house?'   (=(17))

However, this is not excluded by the Chain Conditions in (29), the Case Filter in (27), or any other principle. Therefore, (38) is correctly predicted to be grammatical.

The same account is provided to the example in (18), reproduced as (39).

(39) Cé   ar   cheart dó   é   teach a cheannach?
      who aN+COP.COND correct to.him him house to buy
      'Who ought to buy a house?'   (=(18))

In (39), the subject first undergoes A-movement, leaving a resumptive pronoun. Then, the wh-phrase makes use of the resumptive pronoun strategy, so that it is base-generated in the matrix clause, and another resumptive pronoun is left, which makes up a prepositional pronoun with the preposition. Again, this structure is not excluded by the Chain Conditions in (29), the Case Filter in (27), or any other principle. Therefore, (39) is correctly predicted to be grammatical.

Fifth, and finally, let us consider what the ungrammaticality of (19), reproduced as (40), suggests.

(40) *Do cé   a   ba   cheart *t* teach a   cheannach?
       to   whom aL COP.COND correct   house to buy
       'Who ought to buy a house?'   (=(19))

The structure of the example in (40) is similar to that of the English example in (41).

(41)   For whom is it necessary to buy a house?

(41) is grammatical in English. Therefore, the fact that (40) is ungrammatical in Irish, and does not have the interpretation in (41), indicates that the structure of (40) is not identical to that of (41).

Note here that the PP (*do* NP) itself can be wh-moved, as shown by the examples in (42) and (43).

(42)   D'inis siad [do Mháire] gur cheannaigh Seán carr.
        told   they to Mary   that bought   John car
        'They told Mary that John bought a car.'

(43)   [Do cé]₁ a   d'inis siad *t*₁ [gur cheannaigh Seán carr]?
        to   who aL told   they   that bought   John car
        'To whom did they tell that John bought a car?'

Therefore, the fact that (40) is ungrammatical is not attributed to the fact that the PP *do cé* 'to who' is wh-moved.

Let us now consider the examples in (44) and (45), which employ the resumption strategy for the PP *do cé* 'to who.'[3]

(44) *Do cé   ar   cheart dó   teach a cheannach?
       to   whom aN COP.COND correct to.him house to buy
       'Who ought to buy a house?'

---

[3] The example in (44) is grammatical when it has the interpretation in (i).

   (i)   For whom should he buy a house?

However, this is irrelevant for the present discussion. Note that the example in (45) is ungrammatical with any of the above interpretations.

(45) *Do cé   ar   cheart é   teach a   cheannach?
      to whom aN COP.COND correct him house to buy
      'Who ought to buy a house?'

Both (44) and (45) are ungrammatical. This indicates that wh-movement
is not the main reason for the ungrammaticality of the example in (40).
Rather, the preposition *do* 'to' being attached to the wh-phrase causes the
ungrammaticality of the examples in (40), (44) and (45), as deletion of the
preposition in these examples makes them perfectly grammatical, as shown
in (46)–(48).

(46) Cé   a   ba   cheart *t* teach a   cheannach?
      whom aL COP.COND correct   house to buy
      'Who ought to buy a house?'

(47) Cé   ar   cheart dó   teach a   cheannach?
      whom aN COP.COND correct to.him house to buy
      'Who ought to buy a house?'

(48) Cé   ar   cheart é   teach a   cheannach?
      whom aN COP.COND correct him house to buy
      'Who ought to buy a house?'

Let us now consider what this fact suggests. The structures of the
grammatical examples are those shown in (49a–c) under McCloskey's (2002)
assumption of the wh-interrogative clause construction in Irish.

(49) a. cé$_1$ [$_{CP}$ Op$_1$ aL [$_{IP}$...t_1...]]
         who
     b. cé$_1$ [$_{CP}$ Op$_1$ aN [$_{IP}$...dó$_1$...]]
         who   to.him
     c. cé$_1$ [$_{CP}$ Op$_1$ aN [$_{IP}$...é$_1$...]]
         who   him

As the discussion related to the Chain Conditions shows, the chains in (49a–
c) are all well-formed, and the wh-phrase *cé* 'who' itself is base-generated in
the pre-CP position. The structures in (49a–c) are all well-formed as they
stand. However, in (40), (44) and (45), the preposition *do* 'to' is further
added to the wh-phrase *cé* 'who.' This is a superfluous operation, and we
claim that it is this superfluous operation that makes the examples ungrammatical. The examples in (40), (44) and (45) are all grammatical without
the preposition *do* 'to,' and the grammatical structures are constructed at the

point when the wh-phrase *cé* 'who' is generated in the pre-CP position. At this point, the derivation has already converged, since it does not violate the Chain Conditions, which overrides the Case Filter. Then, the preposition *do* 'to' is further adjoined to the wh-phrase *cé* 'who,' and this operations is not necessary for the derivation to converge, as the derivation has already converged. Therefore, the examples in (40), (44) and (45) are all excluded.

Before closing this section, let us briefly discuss an alternative approach to the mystery with the *ceart* 'correct' construction. Kayne (1984), Ura (1993) and Bošković (1997), among others, based on the Case properties of the *wager* type verbs in English, argue that the wh-phrase in the *wager* construction is assigned Case in an A'-position in the course of the derivation. Consider the examples in (50).

(50) a. *John wagered Peter to be crazy.
    b.   Who did John wager *t* to be crazy?

(50a) shows that the verb *wager* cannot assign accusative Case to the subject of the embedded clause. (50b) shows that the subject of the embedded clause can be successfully wh-moved, which indicates that the wh-phrase *who* gets Case in some way. According to the above researchers, the wh-phrase moves to the SPEC of an agreement phrase before reaching the final destination, and Case assignment/checking takes place in an A'-position in the course of the derivation.

With this analysis in mind, let us turn to the mystery with the *ceart* 'correct' construction. The counterparts of the examples in (50a, b) are (31) and (30), reproduced as (51) and (52), respectively.

(51) *Ba   cheart Seán/é   teach a cheannach.
     COP.COND correct John/him house to buy
     'John/He ought to buy a house.'   (=(11), (21), (31))

(52) Cé a ba   cheart *t* teach a cheannach?
    who aL COP.COND correct   house to buy
    'Who ought to buy a house?'   (=(2), (14), (26), (30))

Suppose that there is an invisible agreement phrase above *ba cheart* 'COP. COND correct.' In (51), since the NP *Seán/é* 'John/him' is in situ, it is not assigned Case, and thus, the example is ruled out. However, in (52), the wh-phrase (the null operator, to be precise) moves to the SPEC of the agreement phrase before reaching the final destination, and Case assignment takes place in the course of the derivation. Therefore, (52) is correctly predicted to be grammatical.

However, the above analysis is faced with a difficulty when examples such as (37), reproduced as (53), are taken into account.

(53) Cé   ar   cheart é   teach a   cheannach?
      who   aN+COP.COND   correct *him* house to buy
      'Who ought to buy a house?'   (=(16), (37))

In (53), the matrix COMP is *aN*, which indicates that no movement has taken place. Therefore, the strategy of Case assignment/checking in the course of the derivation is unavailable for (53). Furthermore, given the structure of (53), shown in (54),

(54) cé$_1$ [$_{CP}$ Op$_1$ aN [$_{AGRP}$...AGR [$_{IP}$...é$_1$...]]]
      who   him

the null operator is base-generated in the SPEC of CP and the resumptive pronoun is base-generated within IP, so that no element can move into or be base-generated at the SPEC of the agreement phrase in the course of the derivation. Therefore, under the analysis of Case assignment/checking in the course of the derivation, (53) is incorrectly predicted to be ungrammatical.

One might argue that the null operator is base-generated in the SPEC of the agreement phrase, and is moved to the SPEC of CP. This operation saves Case assignment/checking of the null operator. However, it would incorrectly change the COMP *aN* to *aL*, as *aN* appears when there is no movement into its SPEC position.

Therefore, based on the above arguments, we conclude that the alternative approach on the basis of the analysis of Case assignment/checking in the course of the derivation does not provide an adequate account for the mystery with the *ceart* 'correct' construction.

5. Conclusion

In this paper, we examined the properties related to the *ceart* 'correct' construction in Irish motivated by a mystery arising from them, and investigated what the properties behind the mystery suggest for the theory of (Irish) syntax. We showed that the data on this construction suggest that the Chain Conditions override the Case Filter in Irish. That is, when the sentence is subject to both the Chain Conditions and the Case Filter, the latter may be violated unless it violates the former. We therefore conclude, based on the properties of the *ceart* 'correct' construction in Irish, that part of the UG principles (such as the Case Filter) may be ignored under well-defined conditions.

Chapter 4

The Genitive Case in Modern Ulster Irish[*]

Hideki Maki and Dónall P. Ó Baoill

Gifu University and *Queen's University Belfast* (Prof. Emeritus)

Keywords: *case, chain, control, genitive, Irish*

1. Introduction

This paper investigates the distribution of genitive case in modern Ulster Irish (Irish, hereafter), and based on the obtained facts, attempts to clarify the nature of chain formation in this language. In Irish, the object of a transitive verb is in principle marked accusative, as shown in (1). When the matrix predicate is a control verb such as *thosaigh* 'to start,' the object of the complement VP is marked either accusative or genitive, as shown in (1) and (2).[1]

(1) Léigh Seán an leabhar/é/*sé.
     read John the book/it.ACC/*it.NOM
     'John read the book/it.ACC/*it.NOM.'

---

* This is a revised version of the paper presented at the 145th Meeting of the Linguistic Society of Japan held at Kyushu University on November 24, 2012. We would like to thank the audience of the meeting, Panos Athanasopoulos, Jessica Dunton, Gilles Guerrin, Sachiko Kudara, Yoichi Miyamoto, Fumikazu Niinuma and Alexandra von Fragstein for their helpful comments on an earlier version of this paper. Our thanks also go to the following native speakers from the eastern borders of Gweedore Parish in North West Donegal with whom the examples have been checked: Donnchadh Mac Fhionnaile, Seán Mac Giolla Chóill, Bríd Bean Mhic Íomhair, Anna Ní Bhaoill, Máire Nic Giolla Chóill, Pádraig Ó Briain, Pádraig Ó Dúgáin (Éamann), Bríd Bean Uí Ghallchóir and Méabha Bean Uí Phíopalaigh. All errors are our own. Research by the first author was supported in part by Japan Society for the Promotion of Science Grant # 21520397 to Gifu University.
[1] VN = verbal noun.

(2)   Thosaigh Seán a léamh   an leabhar/leabhair.
       started   John to read.VN the book.ACC/book.GEN
       'John started to read the book.'

However, when the object is wh-moved, the resulting structure is deviant, if the head noun is marked genitive, as shown in (3) and (4).

(3)   Leabhar le   cé   a   léigh Seán?
       book   with who aL read John
       'Whose book did John read?'

(4) a.   Leabhar   le   cé   a   thosaigh Seán a léamh?
          book.ACC with who aL started John to read.VN
          'Whose book did John start to read?'

    b. *Leabhair le   cé   a   thosaigh Seán a léamh?
          book.GEN with who aL started John to read.VN
          'Whose book did John start to read?'

The ungrammaticality of the example in (4b) with the head of the wh-phrase in CP SPEC being marked genitive is a mystery. In this paper, we investigate what lies behind it. In the following discussion, for the sake of simplicity, we assume, unlike McCloskey (2002), that in wh-interrogative clauses in Irish, the wh-phrase itself rather than the corresponding phonetically null pronoun, moves to CP SPEC, as in (5a), or is base-generated there, as in (5b).

(5) a. $[_{CP}$ Cad é$_1$ $[_{C'}$ a $[_{IP}$ cheannaigh Seán t_1]]]?
          what   aL   bought   John
          'What did John buy?'

    b. $[_{CP}$ Cad é$_1$ $[_{C'}$ ar $[_{IP}$ cheannaigh Seán é$_1$]]]?
          what   aN   bought   John it
          'What did John buy?'

The organization of this paper is as follows. Section 2 reviews properties of the wh-interrogative construction in Irish as background to subsequent sections. Section 3 provides relevant examples with the genitive case in Irish. Based on the properties of the genitive case in Irish, Section 4 discusses what they suggest for the theory of (Irish) syntax. To be specific, it will be claimed that a morphological case mismatch in a given A'-chain does not affect the full interpretation of the chain at LF. Finally, Section 5 concludes this paper.

2.   Background

Let us start by briefly summarizing properties of the wh-interrogative construction in Irish. (See McCloskey (1979, 1990) and Maki and Ó Baoill (2011), among others, for discussion of operator constructions in Irish.) Irish has three types of complementizers: the [−Q] marker, the direct relative marker, and the indirect relative marker. The properties of the three COMPs are summarized in (6).

(6)   Complementizers in Irish[2]

	types of COMPs	non-past form	past form	symbol
a.	the [−Q] marker	*go*	*go/gur*	that
b.	the direct relative marker	*a*	*a*	aL
c.	the indirect relative marker	*a*	*a/ar*	aN

Let us illustrate the properties of the COMPs by relevant examples. (7) is a declarative sentence, and the embedded clause is headed by the [−Q] COMP *gur* 'that.' On the other hand, when the sentence involves wh-interrogative clause formation, as in (8), the embedded COMP must change to the direct relative marker *aL*, and at the same time, another COMP *aL* must be inserted right after the wh-phrase. In this paper, for expository purposes only, we represent A′-chains using the symbols *aL/aN* rather than the wh-phrase itself, as in (aL, *t*) or (aN, RP), where *RP* stands for a resumptive pronoun.

(7)   Creideann Seán gur cheannaigh Máire an carr.
      believe   John that bought   Mary the car
      'John believes that Mary bought the car.'

(8)   Cad é a   chreideann tú   a   cheannaigh Seán *t*?
      what aL believe   you aL bought   John
      'What do you believe that John bought?'   (movement) (aL, aL, *t*)

There is another way to form a wh-interrogative clause. Observe the ex-

---

[2] The complementizer forms used with irregular verbs in the past tense in Irish, namely, the [−Q] marker and indirect relative marker *aN* do not follow the regular usage found with all other verbs. Hence, the regular complementizer forms *gur* 'that' and the indirect relative form *ar* are replaced by *go* 'that' and *a* 'aN,' respectively when used with the following irregular verbs: *bí* 'to be' >> *go/a raibh*; *déan* 'to do' >> *go/a ndearna*; *faigh* 'to get' >> *go/a bhfuair*; *tabhair* 'to give' >> *go/a dtug*; *tar* 'to come' >> *go/a dtáinig* and *téigh* 'to go' >> *go/a ndeachaigh*.

ample in (9).

> (9)   Cad é a   gcreideann tú   gur cheannaigh Seán é/*t?
>   what aN believe   you   that bought   John   it
>   'What do you believe that John bought?'   (resumption) (aN, go, RP)

In (9), the topmost COMP of the wh-interrogative clause is an indirect relative marker *a*, the COMP of the embedded clause is a [−Q] COMP, and the embedded clause contains a resumptive pronoun *é* 'it' instead of a gap. Note that (9) is ungrammatical, if the resumptive pronoun is replaced by a trace, which suggests that *aN* must bind a resumptive pronoun.

McCloskey (2002) provides an account of the distribution of the COMPs by proposing (10).

> (10) a.   C whose specifier is filled by Move is realized as *aL*.
>   b.   C whose specifier is filled by Merge is realized as *aN*.
>   c.   C whose specifier is not filled is realized as *go/gur*.

McCloskey assumes that the SPEC of *aL* contains a null operator/null pronoun (henceforth, null operator) as a result of movement, that in the SPEC of *aN*, there is a base-generated operator, and that in the SPEC of *go/gur*, there is no operator. If this is correct, the structure of the wh-interrogative clause construction in Irish looks like a cleft sentence, as shown in (11).

> (11)   (it is) WH_1 [Op_1 aL/aN [$_{IP}$...t_1/RP_1...]] (where *RP* stands for resumptive pronoun)

In this paper, for expository purposes only, we represent the structure of a wh-interrogative clause by putting a wh-phrase, not its operator, in the SPEC of *aL/aN*.

Having established the particular background, we will observe properties of the genitive case in Irish in the next section.

3.   Data

Let us start by clarifying the nature of control predicates in Irish. There are two types of control predicates based on the position of the object of the complement VP. Control verbs such as *d'fhéach* 'to try' prepose the object of the complement VP before the verb, as shown in (12), while as shown above, control verbs such as *thosaigh* 'to start' leave the object of the complement VP in situ, as shown in (13).

(12) a. D'fhéach Seán an   leabhar   a   léamh.
         tried   John the book.ACC to read.VN
         'John tried to read the book.'

     b. *D'fhéach Seán a   léamh   an   leabhar.
         tried   John to read.VN the book.ACC
         'John tried to read the book.'

(13) a. *Thosaigh Seán an   leabhar   a   léamh.
         started   John the book.ACC to read.VN
         'John started to read the book.'

     b. Thosaigh Seán a   léamh   an   leabhar.
         started   John to read.VN the book.ACC
         'John started to read the book.'

Interestingly enough, the object can only be marked accusative for the former type, and it can be marked either genitive or accusative for the latter type, as shown in (14).

(14) a. *D'fhéach Seán an   leabhair   a   léamh.
         tried   John the book.GEN to read.VN
         'John tried to read the book.'

     b. Thosaigh Seán a   léamh   an   leabhair.
         started   John to read.VN the book.GEN
         'John started to read the book.'

Therefore, in the following discussion, we only focus on examples with the structure in (14b).

Let us now consider the wh-interrogatives of the structure with (14b). In Irish, there is no genitive wh-phrase such as *whose* in English, so that *whose X* is only expressed by *X le cé* 'X with who.' With this in mind, consider the following examples. In multiple wh-questions, the wh-phrase whose head is genitive is allowed, as shown in (15b).

(15) a. Cé   a   thosaigh a   léamh   leabhar le   cé?
         who aL   started   to read.VN book   with who
         'Who started to read whose book?'

     b. Cé   a   thosaigh a   léamh   **leabhair** le   cé?
         who aL   started   to read.VN book.GEN   with who
         'Who started to read whose book?'

However, the wh-phrase whose head is genitive is disallowed, irrespective of whether it is moved to CP SPEC, as shown in (16b), or is base-generated there, as shown in (17b).

(16) a. Leabhar le   cé   a   thosaigh Seán a   léamh?
         book   with who aL   started John to   read.VN
         'Whose book did John start to read?'

     b. ***Leabhair** le   cé   **a**   thosaigh Seán a   léamh?
         book.GEN with who aL   started John to   read.VN
         'Whose book did John start to read?'

(17) a. Leabhar le   cé   ar   thosaigh Seán á   léamh?
         book   with who aN   started John to.its read.VN
         'Whose book did John start to read?'

     b. ***Leabhair** le   cé   **ar** thosaigh Seán á   léamh?
         book.GEN with who aN   started John to.its read.VN
         'Whose book did John start to read?'

4. Discussion

Let us now consider what the observed facts might suggest. The initial generalization on the elements in CP SPEC in Irish seems to be (18).

(18) *Generalization on the Elements in CP SPEC in Irish (First Approximation)*
      No phrase with genitive Case can be adjoined to C′.

However, a close look at the wh-phrases in CP SPEC in Irish suggests that the generalization is (19).

(19) *Generalization on the Elements in CP SPEC in Irish (Second Approximation)*
      No phrase with a particular Case (= a non-default Case) can be adjoined to C′.

The default Case seems to be accusative in Irish, as the following data suggest. Consider first the examples in (20).

(20) a. Is   cuimhin le   Máire gur léigh Seán/sé/*é   an leabhar seo.
         COP memory with Mary that read John/he/him the book   this
         'Mary remembers that John/he read this book.'   (finite clause)

   b. Is   cuimhin le   Máire Seán/*sé/é   an   leabhar seo a
       COP memory with   Mary John/he/him the book   this to
       léamh.
       read.VN
       'Mary remembers that John/he read this book.'   (infinitival clause)

Predicates such as *is cuimhin le* 'COP memory with = remember' in Irish allow two types of complement clauses: finite and infinitival. In infinitival clauses, the subject appears in the accusative Case form as *é* 'him,' as shown in (20b). This suggests that the default Case in Irish is accusative.

    With this in mind, consider the examples in (21).

  (21) a. Cad é atá   *t* ar an bhalla?
          what aL+is   on the wall
          'What is on the wall?'
      b. Cad é a   léigh Seán *t*?
          what aL read John
          'What did John read?'

(21a) involves subject wh-extraction, and (21b) involves object wh-extraction. In Irish, a thing-asking wh-phrase consists of the wh-phrase *cad* 'what' and the resumptive pronoun *é* 'it,' which literally means 'what it.' The exact structure of the wh-phrase is not so clear. However, it is worth noticing that in subject wh-extraction, the resumptive pronoun *é* 'it' cannot be replaced by *sé* 'it.NOM,' as shown in (22). Note that *sé* 'it.NOM' appears in the subject position of a tensed clause, as shown in (23).

  (22) *Cad sé   atá   *t* ar an bhalla?
         what it.NOM aL+is   on the wall
         'What is on the wall?'

  (23) Tá sé/*é   aineolach faoin tsaol.
         be he/him ignorant   about the.world
         'He is ignorant of the world.'

This indicates that the subject wh-phrase in CP SPEC has a default Case, which is accusative.

    Furthermore, there is no subject/object distinction for the wh-phrase *cé* 'who' in Irish, unlike German, as shown in (24) and (25).

(24) a. Cé   a   chonaic *t* Seán?
         who   aL   saw   John
         'Who saw John?'

   b.   Cé   a   chonaic Seán *t*?
         who   aL   saw   John
         'Who did John see?'

(25) a. Wer   hat   Johann gesehen?
         who.NOM   has   John   seen
         'Who saw John?'

   b.   Wen   hat   Johann gesehen?
         who.ACC   has   John   seen
         'Who did John see?'

This fact also fits the generalization in (19) that no phrase with a particular Case (= a non-default Case) can be adjoined to C' in Irish.

With (19) in mind, let us now consider what the ungrammaticality of (16b), reproduced as (26), suggests.

(26) ***Leabhair** le   cé   **a**   thosaigh Seán a   léamh?
       book.GEN   with   who   aL   started   John to read.VN
       'Whose book did John start to read?'   (=(16b))

Under the Case checking analysis (Chomsky (1995: Ch. 3)), the Case that an NP bears is checked off at LF. For expository purposes, let us assume, following Kayne (1984), Ura (1993) and Bošković (1997), among others, that a wh-phrase has its Case checked in an A'-position in the course of the derivation. Then, the genitive Case feature is checked off in the SPEC of *a* 'to' in (26). Then, the wh-phrase moves to CP SPEC, creating an A'-chain shown in (27), where the genitive Case feature has already been checked off, as indicated by (genitive).

(27) (leabhair le cé(genitive), leabhair le cé(genitive))

(27) poses an interesting question, because the head of the chain, which is in CP SPEC, does not have the genitive Case feature, so that the wh-phrase in (26) should be licit in CP SPEC under the generalization in (19).

Therefore, the ungrammaticality of (26) suggests that it is necessary to distinguish between abstract Case and morphological case in the generalization in (19), which is then revised as (28).

(28)   *Generalization on the Elements in CP SPEC in Irish (Final)*
No phrase with a particular morphological case (= a non-default morphological case) can be adjoined to C′.

If (28) is correct, it suggests that in Irish, morphological case plays a crucial role in determination of the grammaticality of the sentences.

With (28) in mind, let us then consider what the grammaticality of (17a), reproduced as (29), suggests.

(29)   Leabhar le   cé   ar   thosaigh Seán á   léamh?
        book   with who aN started John to.its read.VN
        'Whose book did John start to read?'   (=(17a))

(29) uses the complementizer *aN*, which indicates that the wh-phrase is not moved to CP SPEC, but is merged there. Then, the A′-chain has the form in (30).

(30)   (**Op**(default case/Case),
        resumptive pronoun(genitive case/Case evidenced by *á* 'to.its'))

Let us assume that default Case is not checked by anything, and is licit as it stands. As for morphological cases, although it is not clear that their case features are checked off, it is clear that their morphological forms remain identical throughout the derivation, as the above argument suggests. In this paper, we assume that their case features are not checked off, just as their morphological forms are not changed, which does not affect the following arguments. On the other hand, we assume that the feature on a non-default Case must be checked off, as we have assumed. Then, in (30), the genitive Case feature is checked off by *a* 'to.' In terms of morphological case, then, the chain in (30) looks like (31).

(31)   (**Op**(default case), **resumptive pronoun**(genitive case))

Since (29) is a perfectly grammatical sentence in Irish, the chain in (31) should be licit. However, (31) poses an interesting question again. In (31), the operator has no particular morphological case, given (28), while the resumptive pronoun (or variable) has a morphological genitive case. Therefore, the morphological case of the operator is not identical to that of the variable, yet the sentence is grammatical. This, we argue, suggests that the identity of the members in an A′-chain is indifferent to (or not affected by) their morphological case marking. In other words, a morphological case mismatch in a given A′-chain does not affect the full interpretation

(Chomsky (1991)) of the chain at LF. Note here that abstract Case is uninterpretable, thus, it must be elided for the full interpretation of the sentence that contains it. Since morphological case forms remain unchanged in the course of the derivation, it must be concluded that the principle of full interpretation ignores morphological case forms themselves (in the given chains).

The claim that a morphological case mismatch in a given A'-chain does not affect the full interpretation of the chain at LF is further confirmed by other examples of the wh-interrogative construction in Irish, as shown in (32).

(32) a.   Cé$_1$ a   shíl   tú   a   bhí t_1 breoite?
         who aL thought you aL was   ill
         'Who did you think was ill?'   (movement) (aL, aL, t)

   b.   Cé$_1$ ar   shíl   tú   go   raibh   **sé**$_1$ breoite?
         who aN thought you that was   he   ill
         'Who did you think was ill?'   (resumption) (aN, go, RP)

(32a) involves long distance subject wh-extraction, and (32b) makes use of the resumption strategy in the same structure. In (32a), the nominative Case feature is checked off in the embedded clause, and then, the wh-phrase moves to CP SPEC of the matrix clause by way of CP SPEC of the embedded clause, creating an A'-chain shown in (33), where the nominative Case feature has already been checked off, as indicated by (nominative).

(33)   (cé(nominative), cé(nominative), cé(nominative))

This A'-chain is licit, because it does not contain the Case feature, which is uninterpretable.

As for (32b), which does not involve overt wh-movement, the A'-chain in terms of morphological case should look like (34), given (28). (Note that we assume that the abstract nominative Case on the resumptive pronoun in the subject position of the embedded clause has been checked off.)

(34)   (**Op**(default case), **resumptive pronoun**(nominative case))

In (34), the operator has no particular morphological case, given (28), while the resumptive pronoun (or variable) has a morphological nominative case. Therefore, the morphological case of the operator is not identical to that of the variable, yet the sentence is grammatical, just like the example in (29). Therefore, this is another piece of evidence for the claim that a morphological case mismatch in a given A'-chain does not affect the full interpretation (Chomsky (1991)) of the chain at LF.

Let us then consider whether the proposed analysis provides correct predictions for the rest of the core examples in (16a) and (17b), reproduced as (35) and (36), respectively.

(35)   Leabhar le   cé   a   thosaigh Seán a   léamh?
       book   with who aL started   John to read.VN
       'Whose book did John start to read?'   (=(16a))

(36)   *Leabhair le   cé   **ar** thosaigh Seán á   léamh?
       book.GEN with who aN started   John to.its read.VN
       'Whose book did John start to read?'   (=(17b))

(35) involves object wh-extraction. In (35), the accusative Case feature of the wh-phrase *leabhar le cé* 'book with who' is checked off in the complement clause in the course of the derivation. Furthermore, the wh-phrase has a morphologically default case, so that it should be licit in CP SPEC under the generalization in (28). Therefore, (35) is correctly predicted to be grammatical under our analysis.

Let us turn to (36). (36) makes use of the resumption strategy, and the wh-phrase *leabhair le cé* 'book.GEN with who' is base-generated in CP SPEC of the matrix clause. Given (28), the wh-phrase, morphologically marked genitive, should be illicit under the generalization in (28). Therefore, (36) is correctly predicted to be ungrammatical under our analysis.

5. Conclusion

This paper investigated the distribution of genitive case in Irish, and found the generalization on the elements in CP SPEC in Irish shown in (28). With this generalization, we argued that a morphological case mismatch in a given A′-chain does not affect the full interpretation of the chain at LF.

The question remains, however, as to what the generalization in (28) follows from. As pointed out by the German examples in (25), and as further shown by additional German examples in (37) and Greek examples in (38), generalization (28) is not universal.[3]

---

[3] Languages such as French and Italian behave like Irish in the sense that the form of the wh-phrase in CP SPEC remains constant. As an illustration, French examples are provided in (i).

(37) a. Wem   hat   Johann das Buch   gegeben?
         who.DAT   has   John   the book   given
         'To whom did John give the book?'

   b.   Wessen   gedenkt Johann?
         who.GEN   think   John
         'Of whom does John think?'   (German)

(38) a. Poios   eide ton   Gianni?
         who.NOM   saw   the.ACC   John?
         'Who saw John?'

   b.   Poion   eide o   Giannis?
         who.ACC   saw   the.NOM   John
         'Who did John see?'

   c.   Se poion   edose   o   Giannis to   vivlio?
         to who.ACC   gave   the.NOM   John   the.ACC   book
         'To whom did John give the book?'

   d.   Poion   skeftetai o   Giannis?
         who.ACC   think   the.NOM   John
         'Of whom does John think?'   (Greek)

We leave for future research the question as to what principle lies behind the typological differences with respect to generalization (28).

(i) a. Qui est-ce qui a   vu   Jean?
        who   that has   seen John
        'Who saw John?'

   b.   Qui est-ce que Jean a   vu?
        who   that John has   seen
        'Who did John see?'

   c.   A qui   est-ce que Jean a   donné le   livre?
        to who   that John has   given the book
        'To whom did John give the book?'

   d.   A qui   est-ce que Jean pense?
        to who   that John think
        'Of whom does John think?'   (French)

Chapter 5

Scope Ambiguity in WH/Quantifier Interactions in Modern Irish[*]

Hideki Maki and Dónall P. Ó Baoill

Gifu University and *Queen's University Belfast* (Prof. Emeritus)

In this paper, we will investigate scope ambiguity in wh/quantifier interactions in Irish, in comparison with those in English and Japanese, and point out some differences between wh/quantifier interactions in Irish and those in English and Japanese: (i) that the distributive reading of the universal quantifier in Irish that corresponds to *every* in English is allowed when it is in the object position, and the wh-phrase originates from the subject position, and (ii) that the distributive reading of the universal quantifier in Irish is also allowed even when it is in an island, where it is in the subject position, and the wh-phrase originates from the object position. We will claim that these differences are attributed to the fact that the subject position in Irish is within VP, and Irish has resumptive pronouns for wh-phrases, unlike English or Japanese. At the same time, we will show that Japanese, a wh-in-situ language, and Irish share some properties in wh/quantifier interactions, and demonstrate that the analysis of the wh/quantifier interactions in Irish straightforwardly applies to those in Japanese.

Keywords: *English, Irish, Japanese, quantifiers, scope*

1. Introduction

This paper investigates scope ambiguity in wh/quantifier interactions in modern Ulster Irish (Irish, hereafter), in comparison with those in English and Japanese. To our knowledge, no research has been done on wh/quantifier interactions in Irish in the literature. Irish is a verb initial language, and has resumptive pronouns for wh-phrases. In these respects, it is different from English and Japanese. In this paper, we will show some differences between wh/quantifier interactions in Irish and those in English and Japanese, and attribute them to the fact that Irish is a verb initial language,

* We are indebted to Jessica Dunton, Megumi Hasebe, Fumikazu Niinuma, Máire Ó Baoill, Yukiko Ueda, and especially, Anna Bondaruk, the editor of this volume, for their useful comments on an earlier version of this paper. All errors are our own.

59

and has resumptive pronouns for wh-phrases. To be precise, we will show
(i) that the distributive reading of the universal quantifier in Irish that corresponds to *every* in English is allowed when it is in the object position, and
the wh-phrase originates from the subject position, and (ii) that the distributive reading of the universal quantifier in Irish is also allowed even when
it is in an island, in which it is in the subject position, and the wh-phrase
originates from the object position.

The organization of this paper is as follows. Section 2 provides basic
facts about wh/quantifier interactions in English as background to subsequent sections. Section 3 provides relevant examples with wh/quantifier
interactions in Irish. Based on the two remarkable facts in Irish, Section 4
considers why Irish has these properties in terms of wh/quantifier interactions. Section 5 compares Irish facts with the facts in Japanese, and shows
that the analysis of the wh/quantifier interactions in Irish straightforwardly
applies to those in Japanese. Finally, Section 6 concludes the paper.

2.   Background

Let us start by briefly reviewing basic facts about wh/quantifier interactions in English.[1] May (1985) found a contrast in the scope interactions between subject wh-phrase fronting and object wh-phrase fronting, as shown in
(1a, b) and (2a, b).

(1) a.   Who$_1$ t_1 bought everything for Max?
    b.   Who$_1$ t_1 saw everyone at the rally?

(2) a.   What$_1$ did everyone buy t_1 for Max?
    b.   Who$_1$ did everyone see t_1 at the rally?

---

[1] In this paper, we focus on wh/quantifier interactions in Irish as well as English and
Japanese, and do not go into existential quantifier/universal quantifier interactions in these
languages. One of the reasons for this is the fact that in some cases in English, the
similar configurations do not produce the same interpretations. According to Lasnik and
Saito (1992: 155–156), in (i), the universal quantifier *everyone* has a distributive reading. However, in (ii), it does not.

(i)   Someone loves everyone.

(ii) Some woman loves everyone.

In (i) and (ii), *everyone* does not c-command *someone/some woman* at the base-structure,
yet the former can take scope over the latter in (i), but not in (ii).

The examples in (1a, b) only allow the interpretation where the subject wh-phrase *who* takes scope over the universal quantifier *everything/everyone*, so that the distributive reading of the universal quantifier is unavailable. In this paper, we represent the scope relations between wh-phrases and quantifiers using the symbol $\alpha > \beta$, which indicates that α takes scope over β. Then, the scope relations in (1a, b) are represented as (3).

(3) a.   wh > every
    b.   *every > wh

On the other hand, the examples in (2a, b), in which the universal quantifier *everyone* is the subject of the sentence, not only allow the interpretation where the wh-phrase takes scope over the universal quantifier *everyone*, but also the interpretation where the universal quantifier takes scope over the wh-phrase, so that the distributive reading of the universal quantifier is possible, as shown in (4).

(4) a.   wh > every
    b.   every > wh

Therefore, (2a, b) are two-way ambiguous, and (2a), for example, can be answered in two ways, as shown in (5).

(5) a.   They as a group bought a pen for Max.
         (They as a group bought one thing for Max. = group reading)
    b.   John bought a pen for Max, Mary bought a pencil for Max, Bill bought a book for Marx, and so on.
         (Each one of them bought a different thing for Max. = distributive reading)

May (1985) also found the same contrast in wh-interrogative clauses that involve long distance wh-movement, as shown in (6) and (7).

(6)   Who do you think *t* saw everyone at the rally?
      (wh > every, *every > wh)

(7)   Who do you think everyone saw *t* at the rally?
      (wh > every, every > wh)

(6) involves long distance extraction of the subject wh-phrase, and (7) of the object wh-phrase. Only (7) allows the distributive reading.

      Lasnik and Saito (1992: 155) notice that the relative scope of wh-phrases and quantifiers seems to be determined by their D-Structure position.

The one that asymmetrically c-commands the other at D-Structure takes wide scope at LF. Then, they propose the Rigidity Condition in (8), and define Quantifier Raising (QR), as in (9).

(8)   Rigidity Condition
       Suppose that Q_1 and Q_2 are operators (quantified NP or WH).
       Then, Q_1 cannot take wide scope over Q_2 if t_2 c-commands t_1.

(9)   QR adjoins a quantified NP to a minimal node to satisfy (8).

Note here that along the lines proposed in Katz and Postal (1964), Kuroda (1968) and Chomsky (1970), Lasnik and Saito (1992), Sloan (1991) and Murasugi and Saito (1993) suggest the possibility that the wh-phrases involved in wh/quantifier interactions such as those in (6) and (7), are decomposed into the wh part and the indefinite (or existential) part. In other words, the wh/quantifier interactions under consideration are interactions between the existential quantifier *some* in the wh-phrase made up of wh and *some* (wh-*some*), and the universal quantifier *every* in the quantified NP. We will assume this in the following discussion, adhering to the terminology wh/quantifier interactions.

With (8) and (9), let us reconsider (1a), reproduced as (10), and (2a), reproduced as (11).

(10)   Who$_1$ t_1 bought everything for Max?   (=(1a))

(11)   What$_1$ did everyone buy t_1 for Max?   (=(2a))

Given (9), their LF representations are (12) and (13), respectively.

(12)   [$_{CP}$ who$_1$ [$_{IP}$ t_1 [$_{VP}$ everything$_2$ [$_{VP}$ bought t_2 for Max]]]]

(13)   [$_{CP}$ what$_1$ [$_{IP}$ everyone$_2$ [$_{IP}$ t_2 bought t_1 for Max]]]

In (12), *everything* adjoins to VP, and since t_1 c-commands t_2, *everything* cannot take scope over the subject wh-phrase *who*. In (13), *everyone* adjoins to IP, and since t_2 c-commands t_1, *everyone* can take scope over the object wh-phrase *what*. Lasnik and Saito (1992: 155) state that this is in effect the rigidity condition on quantifier scope proposed by Huang (1982) and later by Hoji (1985) for Japanese.

Longobardi (1987) and Cinque (1990) point out that the distributive reading of *everyone* in (7) disappears when the wh-phrase is extracted out of an island.[2] (See Chomsky (1964) for the origin of "wh-island," and Ross (1967) for the other islands, such as a complex NP.) Consider (7), reproduced as (14), and (15).

(14)   Who$_1$ do you think everyone saw t_1 at the rally?   (=(7))
         (every > wh)

(15) ??Who$_1$ do you wonder whether everyone saw t_1 at the rally?
         (*every > wh)

(15) involves extraction of a wh-phrase across a wh-island. Therefore, it has the status of a violation of the Subjacency Condition. However, the point is that while the universal quantifier *everyone* has the distributive reading in (14), such a reading is impossible in (15).

In the analysis of non-D-linked wh-phrases such as *what the hell*, Lasnik and Saito (1992) propose that the wh-phrase first adjoins to the VP in the embedded clause, where it marks a focus position, and then, moves to CP SPEC of the matrix clause. Consider the examples in (16)–(18).

(16)   What the hell$_1$ do you think John [$_{VP}$ t_1' [$_{VP}$ wrote t_1]]?

(17)   *What the hell$_1$ do you wonder who [$_{VP}$ t_1' [$_{VP}$ wrote t_1]]?

(18) ??What$_1$ do you wonder who [$_{VP}$ wrote t_1]?

(16) is perfect, and (17) is totally ungrammatical. Note that (17) is worse than (18), in spite of the fact that both involve extraction out of a wh-clause. Under Lasnik and Saito's (1992) definition of antecedent-government of the Empty Category Principle (ECP), the intermediate trace t_1' adjoined to the VP in the embedded clause is antecedent-governed in (16), but not in (17), because of a barrier due to the intervening wh-phrase in CP SPEC of the embedded clause.[3]

---

[2] Longobardi (1987) is available in Giorgi and Longobardi (1991: Ch. 2), where the original title of Longobardi (1987) is slightly changed.

[3] The Minimalist Program proposed in Chomsky (1995) does not assume the ECP, hence, antecedent-government. Rather, the antecedent-government effect is attributed to (i) Relativized Minimality (Rizzi (1990))/the Attract-F Hypothesis (Chomsky (1995)) for the wh-island effect and (ii) the Minimal Link Condition (MLC) and the ban against adjunction to adjuncts for Ross' (1967) island effects. See Takahashi (1994) for an analysis of Ross' (1967) island effects in terms of the MLC (or Shortest Movement Condition in his terms) and the ban against adjunction to adjuncts. In this paper, we essentially follow Takahashi's (1994) analysis of Ross' island effects. However, for the sake of clarity, we occasionally depend on Lasnik and Saito's (1992) account of the island effects in terms of antecedent-government.

If we assume that a wh-phrase marks a scope position when it interacts with another quantifier, just as a non-D-linked wh-phrase marks a focus position in the course of the derivation, the relevant LF structures of (14) and (15) will look like (19) and (20), respectively.

(19)   [$_{CP}$ Who$_1$ do you think [$_{IP}$ everyone [$_{VP}$ t_1' [$_{VP}$ saw t_1 at the rally]]]]?

(20) ??[$_{CP}$ Who$_1$ do you wonder [$_{CP}$ whether [$_{IP}$ everyone [$_{VP}$ t_1' [$_{VP}$ saw t_1 at the rally]]]]]?

Under Lasnik and Saito's (1992) definition of antecedent-government, the intermediate trace t_1' adjoined to the VP in the embedded clause is antecedent-governed in (19), but not in (20), because of a barrier due to the intervening wh-phrase in CP SPEC of the embedded clause. Following Murasugi and Saito (1993), we assume that the distributive reading of the quantifier *everyone* over another quantifier (*who*, in this case) is impossible when the chain of the other quantifier is not properly formed. In (20), the trace t_1' in the VP-adjoined position in the embedded clause is not properly governed. Therefore, in this configuration, the distributive reading of *everyone* is unavailable.

3.   Irish Data

With the background established in the above section, let us consider Irish data. Before presenting wh/quantifier interaction data, we will first describe basic syntactic properties of Irish in Section 3.1, and then, provide the wh/quantifier data in Section 3.2.

3.1.   Basic Syntactic Properties of Irish

First, Irish is a VSO language. Therefore, in (21a), the subject is *Seán* 'John,' and in (21b), it is *Máire* 'Mary.'

(21) a.   Chonaic Seán Máire.
          saw   John Mary
          'John saw Mary.'
     b.   Chonaic Máire Seán.
          saw   Mary John
          'Mary saw John.'

Second, wh-interrogatives in Irish show complementizer alternations. Irish has three types of complementizers: the [−Q] marker, the direct relative marker, and the indirect relative marker. The properties of the three COMPs are summarized in (22).

(22)   Complementizers in Irish[4]

	types of COMPs	non-past form	past form	symbol
a.	the [−Q] marker	*go*	*go/gur*	that
b.	the direct relative marker	*a*	*a*	aL
c.	the indirect relative marker	*a*	*a/ar*	aN

The properties of the COMPs are illustrated below. (23) is a declarative sentence, and the embedded clause is headed by the [−Q] COMP *gur* 'that.' On the other hand, when the sentence involves wh-interrogative clause formation, as in (24), the embedded COMP must change to the direct relative marker *aL*, and at the same time, another COMP *aL* must be inserted right after the wh-phrase. In this paper, for expository purposes only, we represent A'-chains using the symbols *aL/aN* rather than the wh-phrase itself, as in (aL, *t*) or (aN, RP), where *RP* stands for a resumptive pronoun.

(23)   Creideann Seán gur cheannaigh Máire an carr.
       believe   John that bought   Mary the car
       'John believes that Mary bought the car.'

(24)   Cad é$_1$ a   chreideann tú   a   cheannaigh Seán *t*$_1$?
       what aL believe   you aL bought   John
       'What$_1$ do you believe that John bought *t*$_1$?'   (movement) (aL, aL, *t*)

There is another way to form a wh-interrogative clause in Irish. Observe the example in (25).

(25)   Cad é$_1$ a   gcreideann tú   gur cheannaigh Seán é$_1$/*t_1$?
       what aN believe   you that bought   John it
       'What$_1$ do you believe that John bought it$_1$/t_1?'

                                                    (resumption) (aN, that, RP)

In (25), the topmost COMP of the wh-interrogative clause is an indirect

---

[4] The complementizer forms used with irregular verbs in the past tense in Irish, namely, the [−Q] marker and indirect relative marker *aN* do not follow the regular usage found with all other verbs. Hence, the regular complementizer forms *gur* 'that' and the indirect relative form *ar* are replaced by *go* 'that' and *a* 'aN,' respectively when used with the following irregular verbs: *bí* 'to be' >> *go/a raibh*; *déan* 'to do' >> *go/a ndearna*; *faigh* 'to get' >> *go/a bhfuair*; *tabhair* 'to give' >> *go/a dtug*; *tar* 'to come' >> *go/a dtáinig* and *téigh* 'to go' >> *go/a ndeachaigh*.

relative marker *aN*, the COMP of the embedded clause is a [−Q] COMP, and the embedded clause contains a resumptive pronoun *é* 'it' instead of a gap. Note that (25) is ungrammatical, if the resumptive pronoun is replaced by a trace, which suggests that *aN* must bind a resumptive pronoun.

McCloskey (2002) provides an account of the distribution of the COMPs by proposing (26).

(26) a. C whose specifier is filled by Move is realized as *aL*.
     b. C whose specifier is filled by Merge is realized as *aN*.
     c. C whose specifier is not filled is realized as *go/gur*.

McCloskey assumes that the SPEC of *aL* contains a null operator/null pronoun (henceforth, null operator) as a result of movement, that in the SPEC of *aN*, there is a base-generated operator, and that in the SPEC of *go/gur*, there is no operator. If this is correct, the structure of the wh-interrogative clause construction in Irish looks like a cleft sentence, as shown in (27).

(27) (it is) WH_1 [Op_1 aL/aN [IP...t_1/RP_1...]]

In this paper, for expository purposes only, we represent the structure of a wh-interrogative clause by putting a wh-phrase, not its operator, in the SPEC of *aL/aN*.

3.2. WH/Quantifier Interactions

Let us now consider wh/quantifier interaction data in Irish. Let us start with the example in (28), in which the wh-phrase originates from the object position.

(28) $Cé_1$ a   chonaic achan duine t_1 ag an railí?
      who   aL   saw   every person   at the rally
      'Who_1 did everyone see at the rally t_1?'
      (every > wh, wh > every)

(28) allows the distributive reading of *achan duine* 'everyone,' just like its English counterpart.

Let us then consider the example in (29), in which the wh-phrase originates from the subject position. Note that the surface strings in (28) and (29) are identical, but they have two interpretations based on the original position of the wh-phrase.

(29)   Cé₁   a   chonaic t₁ achan duine   ag an railí?
       who aL saw   every person at the rally
       'Who₁ t₁ saw everyone at the rally?'
       (every > wh, wh > every)

Interestingly enough, contrary to its English counterpart, (29) allows the distributive reading of *achan duine* 'everyone.'

Let us then consider the examples with long distance wh-movement. Consider the example in (30) first, where the object of the embedded clause undergoes wh-movement.

(30)   Cé₁   a   shíleann tú   a   chonaic achan duine t₁   ag an   railí?
       who aL think   you aL saw   every person   at the rally
       'Who₁ do you think everyone saw t₁ at the rally?'
       (every > wh, wh > every)

(30) allows the distributive reading of *achan duine* 'everyone,' just like its English counterpart.

Let us then consider the example in (31), where the subject of the embedded clause undergoes wh-movement.

(31)   Cé₁   a   shíleann tú   a   chonaic t₁ achan duine   ag an   railí?
       who aL think   you aL saw   every person at the rally
       'Who₁ do you think t₁ saw everyone at the rally?'
       (every > wh, wh > every)

Again, contrary to its English counterpart, (31) allows the distributive reading of *achan duine* 'everyone.'

Let us then turn to the examples which contain the universal quantifier *achan duine* 'everyone' in islands. Before presenting the relevant data with wh/quantifier interactions, it is worthwhile showing that in Irish, island violations can be remedied by resumptive pronouns, as pointed out by McCloskey (1979), among others. To see this, consider the examples in (32)–(35), which involve relative clause formation.

(32)   *Sin bean₁   nach   bhfuil fhios agam an bpósfadh   duine
        that woman aL+NEG I.know   if would.marry person
        ar bith t₁.
        any
        'That's a woman₁ that I don't know if anyone would marry t₁.'

(33) *Sin teanga$_1$ a bheadh   meas   agam ar dhuine ar bith atá
 that language aL would.be respect at.me on person any   aL+is
 ábalta t_1 a labhairt.
 able   to speak
 'That's a language$_1$ that I would respect anyone who could speak t_1.'

(34) Sin bean$_1$ nach   bhfuil fhios agam an bpósfadh   duine
 that woman aN+NEG I.know   if would.marry person
 ar bith í$_1$.
 any   her
 'That's a woman$_1$ that I don't know if anyone would marry her$_1$.'

(35) Sin teanga$_1$ a mbeadh meas   agam ar dhuine ar bith atá
 that language aN would.be respect at.me on person any   aL+is
 ábalta í$_1$ a labhairt.
 able   it to speak
 'That's a language$_1$ that I would respect anyone who could speak it$_1$.'
 ((34) and (35) are cited from McCloskey (1979) with slight editing.)

(32) and (33) involve extraction of a wh-phrase out of a wh-island and a
complex NP island, respectively, and these examples are ungrammatical.
However, putting a resumptive pronoun in the position of the trace marked *t*
in each example makes the sentence perfectly grammatical, as shown in (34)
and (35).

The same is true to the examples that involve wh-interrogative clause
formation. Consider the examples in (36)–(39).

(36) *Cén   sagart$_1$ a d'fhiafraigh Seán díot   an bhfaca Máire t_1
 which priest aL asked   John of.you if saw   Mary
 inné?
 yesterday
 'Which priest$_1$ did John ask you if Mary saw t_1 yesterday?'

(37) *Cén   teanga$_1$ a mbeadh meas   agat ar dhuine ar bith
 which language aN would.be respect at.you on person any
 atá   ábalta t_1 a labhairt?
 aL+is able   to speak
 'Which language$_1$ would you respect anyone who could speak t_1?'

(38)   Cén   sagart₁ ar   fhiafraigh Seán díot   an bhfaca Máire
       which priest   aN   asked   John of.you if saw   Mary
       inné   é₁?
       yesterday him
       'Which priest₁ did John ask you if Mary saw him₁ yesterday?'

(39)   Cén   teanga₁   a   mbeadh   meas   agat   ar   dhuine ar bith
       which language aN   would.be respect at.you on   person any
       atá   ábalta í₁ a   labhairt?
       aL+is able   it to   speak
       'Which language₁ would you respect anyone who could speak it₁?'

(36) and (37) involve extraction of a wh-phrase out of a wh-island and
a complex NP island, respectively, and these examples are ungrammatical. However, putting a resumptive pronoun in the position of the trace
marked *t* in each example makes the sentence perfectly grammatical, as
shown in (38) and (39).

With this in mind, let us consider the examples which contain the universal quantifier *achan duine* 'everyone' in islands. First, consider the example in (40), which contains *achan duine* 'everyone' in a wh-island.

(40)   Cén   sagart₁ ar   fhiafraigh Seán díot   an bhfaca achan duine
       which priest   aN   asked   John of.you if saw   every person
       inné   é₁?
       yesterday him
       'Which priest₁ did John ask you if everyone saw him₁ yesterday?'
       (every > wh)

(40), in which the universal quantifier *achan duine* 'everyone,' which is in
a wh-island, and c-commands the resumptive pronoun *é₁* 'him,' which corresponds to the wh-phrase *cén sagart₁* 'which priest,' allows the distributive
reading of *achan duine* 'everyone.'

Note here that when (40) involves overt movement of the object wh-
phrase in the embedded clause to the matrix CP SPEC, the sentence becomes ungrammatical, and the distributive reading of *achan duine* 'everyone'
becomes impossible, as shown in (41).

(41)   *Cén   sagart₁ a   d'fhiafraigh Seán díot   an bhfaca achan
        which priest   aL   asked   John of.you if saw   every
        duine t₁ inné?
        person   yesterday

'Which priest₁ did John ask you if everyone saw t_1 yesterday?'
(*every > wh)

Second, consider the example in (42), which contains *achan duine* 'every-one' in a complex NP island.

(42) Cén   teanga₁   a   mbeadh   meas   agat   ar dhuine ar bith a
      which language aN would.be respect at.you on person any   aL
      bheadh   ag súil   go bhféadfadh   achan duine   í₁ a labhairt?
      be.COND expecting that could.COND every person it to speak
      'Which language₁ would you respect anyone who hopes that every-one could speak it₁?'
      (every > wh)

(42), in which the universal quantifier *achan duine* 'everyone,' which is in a complex NP island, and c-commands the resumptive pronoun $é_1$ 'it,' which corresponds to the wh-phrase *cén teanga₁* 'which language,' allows the distributive reading of *achan duine* 'everyone.'

Note here that when (42) involves overt movement of the object wh-phrase in the complex NP to the matrix CP SPEC, the sentence becomes un-grammatical, and the distributive reading of *achan duine* 'everyone' becomes impossible, as shown in (43).

(43) *Cén   teanga₁   a   bheadh   meas   agat   ar dhuine ar bith a
      which language aL would.be respect at.you on person any   aL
      bheadh   ag súil   go bhféadfadh   achan duine   í₁ a labhairt?
      be.COND expecting that could.COND every person it to speak
      'Which language₁ would you respect anyone who hopes that every-one could speak it₁?'
      (*every > wh)

To sum up, Irish is different from English in two respects. First, in the con-figuration in which the wh-phrase c-commands the universal quantifier *achan duine* 'everyone' in the same clause at the base-structure, the distributive reading of the universal quantifier is allowed in Irish. Second, in the config-uration in which the universal quantifier *achan duine* 'everyone' c-commands the resumptive pronoun that corresponds to the wh-phrase in the matrix CP SPEC, the distributive reading of the universal quantifier is allowed in Irish, even though the wh-phrase is separated from the resumptive pronoun by a syntactic island.

4.   Analysis

Let us now consider why Irish has the two properties in terms of wh/quantifier interactions pointed out in the above section.

4.1.   *Who Saw Everyone?*

Let us start by considering the first case, that is, why the distributive reading of the universal quantifier is allowed in Irish in the configuration in which the wh-phrase c-commands the universal quantifier *achan duine* 'everyone' in the same clause at the base-structure.

Before examining this, let us point out another difference between Irish and English, which arises from the superiority effect. Unlike in English, the superiority effect is not observed in Irish. Consider the examples in (44) and (45).

(44) a.   Who$_1$ t_1 bought what?
    b.   *What$_1$ did who buy t_1?   (Chomsky (1973))

(45) a.   Cé$_1$ a   cheannaigh t_1 cad é?
        who   aL bought   what
        'Who$_1$ t_1 bought what?'
    b.   Cad é$_1$ a   cheannaigh cé t_1?
        what   aL bought   who
        'What$_1$ did who buy t_1?'   (Maki and Ó Baoill (2011: 7))

(44b) is ungrammatical in English, while (45b) is grammatical in Irish. Chomsky (1973) investigates multiple wh-constructions, and proposes the Superiority Condition in (46).

(46)   Superiority Condition
       No rule can involve X, Y in the structure
       ...X...[$_α$...Z...-WYV...]...
       where the rule applies ambiguously to Z and Y and Z is superior to Y.

The notion superior is stated roughly in (47).

(47)   The category A is superior to the category B if every major category dominating A dominates B as well but not conversely.

The Superiority Condition straightforwardly explains the grammaticality of (44a) and the ungrammaticality of (44b) under the assumption that the underlying structure of (44a, b) is (48), because in the structure prior to wh-movement, every major category dominating *who* (IP and CP) dominates *what*, but every major category dominating the latter (VP, IP, and CP) does not dominate the former.

(48)   [$_{CP}$ C [$_{IP}$ who [$_{VP}$ bought what]]]]

Now, slightly simplifying Maki and Ó Baoill's (2011) Irish clause structure, shown in (49), let us consider why the superiority effect does not arise in Irish. Remember that Irish is a verb-initial language.

(49)   [$_{CP}$ C [$_{IP}$ V+I [$_{VP}$ WH$_{SBJ}$ t_V WH$_{OBJ}$]]]]

In (49), subject and object are within the same VP. Then, in the structure prior to wh-movement, every major category dominating WH$_{SBJ}$ (VP, IP and CP) dominates WH$_{OBJ}$, and every major category dominating the latter (VP, IP, and CP) also dominates the former. Therefore, either one of them can be moved to CP SPEC without running afoul of the Superiority Condition in (46). See Maki and Ó Baoill (2011) for the exact analysis of the lack of the superiority effect in Irish.

Suppose then that the structure in (49) is the basic underlying structure in Irish. Let us then reconsider the example in (29), reproduced as (50).

(50)   Cé$_1$ a   chonaic t_1 achan duine   ag an   ralí?
        who   aL   saw   every person at the   rally
        'Who$_1$ t_1 saw everyone at the rally?'   (=(29))
        (every > wh)

The relevant part of the underlying structure of (50) is (51).

(51)   [$_{CP}$ C [$_{IP}$ V+I [$_{VP}$ who t_V everyone]]]]

If we literally adopt Lasnik and Saito's (1992) Rigidity Condition in (8), reproduced as (52),

(52)   Rigidity Condition
        Suppose that Q$_1$ and Q$_2$ are operators (quantified NP or WH).
        Then, Q$_1$ cannot take wide scope over Q$_2$ if t_2 c-commands t_1.
                                                                      (=(8))

it will be predicted that (50) does not allow the distributive reading of *achan duine* 'everyone.' This is because *who* (or its trace) c-commands *everyone* (or its trace) due to the V'-node in the refined structure of (51) shown in (53).

(53) $[_{CP}$ C $[_{IP}$ V+I $[_{VP}$ who $[_{V'}$ t_V everyone]]]]

However, the contrast in the superiority effect between English and Irish and the contrast in the availability of the distributive reading of the universal quantifier between English and Irish do not seem accidental. One of the salient properties of Irish is that the basic structure is verb-initial so that subject and object are not separated by the verb, and probably because of this, subject and object behave in the same fashion with respect to the superiority effect and the wh/quantifier interaction. Since Lasnik and Saito's (1992) Rigidity Condition covers important data in English, we propose to revise it in such a way to cover the Irish data as well. The revised Rigidity Condition is shown in (54).

(54)   Revised Rigidity Condition
        Suppose that Q_1 and Q_2 are operators (quantified NP or WH). Then, Q_1 cannot take wide scope over Q_2 if (i) t_2 c-commands t_1, and (ii) t_1 cannot m-command t_2.

By adding the condition in (ii) that t_1 cannot m-command t_2 to the Rigidity Condition, the contrast between English and Irish in the availability of the distributive reading of 'everyone' is correctly expected. The English example in (1b) is reproduced as (55), and the Irish example in (50) as (56).

(55)   Who$_1$ t_1 saw everyone at the rally?   (=(1b))
        (*every > wh)

(56)   Cé$_1$ a   chonaic t_1 achan duine   ag an   railí?
        who   aL saw   every person at the rally
        'Who$_1$ t_1 saw everyone at the rally?'   (=(29), (50))
        (every > wh)

The relevant structures of (55) and (56) are (57) and (58), respectively.

(57) $[_{CP}$ who$_2$ C $[_{IP}$ t_{who2} $[_{VP}$ everyone$_1$ $[_{VP}$ saw $[_{V'}$ $t_{everyone1}$]]]]]   (English)

(58) $[_{CP}$ who$_2$ C $[_{IP}$ V+I $[_{VP}$ everyone$_1$ $[_{VP}$ t_{who2} $[_{V'}$ t_V $t_{everyone1}$]]]]]   (Irish)

Let us say that Q_1 = everyone$_1$, and Q_2 = who$_2$ in (57) and (58). Then, in (57), (i) t_2 c-commands t_1, and (ii) t_1 cannot m-command t_2 due to the intervening maximal projection VP. Therefore, Q_1 cannot take scope over Q_2 in (57). On the other hand, in (58), (i) t_2 c-commands t_1, but (ii) t_1 can m-command t_2 because there is no intervening maximal projection between them. Therefore, Q_1 can take scope over Q_2 in (58).

Let us then examine whether the Revised Rigidity Condition can correctly predict the possible interpretation of the English example in (2b), reproduced as (59), and of the Irish counterpart in (28), reproduced as (60).

(59)   Who$_1$ did everyone see t_1 at the rally?   (=(2b))
       (every > wh)

(60)   Cé$_1$ a   chonaic achan duine t_1 ag   an   raili?
       who aL saw   every person   at   the rally
       'Who$_1$ did everyone see at the rally t_1?'   (=(28))
       (every > wh)

Both (59) and (60) allow the distributive reading of the universal quantifier 'everyone.' The relevant structures of (59) and (60) are shown in (61) and (62), respectively.

(61)   [$_{CP}$ who$_2$ C [$_{IP}$ everyone$_1$ [$_{IP}$ $t_{everyone1}$ [$_{VP}$ saw [$_{V'}$ t_{who2}]]]]]   (English)

(62)   [$_{CP}$ who$_2$ C [$_{IP}$ V+I [$_{VP}$ everyone$_1$ [$_{VP}$ $t_{everyone1}$ [$_{V'}$ t_V t_{who2}]]]]]   (Irish)

Let us say that Q$_1$ = everyone$_1$, and Q$_2$ = who$_2$ in (61) and (62). Then, in (61), (i) t_2 does not c-command t_1, and (ii) t_1 m-commands t_2. Therefore, Q$_1$ can take scope over Q$_2$ in (61). Likewise, in (62), (i) t_2 does not c-command t_1, and (ii) t_1 m-commands t_2. Therefore, Q$_1$ can take scope over Q$_2$ in (62).

Thus, the Revised Rigidity Condition correctly accounts for the scope interaction facts both in English and Irish, and the difference in scope interactions between the two languages is attributed to the fact that subject and object are within the same maximal projection (VP) in Irish, unlike in English.

Note that the same account is given to other scope interaction facts in both languages, which involve long distance wh-movement.

4.2.   The Resumption Strategy

Let us then turn to the second case, that is, the fact that the distributive reading of the universal quantifier *achan duine* 'everyone' is allowed in Irish in the configuration in which it c-commands the resumptive pronoun that corresponds to the wh-phrase in the matrix CP SPEC, even though the wh-phrase is separated from the resumptive pronoun by a syntactic island.

In the following discussion, we assume the Revised Rigidity Condition. Furthermore, as already shown in Section 2, we also assume, following Murasugi and Saito (1993), that the distributive reading of the quantifier 'everyone' over WH is impossible when the wh-chain is not properly formed.

With this in mind, let us consider the example in (40), reproduced as (63).

(63)   Cén   sagart$_1$ ar fhiafraigh Seán díot   an bhfaca achan duine
       which priest aN asked   John of.you if saw   every person
       inné   é$_1$?
       yesterday him
       'Which priest$_1$ did John ask you if everyone saw him$_1$ yesterday?'
       (every > wh)   (=(40))

The relevant structure of (63) is shown in (64).

(64)   WH$_1$...[$_{ISLAND}$ everyone RP$_{WH1}$]

Under the assumption that subject and object are within the same VP in Irish, the more precise structure of (64) is (65).

(65)   WH$_1$...[$_{ISLAND}$ [$_{VP}$ everyone [$_{V'}$ RP$_{WH1}$]]]

Note here that the properties of the resumptive pronoun are fundamentally identical to those of the corresponding wh-phrase, except for the fact that it may not contain a wh-feature. Therefore, it should have the existential part of the wh-phrase within it. Suppose then that a resumptive pronoun containing the existential part of a wh-phrase undergoes LF raising. Then, (63) will have the LF representation in (66), where the universal quantifier also undergoes LF raising.

(66)   WH$_1$...[$_{ISLAND}$ [$_{VP}$ everyone$_2$ [$_{VP}$ RP$_{WH1}$ [$_{VP}$ $t_{everyone2}$ [$_{V'}$ t_{RPWH1}]]]]]

The Revised Rigidity Condition predicts that (66) allows the interpretation in which the universal quantifier *everyone* takes scope over the resumptive pronoun, which is fundamentally identical to the wh-phrase, because (i) t_2 c-commands t_1, but (ii) t_1 can m-command t_2 due to the fact that there is no intervening maximal projection between them. Therefore, the distributive reading of *everyone* is possible in (63). Furthermore, in (66), the wh-chain (WH$_1$, RP$_{WH1}$) is well-formed, because no movement is involved in the chain, and the resumptive pronoun is correctly bound by the wh-phrase in the SPEC of the [+Q] COMP. Remember that in wh-interrogatives created by the resumption strategy, no wh-trace is created in the course of the derivation within overt syntax, although traces may be created by raising of resumptive pronouns at LF in some cases such as (63). Therefore, while the LF traces, if any, need to be licensed (properly governed), the resumptive pronoun itself must be licensed by being bound by its corresponding wh-phrase base-generated in the SPEC of the [+Q] COMP. Then, as it does not contain a wh-trace, the wh-chain (WH$_1$, RP$_{WH1}$) in (66) does not violate the condition on wh-chains regarding the interpretation of the universal quantifier suggested by Murasugi and Saito (1993). Hence, the example in (63) is correctly predicted to allow the distributive reading of the universal quantifier *achan duine* 'everyone' under the two conditions, namely, the Revised Rigidity Condition and the condition on wh-chains regarding the interpretation of the universal quantifier.

The same account is also given to the example in (42), reproduced as (67), which contains *achan duine* 'everyone' in a complex NP island.

(67)   Cén   teanga$_1$ a   mbeadh   meas   agat   ar dhuine ar bith a
       which language aN would.be respect at.you on person any   aL
       bheadh   ag súil   go   bhféadfadh   achan duine   í$_1$ a labhairt?
       be.COND expecting that could.COND every person it to speak
       'Which language$_1$ would you respect anyone who hopes that every-
       one could speak it$_1$?'   (=(42))
       (every > wh)

Again, the Revised Rigidity Condition predicts that (67) allows the interpretation in which the universal quantifier *achan duine* 'everyone' takes scope over the wh-phrase, and thus, the distributive reading of 'everyone' is possible. Furthermore, in (67), the wh-chain (WH$_1$, RP$_{WH1}$) is a well-formed chain, and does not run afoul of the condition on wh-chains regarding the interpretation of the universal quantifier suggested by Murasugi and Saito (1993). Therefore, the example in (67) is correctly predicted to allow the distributive reading of the universal quantifier *achan duine* 'everyone' under the two conditions.

5.   WH/Quantifier Interactions in Japanese

This section shows that the analysis of the wh/quantifier interactions in Irish presented above straightforwardly applies to the wh/quantifier interactions in Japanese, a wh-in-situ and head-final language.

Let us start by reviewing basic properties of the wh-construction in Japanese. As shown in (68)–(71), a wh-in-situ in Japanese is not subject to Ross' (1967) Complex NP Constraint, but is subject to the Wh-Island

Condition.[5]

(68)   Sono rarii-de Taroo-ga   dare-o   mita no?
       that   rally-at Taro-NOM who-ACC saw   Q
       '[Q [Taro saw who at the rally]].'

(69)   Kimi-wa [sono rarii-de Taroo-ga   dare-o   mita to]   omotteru
       you-TOP that   rally-at Taro-NOM who-ACC saw   that   think
       no?
       Q
       '[Q [you think [that Taro saw who at the rally]]].'

(70)   Kimi-wa [sono rarii-de Taroo-ga   dare-o   mita to]   omotteiru
       you-TOP that   rally-at Taro-NOM who-ACC saw   that   think
       hito-ni atta no?
       man-to met Q
       '[Q [you met [the man who thinks [that Taro saw who at the ral-
       ly]]]].'

(71)   *Kimi-wa [sono rarii-de Taroo-ga   dare-o   mita kadooka]
       you-TOP that   rally-at Taro-NOM who-ACC saw   whether
       shitteru no?
       know   Q
       '[Q [you know [whether Taro saw who at the rally]]].'

In (68) and (69), there is no island between the wh-in-situ and the [+Q]
COMP where it takes scope. Therefore, the examples are correctly predicted
to be grammatical. In (70), a complex NP intervenes between the wh-phrase
and the [+Q] COMP where it takes scope, but the example is perfectly
grammatical. On the other hand, in (71), a wh-island intervenes between
the wh-phrase and the [+Q] COMP where it takes scope, and the example
is ungrammatical. There are many important approaches to the above facts
in Japanese. See Nishigauchi (1986, 1990), Lasnik and Saito (1984, 1992),
Watanabe (1992a) and Maki (1995), among others. In this paper, we adopt
Maki's (1995) approach with a certain revision.

    Maki (1995) proposes, following Chomsky's (1995) Minimalist
Program, that what moves in the wh-construction with an argument wh-
phrase in Japanese is not the entire wh-phrase but just the wh-feature in the

---

[5] The abbreviations used in the following examples are as follows: ACC = accusative,
NOM = nominative, Q = Question and TOP = topic.

wh-phrase, and the movement takes place at LF. The operation Attract-F proposed in Chomsky (1995) attracts the closest relevant feature to the attractor. Given this, in (71), the matrix [+Q] COMP targets the higher wh-feature in the embedded [+Q] COMP, not the one in the wh-in-situ in the embedded clause, so that it cannot attract the proper wh-feature. Therefore, (71) is excluded. On the other hand, in (70), there is no wh-feature other than the one in the wh-phrase in the complex NP, so that the matrix [+Q] COMP can attract the proper wh-feature. Therefore, (70) is not excluded under the theory with Attract-F.

Maki (1995) attributes the difference between Japanese and English in terms of the Complex NP Constraint effect on wh-extraction, shown in (70) and (72),

(72) *Who$_1$ did you see [the man [who thinks [that Taro saw t_1 at the rally]]]?

to the difference in the size of what moves and the ban against adjunction to adjuncts proposed in Takahashi (1994). In the wh-construction in English, what moves is a phrase, and it moves to the target CP SPEC by successive adjunction to every maximal projection it passes. Then, in (72), the wh-phrase necessarily adjoins to the relative clause, which is an adjunct, so that this adjunction operation runs afoul of the ban against adjunction to adjuncts. On the other hand, in the wh-construction in Japanese, what moves is the wh-feature in the wh-phrase, which moves to the target COMP by successive adjunction to every head it passes. Since a head is a head, not an adjunct, the head of the relative clause in (70) is not an adjunct. Therefore, this LF feature movement does not run afoul of the ban against adjunction to adjuncts, and (70) is correctly predicted to be grammatical.

Chomsky (2000, 2001) reformulates feature movement in terms of Agree. In this paper, we adopt a revised version of Maki's (1995) feature movement analysis in terms of Agree. However, his essential account of the phenomenon is kept under the revision.

With this background, let us consider wh/quantifier interaction facts in Japanese. In this paper, we use the expression *daremo hitori hitori* 'everyone one one' as a representative case of the universal quantifier meaning 'every' in Japanese, because *daremo* alone is ambiguous between the universal quantifier meaning 'every' and the negative quantifier meaning '(not) any.' In (73), the universal quantifier c-commands the wh-phrase, and the distributive reading of the universal quantifier is possible.

(73)   Sono rarii-de daremo-ga   hitori hitori dare-o   mita no?
        that rally-at everyone-NOM one   one   who-ACC saw Q
        '[Q [everyone saw who at the rally]].'
        (every > wh)

On the other hand, in (74), the universal quantifier is c-commanded by the wh-phrase in the subject position, and the distributive reading of the universal quantifier is impossible.

(74)   Sono rarii-de dare-ga   daremo-o   hitori hitori mita no?
        that rally-at who-NOM everyone-ACC one   one   saw   Q
        '[Q [who saw everyone at the rally]].'
        (*every > wh)

In (75) and (76), the universal quantifier and the wh-phrase are embedded in a complement clause, and the [+Q] COMP where the wh-phrase takes scope is in the matrix clause. In (75), the universal quantifier c-commands the wh-phrase, and in (76), the former is c-commanded by the latter.

(75)   Kimi-wa [sono rarii-de daremo-ga   hitori hitori dare-o
        you-TOP that rally-at everyone-NOM one   one   who-ACC
        mita to]   omotteru no?
        saw   that think   Q
        '[Q [you think [that everyone saw who at the rally]]].'
        (every > wh)

(76)   Kimi-wa [sono rarii-de dare-ga   daremo-o   hitori hitori
        you-TOP that rally-at who-NOM everyone-ACC one   one
        mita to]   omotteru no?
        saw   that think   Q
        '[Q [you think [that who saw everyone at the rally]]].'
        (*every > wh)

Just like (73) and (74), the distributive reading of the universal quantifier is possible in (75), and impossible in (76).

Let us then turn to the case in which the two quantifiers are embedded in a complex NP. Consider (77). See Saito (1994) and Maki and Ochi (1998) for related data.

(77)   Kimi-wa   [sono rarii-de   daremo-ga   hitori   hitori   dare-o
        you-TOP   that   rally-at   everyone-NOM   one   one   who-ACC
        mita to]   omotteiru   hito-ni   atta   no?
        saw   that   think   man-to   met   Q
        '[Q [you met [the man who thinks [that everyone saw who at the
        rally]]]].'
        (every > wh)

In (77), the universal quantifier c-commands the wh-phrase, and the distributive reading of the universal quantifier is possible.

Let us finally consider the case in which the two quantifiers are embedded in a wh-clause. Consider (78). See Saito (1994, 1999) for related data.

(78)   *Kimi-wa   [sono rarii-de   daremo-ga   hitori   hitori   dare-o
        you-TOP   that   rally-at   everyone-NOM   one   one   who-ACC
        mita kadooka]   shitteru   no?
        saw   whether   know   Q
        '[Q [you know [whether everyone saw who at the rally]]].'
        (*every > wh)

To begin with, (78) is ungrammatical due to the wh-island condition effect. The question is whether the distributive reading of the universal quantifier is possible. There is not a consensus regarding this. Saito (1994, 1999) states that the distributive reading of the universal quantifier is possible in examples such as (78). However, for some other native speakers of Japanese who we consulted about the data, the intended reading was impossible. For us, the intended reading is also impossible. In this paper, we deal with the variety of Japanese in which the distributive reading of the universal quantifier is impossible in examples such as (78), leaving the issue of the difference in grammaticality judgments for future research.[6]

Let us now consider the data under the revised version of Maki's (1995) analysis, the Revised Rigidity Condition, and the condition on wh-

---

[6] Note that Saito's (1994, 1999) main point is the contrast between (i) and (ii). The data are from Saito (1999: 593) with slight editing.

(i) ??[Yamada-ga   [karera-ga   dare-kara   wairo-o   uketotta   kadooka]
     Yamada-NOM   they-NOM   who-from   bribe-ACC   received   whether
     shirabete iru   ka]   oshiete   kudasai.
     is-investigating   Q   tell.me   please
     'Please tell me [Q Yamada is investigating [whether they received bribes from whom]].'

chains regarding the interpretation of the universal quantifier suggested by Murasugi and Saito (1993). First, consider (73), in which the universal quantifier c-commands the wh-phrase. Under the revised version of Maki's (1995) analysis, the [+Q] COMP agrees with the wh-feature in the wh-phrase in the base-generated position. Therefore, no wh-(feature) movement takes place. Then, suppose that the universal quantifier and the wh-phrase adjoin to the minimal maximal projections for scope-taking at LF. Then, the relevant LF structure of (73) will be (79).

(79) $[_{CP} [_{IP} \text{everyone}_1 [_{IP} t_{everyone1} [_{VP} \text{who}_2 [_{VP} [_{V'} t_{who2} \text{saw}]]] I]] C]$

The Revised Rigidity Condition predicts that (73) allows the interpretation in which the universal quantifier takes scope over the wh-phrase, because (i) t_2 does not c-command t_1, and (ii) t_1 m-commands t_2. Therefore, the distributive reading of the universal quantifier is possible. Furthermore, in (73), the wh-chain formed by Agree is a well-formed chain, and does not run afoul of the condition on wh-chains regarding the interpretation of the universal quantifier suggested by Murasugi and Saito (1993). Therefore, the example in (73) is correctly predicted to allow the distributive reading of the universal quantifier.

Second, consider (74), in which the universal quantifier is c-commanded by the wh-phrase. The relevant LF structure of (74) will be (80).

(80) $[_{CP} [_{IP} \text{who}_1 [_{IP} t_{who1} [_{VP} \text{eveyone}_2 [_{VP} [_{V'} t_{everyone2} \text{saw}]]] I]] C]$

The Revised Rigidity Condition predicts that (74) does not allow the interpretation in which the universal quantifier takes scope over the wh-

---

(ii) ?[Dare-kara₁ [Yamada-ga   [karera-ga t_1 wairo-o   uketotta kadooka]
    who-from   Yamada-NOM   they-NOM   bribe-ACC received whether
    shirabete iru   ka]] oshiete kudasai.
    is-investigating Q   tell.me please
    'Please tell me [Q from whom₁, Yamada is investigating [whether they received bribes t_1]].'

According to Saito (1999), there is a clear contrast between (i) and (ii) with respect to the availability of the distributive reading of *karera* 'they.' In (i), the wh-phrase is in a wh-clause, and the distributive reading of *karera* 'they' is allowed. However, in (ii), the wh-phrase is moved out of the wh-clause by scrambling, and is in the sentence-initial position of the clause headed by a [+Q] COMP. Then, the distributive reading of *karera* 'they' is totally disallowed, just like its pseudo-counterpart in English, such as (iii).

(iii)??Who₁ do you wonder [whether everyone saw t_1 at the rally]?

See Takahashi (1993) for relevant discussion on scrambled wh-phrases.

phrase, because t_1 c-commands t_2, and (ii) t_2 cannot m-command t_1 in (80). Therefore, the example in (74) is correctly predicted to disallow the distributive reading of the universal quantifier.

The accounts provided for (73) and (74) are applicable to the examples in (75) and (76), because the universal quantifier c-commands the wh-phrase in (75), just as in (73), and the universal quantifier is c-commanded by the wh-phrase in (76), just as in (74).

Let us now consider (77), in which the universal quantifier and the wh-phrase are in a complex NP. Under the revised version of Maki's (1995) analysis, the [+Q] COMP agrees with the wh-feature in the wh-phrase in the base-generated position. Therefore, no wh-(feature) movement takes place. Then, suppose that the universal quantifier and the wh-phrase adjoin to the minimal maximal projections for scope-taking at LF. Then, the relevant LF structure of (77) will be (81).

(81) $[_{CP} [_{IP}...[_{NP}...[_{CP} [_{IP}$ everyone$_1$ $[_{IP} t_{everyone1} [_{VP}$ who$_2$ $[_{VP} [_{V'} t_{who2}$ saw]]] I]] C]...N]...I...C]$

The Revised Rigidity Condition predicts that (77) allows the interpretation in which the universal quantifier takes scope over the wh-phrase, because (i) t_2 does not c-command t_1, and (ii) t_1 m-commands t_2. Therefore, the distributive reading of the universal quantifier is possible. Furthermore, in (77), the wh-chain formed by Agree is a well-formed chain, and does not run afoul of the condition on wh-chains regarding the interpretation of the universal quantifier suggested by Murasugi and Saito (1993). Therefore, the example in (77) is correctly predicted to allow the distributive reading of the universal quantifier.

Let us finally consider (78), in which the universal quantifier and the wh-phrase are in a wh-clause. Under the revised version of Maki's (1995) analysis, the [+Q] COMP cannot agree with the wh-feature in the wh-phrase in the base-generated position due to the intervening wh-feature in the COMP of the embedded clause. Suppose then that the universal quantifier and the wh-phrase adjoin to the minimal maximal projections for scope-taking at LF. Then, the relevant LF structure of (78) will be (82).

(82) $[_{CP} [_{IP}...[_{CP} [_{IP}$ everyone$_1$ $[_{IP} t_{everyone1} [_{VP}$ who$_2$ $[_{VP} [_{V'} t_{who2}$ saw]]] I]] C_Q]...I...C]$

The Revised Rigidity Condition is not violated in (82). However, in (78), the wh-chain has not been properly created by Agree. Therefore, (78) runs afoul of the condition on wh-chains regarding the interpretation of the universal quantifier suggested by Murasugi and Saito (1993). Therefore, the example in (78) is correctly predicted to disallow the distributive reading of the universal quantifier.

6.   Conclusion

This paper investigated scope ambiguity in wh/quantifier interactions in Irish, and found the following: (i) that the distributive reading of the universal quantifier in Irish that corresponds to *every* in English is allowed when it is in the object position, and the wh-phrase originates from the subject position, and (ii) that the distributive reading of the universal quantifier in Irish is also allowed even when it is in an island, in which it is in the subject position, and the wh-phrase originates from the object position. We suggested that these properties follow from the fact that the subject position in Irish is within VP, and Irish has resumptive pronouns for wh-phrases. We also investigated scope ambiguity in wh/quantifier interactions in Japanese, a wh-in-situ language, and demonstrated that the analysis of the wh/quantifier interactions in Irish straightforwardly applies to those in Japanese.

Chapter 6

Cad é an Dóigh 'How' in Irish[*]

Dónall P. Ó Baoill and Hideki Maki

Queen's University Belfast (Prof. Emeritus) and *Gifu University*

Keywords: *adjunct wh-phrases*, cad é an dóigh *'how,'* cén fáth *'why,'* chain, COMP

1. Introduction

This paper investigates chain properties of the manner adverbial wh-phrase *cad é an dóigh* 'what it the way = how' in modern Ulster Irish (Irish, hereafter), as seen in examples such as (1).[1]

(1) Cad é an dóigh ar chóirigh Seán an carr?
     what the way aN fixed   John the car
     'How did John fix the car?'

The nature of *cad é an dóigh* 'how' has not been fully examined in the literature. Based on the newly found data, we will argue (i) that the data lend support to Lasnik and Saito's (1992) claim that an adjunct wh-phrase only creates variables/traces at LF, (ii) that adjunct wh-phrases do not constitute

---

  * This is a revised version of the paper presented at the 147th Meeting of the Linguistic Society of Japan held at Kobe City University of Foreign Studies on November 24, 2013. We would like to thank the audience of the meeting, Jessica Dunton and Fumikazu Niinuma for their helpful comments on an earlier version of this paper. Our thanks also go to the following native speakers from the eastern borders of Gweedore Parish in North West Donegal with whom the examples have been checked: Donnchadh Mac Fhionnaile, Seán Mac Giolla Chóill, Bríd Bean Mhic Íomhair, Anna Ní Bhaoill, Máire Nic Giolla Chóill, Pádraig Ó Briain, Pádraig Ó Dúgáin (Éamann), Bríd Bean Uí Ghallchóir and Méabha Bean Uí Phíopalaigh. All errors are our own. Research by the second author was supported in part by Japan Society for the Promotion of Science Grant # 25370428 to Gifu University.

  [1] The abbreviations used in this paper are as follows: 2 = second person, ACC = accusative, ASP = aspect, COND = conditional, GEN = genitive, NEG = negation, NOM = nominative, PAST = past tense, PP3 = third person possessive pronoun, Q = question, RP = resumptive pronoun, SG = singular, TOP = topic and VN = verbal noun.

a uniform category, but fall into two categories in Irish: the *how*-type and the *why*-type, (iii) that non-genuine argument operators (*how*, *why*, and the comparative operator) do not simply constitute a uniform category in Irish, and (iv) that Irish has two types of [+Q] COMPs (one found in English and another found in Chinese).

The organization of this paper is as follows. Section 2 reviews properties of the wh-interrogative construction in Irish as background to subsequent sections. Section 3 provides the data with the manner adverbial wh-phrase *cad é an dóigh* 'how' in Irish. Based on the properties of *cad é an dóigh* 'how,' Section 4 discusses what they might suggest for the theory of (Irish) syntax. Finally, Section 5 concludes this paper.

2. Background

Let us start by briefly summarizing properties of the wh-interrogative construction in Irish. (See McCloskey (1979, 1990) and Maki and Ó Baoill (2011), among others, for discussion of operator constructions in Irish.) Irish has three types of complementizers: the [−Q] marker, the direct relative marker, and the indirect relative marker. The properties of the three COMPs are summarized in (2).

(2)   Complementizers in Irish[2]

	types of COMPs	non-past form	past form	symbol
a.	the [−Q] marker	*go*	*go/gur*	that
b.	the direct relative marker	*a*	*a*	aL
c.	the indirect relative marker	*a*	*a/ar*	aN

Let us illustrate the properties of the COMPs by relevant examples. (3) is a declarative sentence, and the embedded clause is headed by the [−Q] COMP *gur* 'that.' When the sentence involves wh-interrogative clause formation, as in (4), the embedded COMP must change to the direct relative marker *aL*, and at the same time, another COMP *aL* must be inserted right

---

[2] The complementizer forms used with irregular verbs in the past tense in Irish, namely, the [−Q] marker and indirect relative marker *aN* do not follow the regular usage found with all other verbs. Hence, the regular complementizer forms *gur* 'that' and the indirect relative form *ar* are replaced by *go* 'that' and *a* 'aN,' respectively when used with the following irregular verbs: *bí* 'to be' >> *go/a raibh*; *déan* 'to do' >> *go/a ndearna*; *faigh* 'to get' >> *go/a bhfuair*; *tabhair* 'to give' >> *go/a dtug*; *tar* 'to come' >> *go/a dtáinig* and *téigh* 'to go' >> *go/a ndeachaigh*.

after the wh-phrase. In this paper, for expository purposes only, we represent A'-chains using the symbols *aL/aN* rather than the wh-phrase itself, as in (aL, *t*) or (aN, RP), where *RP* stands for a resumptive pronoun.

(3) Creideann Seán gur cheannaigh Máire an carr.
     believe   John that bought   Mary the car
     'John believes that Mary bought the car.'

(4) Cad é a chreideann tú   a   cheannaigh Seán *t*?
     what aL believe   you aL bought   John
     'What do you believe that John bought?'   (movement) (aL, aL, *t*)

There is another way to form a wh-interrogative clause in Irish, as shown in (5).

(5) Cad é a gcreideann tú   gur cheannaigh Seán é/*t*?
     what aN believe   you that bought   John it
     'What do you believe that John bought?'

                                              (resumption) (aN, that, RP)

In (5), the topmost COMP of the wh-interrogative clause is an indirect relative marker *a*, the COMP of the embedded clause is a [−Q] COMP, and the embedded clause contains a resumptive pronoun *é* 'it' instead of a gap. Note that (5) is ungrammatical, if the resumptive pronoun is replaced by a trace, which suggests that *aN* must bind a resumptive pronoun.

McCloskey (2002) provides an account of the distribution of the COMPs by proposing (6).

(6) a. C whose specifier is filled by Move is realized as *aL*.
    b. C whose specifier is filled by Merge is realized as *aN*.
    c. C whose specifier is not filled is realized as *go/gur*.

McCloskey assumes that the SPEC of *aL* contains a null operator/null pronoun (henceforth, null operator) as a result of movement, that in the SPEC of *aN*, there is a base-generated operator, and that in the SPEC of *go/gur*, there is no operator. If this is correct, the structure of the wh-interrogative clause construction in Irish looks like a cleft sentence, as shown in (7).

(7) (it is) WH_1 [$\mathbf{Op_1}$ aL/aN [$_{IP}...t_1/RP_1...$]]
     (where *RP* stands for resumptive pronoun)

In this paper, for expository purposes only, we represent the structure of a wh-interrogative clause by putting a wh-phrase, not its operator, in the SPEC of *aL/aN*.

Let us then review the basic chain properties of argument wh-phrases in Irish for the investigation of the properties of the adjunct wh-phrase *cad é an dóigh* 'how.' We have seen above that A'-chains in Irish headed by the argument wh-phrase *cad é* 'what' allow two patterns, when the sentence contains one embedding, as shown in (4) and (5).

(4) Cad é a   chreideann tú   a   cheannaigh Seán *t*?
     what aL believe   you aL bought   John
     'What do you believe that John bought?'   (movement) (aL, aL, *t*)

(5) Cad é a   gcreideann tú   gur cheannaigh Seán é/*t?
     what aN believe   you that bought   John it
     'What do you believe that John bought?'

                                            (resumption) (aN, that, RP)

A'-chains in Irish headed by the argument wh-phrase *cad é* 'what' allow four more patterns, as shown in (8)–(11).

(8) Cad é a   gcreideann tú   ar   cheannaigh Seán é?
     what aN believe   you aN bought   John it
     'What do you believe [that John bought *t*]?'   (aN, aN, RP)

(9) Cad é a   chreideann tú   ar   cheannaigh Seán é?
     what aL believe   you aN bought   John it
     'What do you believe [that John bought *t*]?'   (aL, aN, RP)

(10) Cad é a   raibh súil agat   a   cheannófá   *t*?
     what aN was hope at.you aL buy.COND
     'What did you hope [that you would buy *t*]?'   (aN, aL, *t*)

(11) Cad é a   chreideann tú   gur cheannaigh Seán é?
     what aL believe   you that bought   John it
     'What do you believe [that John bought *t*]?'   (aL, that, RP)

Note that *aN* is an indirect relative marker, and binds either an operator that is moved to CP SPEC or a resumptive pronoun in situ.

3. Data

Having established the particular background, let us now examine the properties of the adjunct wh-phrase *cad é an dóigh* 'how' in Irish. Firstly, the contrast between (1) and (12) indicates that *cad é an dóigh* 'how' does not involve movement in overt syntax.

(1)   Cad é an dóigh ar chóirigh Seán an   carr?
      what the way   aN fixed   John the car
      'How did John fix the car?'   (aN)

(12) *Cad é an dóigh a chóirigh Seán an   carr?
      what   the way   aL fixed   John the car
      'How did John fix the car?'   (aL, *t*)

Secondly, *cad é an dóigh* 'how' exhibits some interesting properties in wh-questions with one embedding, as shown in (13)–(18).

(13) *Cad é an dóigh a chreid   tú   a   chóirigh Seán an carr?
      what   the way   aL believed you aL fixed   John the car
      'How did you believe [that John fixed the car]?'   (aL, aL, *t*)

(14) Cad é an dóigh ar chreid   tú   gur chóirigh Seán an carr?
      what the way   aN believed you that fixed   John the car
      'How did you believe [that John fixed the car]?'   (aN, that)

(15) Cad é an dóigh ar chreid   tú   ar chóirigh Seán an carr?
      what the way   aN believed you aN fixed   John the car
      'How did you believe [that John fixed the car]?'   (aN, aN)

(16) *Cad é an dóigh a chreid   tú   ar chóirigh Seán an carr?
      what   the way   aL believed you aN fixed   John the car
      'How did you believe [that John fixed the car]?'   (aL, aN)

(17) Cad é an dóigh a raibh súil agat   a chóireofá   an carr?
      what the way   aN was   hope at.you aL fix.COND.2.SG the car
      'How did you hope [that you would fix the car]?'   (aN, aL, *t*)

(18) *Cad é an dóigh a mheas   tú   gur cheart dúinn an carr a
      what   the way   aL thought you that right   for.us the car to
      chóiriú?
      fix.VN
      'How did you think [that we ought to fix the car]?'   (aL, that)

(13), (16) and (18) are ungrammatical, where the topmost COMP is *aL*, no matter what interpretations they may have. (14) is ambiguous: it has both the interpretation where *cad é an dóigh* 'how' modifies the matrix predicate and the interpretation where it modifies the embedded predicate. (15) has only one interpretation where it modifies the embedded predicate. Finally, (17) also has only one interpretation where it modifies the embedded predicate.

Thirdly, as Ó Baoill and Maki (2014a) show, the manner adverbial wh-phrase *cad é an dóigh* 'how' may appear in an embedded clause or a complex NP, as shown in (19b) and (20b).

(19) a. Cad é an dóigh a síleann tú gur chóirigh Seán an carr?
   what the way aN think you that fixed John the car
   'How do you think [that John fixed the car *t*]?'

   b. Síleann tú gur chóirigh Seán an carr (ar) cad é an dóigh?
   think you that fixed John the car on what the way
   'How do you think [that John fixed the car *t*]?'

(20) a. Cad é an dóigh a bhfaca siad [an fear a chóirigh an
   what the way aN saw they the man aL fixed the
   carr *t*]?
   car
   '[Q [they saw [the man who fixed the car how]]].'

   b. Chonaic siad [an fear a chóirigh an carr (ar) cad é an
   saw they the man aL fixed the car on what the
   dóigh]?
   way
   '[Q [they saw [the man who fixed the car how]]].'

Note that both sentences in (20) are grammatical. In (20a), *cad é an dóigh* 'how' modifies the matrix clause, but it cannot modify the clause in the complex NP. In (20b), *cad é an dóigh* 'how' only modifies the clause in the complex NP.

4.   Discussion

Let us now consider what the observed facts might suggest for the theory of (Irish) syntax. Firstly, the fact that (14) is ambiguous, and thus, has the interpretation in which *cad é an dóigh* 'how' modifies the embedded predicate,

(14) Cad é an dóigh ar chreid tú gur chóirigh Seán an carr?
   what the way aN believed you that fixed John the car
   'How did you believe [that John fixed the car]?'   (aN, that)

suggests that it should create a variable/trace in the embedded clause, and this is possible only at LF. This is because the topmost COMP is *aN*, so that *cad é an dóigh* 'how' is base-generated in CP SPEC in overt syntax rather than is moved into that position in overt syntax. This then lends direct support to Lasnik and Saito's (1992) hypothesis that traces of adjunct wh-phrases do not exist at the pre-LF level, and are only created at LF.

Secondly, a comparative study between *cad é an dóigh* 'how' and *cén fáth* 'why' suggests that these two adjunct wh-phrases do not behave in the same fashion, and thus, adjunct wh-phrases fall into two categories in Irish. Consider the examples with *cén fáth* 'why' in (21)–(23).

(21)   Cén   fáth   do   bharúil ar chreid   Pól go ndearna
       what.the reason in.your opinion aN believed Paul that did
       sé   é?
       he   it
       'Why in your opinion did Paul believe that he did it?'   (aN, that)

(22)   Cén   fáth   do   bharúil ar chreid   Pól a   ndearna
       what.the reason in.your opinion aN believed Paul aN did
       sé   é?
       he   it
       'Why in your opinion did Paul believe that he did it?'   (aN, aN)

(23)   Cén   fáth   do   bharúil a   chreid   Pól a   ndearna
       what.the reason in.your opinion aL believed Paul aN did
       sé   é?
       he   it
       'Why in your opinion did Paul believe that he did it?'   (aL, aN)

The embedded COMP is realized as *go* 'that' in (21), and as *a* 'aN' in (22) and (23). Each sentence is unambiguous: (21) only has the reading in which *cén fáth* 'why' modifies the matrix predicate, and (22) and (23) only have the reading in which *cén fáth* 'why' modifies the embedded predicate. Now, the fact that (21) is unambiguous, while (14) is ambiguous, suggests that the behavior of *cén fáth* 'why' is different from that of *cad é an dóigh* 'how.' Furthermore, McCloskey (2002) claims that (23) shows that *cén fáth* 'why' is base-generated in the SPEC of *aN*, and moves to the SPEC of *aL*. This indicates that *cén fáth* 'why' may undergo overt movement. However, *cad é an dóigh* 'how' does not appear in the SPEC of *aL* in any of the examples in (12), (13), (16) and (18). Thus, *cad é an dóigh* 'how' is only base-generated in the SPEC of *aN*, and does not move to CP SPEC in overt syntax. Therefore, these facts indicate that there are two types of adjunct wh-phrases in Irish.

This dichotomy is also supported by the data in (24) and (25).

(24) a. Cad é an   dóigh ar   chóirigh Seán an carr?
         what the way aN fixed   John the car
         'How did John fix the car?'

    b. Chóirigh Seán an carr (ar) cad é an   dóigh?
         fixed   John the car on what the way
         'How did John fix the car?'

(25) a. Cén   fáth   ar chóirigh Seán an carr?
         what.the reason aN fixed   John the car
         'Why did John fix the car?'

    b. *Chóirigh Seán an carr cén   fáth?
         fixed   John the car what.the reason
         'Why did John fix the car?'

(24b) shows that the manner adverbial wh-phrase *cad é an dóigh* 'how' can
be in situ, while (25b) shows that the reason adverbial wh-phrase *cén fáth*
'why' cannot be in situ.

This distinction is also observed in other languages such as French.
Consider the examples in (26) and (27).

(26) a. Comment Jean a   réparé la voiture?
         how   Jean has fixed the car
         'How did Jean fix the car?'
                          (personal communication with Gilles Guerrin)

    b. Jean a   réparé la voiture comment?
         Jean has fixed the car   how
         'How did Jean fix the car?'   (Bošković (2000: 56))

(27) a. Pourquoi Jean a   réparé la voiture?
         why   Jean has fixed the car
         'Why did Jean fix the car?'

    b. *Jean a   réparé la voiture pourquoi?
         Jean has fixed the car   why
         'Why did Jean fix the car?'

The contrast between (26b) and (27b) in French corresponds exactly to the
contrast between (24b) and (25b) in Irish, strengthening the dichotomy between the manner adverbial wh-phrase and the reason adverbial wh-phrase.

The fact that there are two types of adjunct wh-phrases in Irish, has
a further cross-linguistic implication. Yoshida and Yoshida (1996) and Ko

(2005) show an argument/adjunct asymmetry with respect to the selectability of the sentence-final question marker in Japanese and Korean, respectively. Consider the Japanese examples in (28). The question marker *no* cannot be deleted in questions with *naze* 'why.'

(28) a. Taroo-wa   nani-o   kata   (no)?
         Taro-TOP   what-ACC bought   Q
         'What did Taro buy?'
     b. Taroo-wa   naze   kaetta   *(no)?
         Taro-TOP   why   left   Q
         'Why did Taro leave?'

Interestingly enough, (29) shows that the question marker *no* can be elided in questions with *doo* 'how.'

(29) Taroo-wa   doo   furumatta   (no)?
      Taro-TOP   how   behaved   Q
      'How did Taro behave?'

Therefore, the Japanese data also provide evidence for the claim that adjunct wh-phrases do not constitute a uniform category.

  Thirdly, a comparative study among the wh-construction headed by an argument wh-phrase such as *cad é* 'what,' the wh-construction headed by the adjunct wh-phrase *cad é an dóigh* 'how,' the wh-construction headed by the adjunct wh-phrase *cén fáth* 'why,' and the comparative construction, reveals the nature of non-genuine argument operators in Irish. Firstly, the wh-construction headed by an argument wh-phrase such as *cad é* 'what' allows a chain to start with either *aL* or *aN*, and to terminate with either a trace or a resumptive pronoun, as shown in (4), (5) and (8)–(11).

(4) Cad é   a   chreideann   tú   a   cheannaigh   Seán   *t*?
     what   aL   believe   you   aL   bought   John
     'What do you believe that John bought?'   (movement) (aL, aL, *t*)

(5) Cad é   a   gcreideann   tú   gur   cheannaigh   Seán   é/*t*?
     what   aN   believe   you   that bought   John   it
     'What do you believe that John bought?'
                                              (resumption) (aN, that, RP)

(8) Cad é   a   gcreideann   tú   ar   cheannaigh   Seán   é?
     what   aN   believe   you   aN   bought   John   it
     'What do you believe [that John bought *t*]?'   (aN, aN, RP)

(9) Cad é a chreideann tú ar cheannaigh Seán é?
what aL believe you aN bought John it
'What do you believe [that John bought *t*]?' (aL, aN, RP)

(10) Cad é a raibh súil agat a cheannófá *t*?
what aN was hope at.you aL buy.COND
'What did you hope [that you would buy *t*]?' (aN, aL, *t*)

(11) Cad é a chreideann tú gur cheannaigh Seán é?
what aL believe you that bought John it
'What do you believe [that John bought *t*]?' (aL, that, RP)

Secondly, the wh-construction headed by the adjunct wh-phrase *cad é an dóigh* 'how' only allows a chain to start with *aN*, when the wh-phrase modifies the embedded predicate, although it allows a chain to terminate with either a trace or a resumptive pronoun, as shown in (14), (15) and (17).

(14) Cad é an dóigh ar chreid tú gur chóirigh Seán an carr?
what the way aN believed you that fixed John the car
'How did you believe [that John fixed the car]?' (aN, that)

(15) Cad é an dóigh ar chreid tú ar chóirigh Seán an carr?
what the way aN believed you aN fixed John the car
'How did you believe [that John fixed the car]?' (aN, aN)

(17) Cad é an dóigh a raibh súil agat a chóireofá an carr?
what the way aN was hope at.you aL fix.COND.2.SG the car
'How did you hope [that you would fix the car]?' (aN, aL, *t*)

Thirdly, the wh-construction headed by the adjunct wh-phrase *cén fáth* 'why' only allows a chain in which the COMP of the embedded clause is *aN*, when the wh-phrase modifies the embedded predicate, as shown in (22) and (23).

(22) Cén fáth do bharúil ar chreid Pól a ndearna sé é?
what.the reason in.your opinion aN believed Paul aN did he it
'Why in your opinion did Paul believe that he did it?' (aN, aN)

(23) Cén   fáth   do   bharúil a   chreid   Pól   a   ndearna
    what.the reason in.your opinion aL believed Paul aN did
    sé   é?
    he   it
    'Why in your opinion did Paul believe that he did it?'   (aL, aN)

Fourthly, the comparative construction only allows a chain to terminate with a trace, although it allows a chain to start with either *aL* or *aN*, as shown in (30)–(37). (The data are from Maki and Ó Baoill (2011).)

(30) Cheannaigh sí   níos mó úllaí   ná   a   chreideann tú   a
    bought   she more   apples than aL believe   you aL
    cheannaigh Seán   *t*.
    bought   John
    'She bought more apples than you believe that John bought.'
                                                    (aL, aL, *t*)

(31) Cheannaigh sí   níos mó úllaí   ná   a   raibh súil   agam a
    bought   she more   apples than aN was   hope at.me aL
    cheannófá   *t*.
    buy.COND.2.SG
    'She bought more apples than I hoped you would buy.'   (aN, aL, *t*)

(32) *Cheannaigh sí   níos mó úllaí   ná   a   chreideann tú   ar
    bought   she more   apples than aL believe   you aN
    cheannaigh Seán   iad.
    bought   John them
    'She bought more apples than you believe that John bought them.'
                                                    (aL, aN, RP)

(33) *Cheannaigh sí   níos mó úllaí   ná   a   chreideann tú   gur
    bought   she more   apples than aL believe   you that
    cheannaigh Seán   iad.
    bought   John them
    'She bought more apples than you believe that John bought them.'
                                                    (aL, that, RP)

(34) *Cheannaigh sí   níos mó úllaí   ná   a   gcreideann tú   gur
    bought   she more   apples than aN believe   you that
    cheannaigh Seán   iad.
    bought   John them
    'She bought more apples than you believe that John bought them.'

(aN, that, RP)

(35) *Cheannaigh sí níos mó úllaí   ná   a   gcreideann tú   ar
       bought   she more   apples than aN believe   you aN
       cheannaigh Seán iad.
       bought   John them
       'She bought more apples than you believe that John bought them.'

(aN, aN, RP)

(36) *Cheannaigh sí níos mó úllaí   ná   a   chreideann tú   ar
       bought   she more   apples than aL believe   you aN
       cheannaigh Seán.
       bought   John
       'She bought more apples than you believe that John bought.'

(aL, aN)

(37) *Cheannaigh sí níos mó úllaí   ná   a   gcreideann tú   ar
       bought   she more   apples than aN believe   you aN
       cheannaigh Seán.
       bought   John
       'She bought more apples than you believe that John bought.'

(aN, aN)

Thus, the wh-construction headed by the adjunct wh-phrase *cad é an dóigh* 'how' only allows the chain patterns in (38), the wh-construction headed by the adjunct wh-phrase *cén fáth* 'why' only allows the chain patterns in (39), and the comparative construction only allows the chain patterns in (40).

(38)   The Wh-Construction Headed by the Adjunct Wh-Phrase *Cad é an Dóigh* 'How'
   a.   (aN, that)
   b.   (aN, aN)
   c.   (aN, aL, *t*)

(39)   The Wh-Construction Headed by the Adjunct Wh-Phrase *Cén Fáth* 'Why'
   a.   (aN, aN)
   b.   (aL, aN)

(40)   The Comparative Construction
   a.   (aL, aL, *t*)

b. (aN, aL, *t*)

The patterns in (40) are totally different from those in (38). This is rather surprising, given the fact that the comparative construction seems to involve movement of an operator that contains an amount expression such as *x much/x many*, which is not referential/nominal like *cad é* 'what,' but rather is non-referential/non-nominal like *cad é an dóigh* 'how.' The above facts about the chain patterns allowed by the four types of structures thus reveal that while there is a clear difference between the chains headed by an argument operator and the chains headed by a non-genuine argument operator, there is still a difference among the chains allowed by the three types of non-genuine argument operators, which in turn indicates that non-genuine argument operators do not simply constitute a uniform category in Irish, and probably in human language.

Fourthly, the fact that the manner adverbial wh-phrase *cad é an dóigh* 'how' may appear in an embedded clause or a complex NP, as shown in (19b) and (20b),

(19) b. Síleann tú   gur chóirigh Seán an carr (ar) cad é an dóigh?
         think   you that fixed   John the car on what the way
         'How do you think [that John fixed the car *t*]?'

(20) b. Chonaic siad [an fear a   chóirigh an carr (ar) cad é an dóigh]?
         saw   they the man aL fixed   the car on what the way
         '[Q [they saw [the man who fixed the car how]]].'

suggests that the COMP that licenses *cad é an dóigh* 'how' in situ is similar to the one found in Chinese and Mongolian, as shown in (41)–(46).

(41) Lisi zenme xiuli-le nabu che?
      Lisi how   fix-ASP that car
      '[Q Lisi fixed the car how]]].'   (Chinese)

(42) Ni renwei Lisi zenme xiuli-le nabu che?
      you think Lisi how   fix-ASP that car
      '[Q [you think [Lisi fixed the car how]]].'   (Chinese)
                                  (personal communication with Ling-Yun Fan)

(43) Ni bu yuanyi yong [[ta zenmeyang zhuan-lai de] qian]?
      you not willing use he how   earn-come DE money
      '[Q [you are reluctant to use [the money he earns how]]].'   (Chinese)
                                                          (Lin (1992: 295))

(44)   Baɣatur-ø   yaɣaqiju   tere   terge-gi   jasa-ɣsan   boi?
       Bagatur-NOM   how   that   car-ACC   repair-PAST   Q
       '[Q [Bagatur fixed the car how]]].'   (Mongolian)

(45)   Či-ø   Baɣatur-ø/-i   yaɣaqiju   tere   terge-gi
       you-NOM   Bagatur-NOM/-ACC   how   that   car-ACC
       jasa-ɣsan   gejü   boduju   baiqu   boi?
       repair-PAST   that   think   be   Q
       '[Q [you think [Bagatur fixed the car how]]].'   (Mongolian)

(46)   Či-ø   [tegün-nü   yaɣaqiju   olu-ɣsan   joɣus-i-ni]
       you-NOM   he-GEN   how   earn-PAST   money-GEN-PP3
       jaruqu   dura   ügei   boi?
       use   preference   NEG   Q
       '[Q [you are reluctant to use [the money he earns how]]].'
                                                               (Mongolian)
                     (personal communication with Lina Bao)

Therefore, the Irish [+Q] COMP optionally has a [strong] feature that triggers overt wh-movement, as shown in (47),

(47)   Cad é   a   cheannaigh Seán   *t*?
       what   aL   bought   John
       'What did John buy?'   (movement) (aL, *t*)

or base-generation of a wh-phrase in CP SPEC, as shown in (1).

(1)   Cad é   an   dóigh   ar   chóirigh   Seán   an   carr?
       what   the   way   aN   fixed   John   the   car
       'How did John fix the car?'   (base-generation) (aN)

If it does not have a [strong] feature, it allows a wh-phrase to be in situ, licensing it by binding, as shown in (20b).

(20) b.   Chonaic   siad   [an   fear   a   chóirigh   an   carr   (ar)   cad é   an
          saw   they   the   man   aL   fixed   the   car   on   what   the
          dóigh]?
          way
          '[Q [they saw [the man who fixed the car how]]].'

This indicates that Irish has two types of [+Q] COMPs (one found in English and another found in Chinese). See Ó Baoill and Maki (2014a) for more detailed discussion of the phenomenon.

5. Conclusion

In this paper, based on the newly found data on *cad é an dóigh* 'how' in Irish, we argued (i) that an adjunct wh-phrase only creates variables/traces at LF, (ii) that adjunct wh-phrases fall into two categories in Irish: the *how*-type and the *why*-type, (iii) that non-genuine argument operators (*how*, *why*, and the comparative operator) do not simply constitute a uniform category in Irish, and (iv) that Irish has two types of [+Q] COMPs.

Chapter 7

Irish [+Q] COMPs[*]

Dónall P. Ó Baoill and Hideki Maki

Queen's University Belfast (Prof. Emeritus) and *Gifu University*

Keywords: Chinese, English, Irish, [+Q] COMPs, wh-construction

1. Introduction

This paper closely investigates the wh-construction in Modern Irish (Irish, hereafter), and points out that in terms of the wh-construction, Irish is a typologically unique language in the sense that it has two different types of [+Q] COMPs: one type of [+Q] COMP has a [strong] feature that needs to be deleted in overt syntax, which necessarily involves overt wh-movement; and another type that does not have this feature, and binds a wh-phrase in situ, so that no wh-movement takes place with this COMP. If this is correct, Irish is different from (i) English, which has a [+Q] COMP with a [strong] feature, which is inserted only in overt syntax, (ii) French, which has a [+Q] COMP with a [strong] feature, which is inserted either in overt syntax or in LF, according to Bošković (2000), and (iii) Chinese, which seems to have a [+Q] COMP without a [strong] feature. The present research thus shows that a given language picks up a certain type of [+Q] COMP or certain types of [+Q] COMPs out of the list of possible [+Q]

* An earlier version of this paper was presented at the 31st Conference of the English Linguistic Society of Japan held at Fukuoka University on November 9, 2013. We would like to thank the audience of the conference, Lina Bao, Jessica Dunton, Ling-Yun Fan, Alexandra von Fragstein, Gilles Guerrin, Megumi Hasebe, Luisa Martí and two anonymous *EL* referees for their valuable comments. Our thanks also go to the following native speakers from the eastern borders of Gweedore Parish in North West Donegal with whom the examples have been checked: Donnchadh Mac Fhionnaile, Seán Mac Giolla Chóill, Bríd Bean Mhic Íomhair, Anna Ní Bhaoill, Máire Nic Giolla Chóill, Pádraig Ó Briain, Pádraig Ó Dúgáin (Éamann), Bríd Bean Uí Ghallchóir and Méabha Bean Uí Phíopalaigh. All errors are our own. Research by the second author was supported in part by Japan Society for the Promotion of Science Grant # 25370428 to Gifu University.

COMPs, and Irish has picked up two types of [+Q] COMPs (one found in English and another found in Chinese). The Irish data in point are shown in (1).[1]

> (1) a. Cad é a chreideann tú a cheannaigh Seán *t*?
>   what aL believe   you aL bought   John
>   'What do you believe that John bought?'
>   b. Creideann tú gur ceannaigh Seán cad é?
>   believe   you that bought   John what
>   'What do you believe that John bought?'

(1a) is a non-echo wh-question which involves overt wh-movement. (See McCloskey (1979, 2002), among others.) (1b) is also well-formed as a non-echo wh-question, and the wh-phrase is in situ in the embedded clause. We will provide more examples of type (1b) in this paper, and based on the newly found data, we will argue (i) that Irish has two types of [+Q] COMPs, one with a [strong] feature, and another with a [weak] feature, (ii) that adjunct wh-phrases in Irish are categorized into two groups: the manner class and the reason class, and the manner class wh-phrases pattern together with argument wh-phrases, and (iii) that the differences in the A'-chain patterns suggest that there are actually three types of wh-phrases in Irish: argument, manner and reason wh-phrases.

The organization of this paper is as follows. Section 2 reviews properties of (i) the wh-construction in French and (ii) complementizers in Irish as background to subsequent sections. Section 3 provides the wh-interrogative data in Irish. Based on the newly found data, Section 4 discusses what they suggest for the theory of (Irish) syntax. Finally, Section 5 concludes this paper.

2. Background

2.1. French

Bošković (2000) argues that French [+Q] COMP with a [strong] feature is inserted in overt syntax or in LF based on abundant data including (2)–(4). In French, both (2a) and (2b) are grammatical, suggesting that a wh-

---

[1] The abbreviations used in this paper are as follows: ACC = accusative, ADN = adnominal, ASP = aspect, GEN = genitive, NEG = negation, NOM = nominative, PAST = past tense, PP3 = third person possessive pronoun, PRES = present tense, Q = question, RP = resumptive pronoun and TOP = topic.

phrase can be in CP SPEC or in situ.

(2) a.   Qui as-tu   vu?
         who have-you seen
         'Who did you see?'

   b.   Tu   as   vu   qui?
        you have seen who
        'Who did you see?'

However, the ungrammaticality of (3b) and (4b) indicates that a wh-phrase cannot always be in situ.

(3) a.   Qui Jean et   Pierre croient-ils   que Marie a   vu?
         who Jean and Pierre believe-they that Marie has seen
         'Who do Jean and Pierre believe that Marie saw?'

   b. ?*Jean et   Pierre croient que Marie a   vu   qui?
         Jean and Pierre believe that Marie has seen who
         'Who do Jean and Pierre believe that Marie saw?'

(4) a.   Que ne   mange-t-il pas?
         what NEG eat-he   NEG
         'What doesn't Jean eat?'

   b. ?*Jean ne   mange pas   quoi?
         Jean NEG eat   NEG what
         'What doesn't Jean eat?'

Bošković (2000) claims that the above data suggest (i) that a [+Q] COMP with a [strong] feature is derivationally inserted, so that it can be inserted in LF, and (ii) that LF wh-movement is restricted to head-movement, which cannot move across an A'-head, such as COMP in (3b) or NEG in (4b). To summarize, if Bošković (2000) is correct, French has one type of [+Q] COMP with a [strong] feature, which can be inserted either in overt syntax or in LF.

2.2. Irish

Second, let us review the properties of complementizers in Irish. Irish has three types of complementizers: the [−Q] marker, the direct relative marker, and the indirect relative marker. The properties of the three COMPs are summarized in (5).

(5)   Complementizers in Irish[2]

	types of COMPs	non-past form	past form	symbol
a.	the [−Q] marker	*go*	*go/gur*	that
b.	the direct relative marker	*a*	*a*	aL
c.	the indirect relative marker	*a*	*a/ar*	aN

Let us illustrate the properties of the COMPs by relevant examples. (6) is a declarative sentence, and the embedded clause is headed by the [−Q] COMP *gur* 'that.' On the other hand, when the sentence involves wh-interrogative clause formation, as in (7), the embedded COMP must change to the direct relative marker *aL*, and at the same time, another COMP *aL* must be inserted right after the wh-phrase.

(6)   Creideann Seán gur cheannaigh Máire an   carr.
       believe   John that bought   Mary   the car
       'John believes that Mary bought the car.'

(7)   Cad é a   chreideann tú   a   cheannaigh Seán *t*?
       what   aL believe   you   aL bought   John
       'What do you believe that John bought?'   (movement) (aL, aL, *t*)

There is another way to form a wh-interrogative clause in Irish. Observe the example in (8).

(8)   Cad é a   gcreideann tú   gur cheannaigh Seán é/*t*?
       what   aN believe   you   that bought   John it
       'What do you believe that John bought?'

                                                  (resumption) (aN, that, RP)

In (8), the topmost COMP of the wh-interrogative clause is an indirect relative marker *aN*, the COMP of the embedded clause is a [−Q] COMP, and the embedded clause contains a resumptive pronoun (RP) *é* 'it' instead of a gap. Note that (8) becomes ungrammatical, if the resumptive pronoun is replaced by a trace, which suggests that *aN* must bind a resumptive pronoun.

---

[2] The complementizer forms used with irregular verbs in the past tense in Irish, namely, the [−Q] marker and indirect relative marker *aN* do not follow the regular usage found with all other verbs. Hence, the regular complementizer forms *gur* 'that' and the indirect relative form *ar* are replaced by *go* 'that' and *a* 'aN,' respectively when used with the following irregular verbs: *bí* 'to be' >> *go/a raibh*; *déan* 'to do' >> *go/a ndearna*; *faigh* 'to get' >> *go/a bhfuair*; *tabhair* 'to give' >> *go/a dtug*; *tar* 'to come' >> *go/a dtáinig* and *téigh* 'to go' >> *go/a ndeachaigh*.

McCloskey (2002) provides an account of the distribution of the COMPs by proposing (9).

(9) a.   C whose specifier is filled by Move is realized as *aL*.
   b.   C whose specifier is filled by Merge is realized as *aN*.
   c.   C whose specifier is not filled is realized as *go/gur*.

McCloskey assumes that the SPEC of *aL* contains a null operator/null pronoun (henceforth, null operator) as a result of movement, that in the SPEC of *aN*, there is a base-generated operator, and that in the SPEC of *go/gur*, there is no operator. In this paper, for expository purposes only, we represent the structure of a wh-interrogative clause by putting a wh-phrase, not its operator, in the SPEC of *aL/aN*, as shown in (10).

(10)   [WH$_1$ aL/aN [$_{IP}$...t_1/RP$_1$...]]]

3.   Irish Data

Having outlined the particular background, let us consider the Irish wh-construction. Firstly, (11) and (1) show that wh-in-situ is possible in matrix clauses and embedded complement clauses, respectively.

(11) a.   Cad é a   cheannaigh Seán   *t*?   (movement)
         what aL bought   John
         'What did John buy?'
   b.   Cheannaigh Seán cad é?   (in-situ)
         bought   John what
         'What did John buy?'

(1) a.   Cad é a   chreideann tú   a   cheannaigh Seán   *t*?
         what aL believe   you aL bought   John
         'What do you believe that John bought?'
   b.   Creideann tú   gur ceannaigh Seán cad é?
         believe   you that bought   John what
         'What do you believe that John bought?'

Secondly, wh-in-situ is possible within a complex NP island, while wh-movement out of it is not, as shown in (12) and (13).

(12) a. *Cad é a   chreideann siad [an ráfla   gur cheannaigh Seán *t*]?
       what aL believe   they the rumor that bought   John
       '[Q [they believe [the rumor that John bought what]]].'

   b. Creideann siad [an ráfla   gur cheannaigh Seán cad é]?
       believe   they the rumor that bought   John what
       '[Q [they believe [the rumor that John bought what]]].'

(13) a. *Cad é a   chonaic siad [an   fear a   cheannaigh *t*]?
       what aL saw   they   the man aL bought
       '[Q [they saw [the man who bought what]]].'

   b. Chonaic siad [an   fear a   cheannaigh cad é]?
       saw   they the man aL bought   what
       '[Q [they saw [the man who bought what]]].'

Thirdly, wh-in-situ is possible within an adjunct island, while wh-movement out of it is not. See the examples in (14).

(14) a. *Cad é a   dúirt tú   a   bhí   iontas   ar Mháire [cionnas
       what aL said you aL be.PAST surprise on Mary   because
       gur cheannaigh Seán *t*]?
       that bought   John
       '[Q [you said that Mary was surprised [because John bought what]]].'

   b. Dúirt tú   go   raibh   iontas   ar Mháire [cionnas
       said you that.PAST be.PAST surprise on Mary   because
       gur cheannaigh Seán cad é]?
       that bought   John what
       '[Q [you said that Mary was surprised [because John bought what]]].'

Fourthly, wh-in-situ is possible within a wh-island, while wh-movement out of it is not. See the examples in (15).

(15) a. *Cad é atá   a   fhios   agat   [ar cheannaigh
       what aL.be.PRES the knowledge with.you Q bought
       Seán *t*]?
       John
       '[Q [you know [whether John bought what]]].'

b. An bhfuil   a   fhios   agat   [ar cheannaigh Seán
    Q   be.PRES   the   knowledge   with.you   Q   bought   John
    cad é]?
    what
    '[Q [you know [whether John bought what]]].'

Fifthly, and finally, wh-movement across a negation head is possible, and wh-in-situ is also possible within a negation island, as shown in (16) and (17).

(16) a. Cad é nár   cheannaigh Seán *t*?
         what aL.NEG bought   John
         'What didn't John buy?'

    b. Níor   cheannaigh Seán cad é?
        NEG.PAST bought   John   what
        'What didn't John buy?'

(17) a. Cad é a   shíleann tú   nár   cheannaigh Seán *t*?
         what aL think   you aL.NEG bought   John
         'What don't you think that John bought?'

    b. Ní   shíleann tú   gur cheannaigh Seán cad é?
        NEG.PRES think   you that bought   John   what
        'What don't you think that John bought?'

4.   Discussion

Let us now consider what the above findings suggest for the theory of (Irish) syntax. Firstly, Irish has two types of [+Q] COMPs. The contrast between (1b) in Irish and (3b) in French suggests that unlike French, a wh-phrase in situ does not undergo LF head movement. Furthermore, the fact that the *b*-examples in (12)–(15) are grammatical in Irish suggests that a wh-phrase in situ does not undergo LF movement in general. Rather, these facts suggest that in the wh-construction with a wh-in-situ, Irish has a [+Q] COMP that is not found in French or English. The [+Q] COMP seems to pattern with the one found in Chinese. Consider the examples in (18)–(20). (19) and (20) are from Huang (1982: 530, 493).

(18)   Ni   renwei [Lisi   piping-le   shei]?
       you think   Lisi   criticize-ASP who
       '[Q [you think [Lisi criticized who]]].'

                        (personal communication with Ling-Yun Fan)

(19) Ni   xiang-zhidao [shei xi-bu-xihuan ni]?
      you wonder   who like-not-like you
      '[Q [you wonder [whether who likes you or not]]].'

(20) Ni   xihuan [NP [S wo piping   shei] de   wenzhang]?
      you like   I criticize who DE   article
      '[Q [you like [the articles in which I criticize who]]].'

Huang (1982) claims that a wh-phrase in situ in Chinese undergoes LF movement, and Subjacency is not in operation in LF. This can be restated as follows. Chinese [+Q] COMP binds an argument wh-phrase in situ, which does not move in LF.

Note in passing that Mongolian, a wh-in-situ language, patterns exactly like Chinese with respect to the behaviour of wh-in-situ, as shown in the examples in (21)–(23), which are from Lina Bao (personal communication).

(21) Či-ø   [Baγatur-un   yaγu-ø   qudaldun abu-γsan
      you-NOM   Bagatur-GEN what-ACC buy   take-PAST.ADN
      gezü] bodu-γsan   boi?
      that   think-PAST.ADN Q
      '[Q [you thought [that Bagatur bought what]]].'

(22) Či-ø   [Baγatur-un   yaγu-ø   qudaldun abu-γsan
      you-NOM   Bagatur-GEN what-ACC buy   take-PAST.ADN
      esekü-gi-ni]   medekü boi?
      not-ACC-PP3   know   Q
      '[Q [you know [whether Bagatur bought what]]].'

                                            (*ni*= 3rd person possessive pronoun)

(23) Či-ø   [[bi-ø/minu   ken-i   šigumjile-gsen]
      you-NOM   I-NOM/I.GEN who-ACC criticize-PAST.ADN
      joqiyal]-du duratai boi?
      article-to   like   Q
      '[Q [you like [the articles in which I criticize who]]].'

Now, it has turned out that Irish [+Q] COMP for an argument wh-phrase is exactly like the one found in Chinese and Mongolian, as exemplified by the *b*-examples in (12)–(15). At the same time, all the *a*-examples show that Irish also has another [+Q] COMP, which is like the one found in English, as shown by the examples in (24)–(28).

(24) What do you believe that John bought?

(25)   *What do they believe [the rumor that John bought *t*]?

(26)   *What did they see [the man who bought *t*]?

(27)   *What did you say that Mary was surprised [because John bought *t*]?

(28)   *What do you know [whether John bought *t*]?

Thus, the present research made it explicit that a language can have two types of [+Q] COMPs, and its manifestation is Irish.

Secondly, the contrast between (29) and (30) shows that adjunct wh-phrases are categorized into two groups: the manner class and the reason class.

(29) a.   Cad é an dóigh   ar   chóirigh Seán an   carr?
          what the way   aN fixed   John the car
          'How did John fix the car?'

     b.   Chóirigh Seán an   carr (ar) cad é an   dóigh?
          fixed   John the car   (on) what the way
          'How did John fix the car?'

(30) a.   Cén   fáth   ar   chóirigh Seán an   carr?
          what.the reason aN fixed   John the car
          'Why did John fix the car?'

     b. *Chóirigh Seán an   carr cén   fáth?
          fixed   John the car   what.the reason
          'Why did John fix the car?'

(29b) shows that the manner adverbial wh-phrase *cad é an dóigh* 'what it the way = how' can be in situ, while (30b) shows that the reason adverbial wh-phrase *cén fáth* 'what.the reason = why' cannot be in situ. This dichotomy is further confirmed by the corresponding examples in French, as shown in (31) and (32).

(31) a.   Comment Jean a   réparé la   voiture?
          how   Jean has fixed   the car
          'How did Jean fix the car?'
                              (personal communication with Gilles Guerrin)

     b.   Jean a   réparé la   voiture comment?
          Jean has fixed   the car   how
          'How did Jean fix the car?'   (Bošković (2000: 56))

(32) a. Pourquoi Jean a réparé la voiture?
         why   Jean has fixed the car
         'Why did Jean fix the car?'
     b. *Jean a réparé la voiture pourquoi?
         Jean has fixed the car   why
         'Why did Jean fix the car?'

Note further that the manner adverbial wh-phrase *cad é an dóigh* 'how' can
be in the embedded clause, as shown in (33b).

(33) a. Cad é an dóigh a síleann tú gur chóirigh Seán an carr?
         what the way aN think you that fixed   John the car
         'How do you think [that John fixed the car *t*]?'
     b. Síleann tú gur chóirigh Seán an carr (ar) cad é an dóigh?
         think you that fixed   John the car on what the way
         'How do you think [that John fixed the car *t*]?'

In this sense, the COMP that licenses *cad é an dóigh* 'how' in situ is similar
to the one found in Chinese and Mongolian, as shown in (34)–(37).

(34) Lisi zenme xiuli-le nabu che?
      Lisi how   fix-ASP that car
      '[Q [Lisi fixed the car how]].'   (C)

(35) Ni   renwei Lisi zenme xiuli-le nabu che?
      you think Lisi how   fix-ASP that car
      '[Q [you think [Lisi fixed the car how]]].'   (C)
                            (personal communication with Ling-Yun Fan)

(36) Baɣatur-ø   yaɣaqiju tere terge-gi jasa-ɣsan   boi?
      Bagatur-NOM how   that car-ACC repair-PAST Q
      '[Q [Bagatur fixed the car how]]].'   (M)

(37) Či-ø   Baɣatur-ø/-i   yaɣaqiju tere terge-gi jasa-ɣsan
      you-NOM Bagatur-NOM/-ACC how   that car-ACC repair-PAST
      gejü boduju baiqu boi?
      that think be   Q
      '[Q [you think [Bagatur fixed the car how]]].'   (M)

Furthermore, the manner adverbial wh-phrase *cad é an dóigh* 'how' can
be in a complex NP, as shown in (38b).

(38) a. Cad é an dóigh a   bhfaca siad [an fear a   chóirigh an
    what the way aN saw   they the man aL fixed   the
    carr *t*]?
    car
    '[Q [they saw [the man who fixed the car how]]].'

   b. Chonaic siad [an fear a   chóirigh an carr (ar) cad é an
    saw   they the man aL fixed   the car on what the
    dóigh]?
    way
    '[Q [they saw [the man who fixed the car how]]].'

Both sentences in (38) are grammatical. In (38a), *cad é an dóigh* 'how' modifies the matrix clause, but it cannot modify the clause in the complex NP. In (38b), *cad é an dóigh* 'how' only modifies the clause in the complex NP.

Again, this is what takes place in Chinese and Mongolian, as shown in (39) and (40).

(39) Ni   bu   yuanyi yong [[ta zenmeyang zhuan-lai de] qian]?
    you not willing use he   how   earn-come DE money
    '[Q [you are reluctant to use [the money he earns how]]].'   (C)
    (Lin (1992: 295))

(40) Či-ø   [tegün-nü yaɣaqiju olu-ɣsan   joɣus-i-ni]
    you-NOM he-GEN how   earn-PAST.ADN money-GEN-PP3
    jaruqu dura   ügei boi?
    use   preference NEG Q
    '[Q [you are reluctant to use [the money he earns how]]].'   (M)
    (personal communication with Lina Bao)

Thus, the above data clearly show that adjunct wh-phrases are categorized into two groups: the manner class and the reason class. This then provides support for the essential claim by Bošković (2000) for French. See also Lin (1992) for the same claim based on Chinese data.

Note, however, that there is a major difference between Chinese *weishenme* 'why' and Irish *cén fáth* 'why.' The examples in (30) show that *cén fáth* 'why' in Irish must be base-generated in CP SPEC.

(30) a. Cén   fáth ar chóirigh Seán an carr?
    what.the reason aN fixed   John the car
    'Why did John fix the car?'

   b. *Chóirigh Seán an carr cén   fáth?
      fixed   John the car what.the reason
      'Why did John fix the car?'

The Chinese counterpart of (30b) is perfect, as shown in (41).

(41)   Lisi weishenme xiuli-le   nabu che?
      Lisi why   fix-ASP that car
      '[Q Lisi fixed the car why]]].'   (C)

At first sight, *weishenme* 'why' is base-generated within TP. However, Lin (1992) and Ko (2005) argue that it is actually base-generated in CP SPEC, just like Irish and English. Ko (2005) claims the External-Merge Hypothesis, which states that in the overt syntax, 'why' in Chinese/Japanese/ Korean is externally-merged into the [Spec,CP] of the clause it modifies, and that the CP that 'why' merges with may be declarative or interrogative. Therefore, (42), which is grammatical, has *weishenme* 'why' in CP SPEC of the embedded clause, with the subject *Lisi* topicalized across it, as schematically shown in (43).

(42)   Ni   renwei Lisi weishenme cizhi?
      you think Lisi why   resign
      'Why$_1$ do you think [Lisi resigned t_1]?'   (Soh (2001))

(43) a.   you think [$_{CP}$ why [$_{IP}$ Lisi resigned]]
     b.   you think [$_{CP}$ Lisi [$_{CP}$ why [$_{IP}$ t_{Lisi} resigned]]]

The point is that in (42), the reason adjunct wh-phrase is in the embedded clause at the surface level, although it takes matrix scope.

   However, this is impossible in Irish, as shown in (44).

(44)   *Dúirt Pól cén   fáth a raibh   Seán ann?
      said Paul what.the reason aN be.PAST John there
      'Why$_1$ did Paul say [that John was there t_1]?'

In (44), the reason adjunct wh-phrase *cén fáth* 'why' is in CP SPEC of the embedded clause. The COMP *aN* indicates that the wh-phrase is base-generated in that position. In order for (44) to be grammatical, *cén fáth* 'why' must be in CP SPEC where it takes scope at the surface level, as shown in (45), cited from McCloskey (2002, ex. 69).

(45)   Cén   fáth   a   dúirt Pól   a   raibh   Seán ann?
       what.the reason aL   said Paul   aN   be.PAST John there
       'Why₁ did Paul say [that John was there t₁]?'

In (45), the embedded COMP is *aN*, and the matrix COMP is *aL*.
Therefore, *cén fáth* 'why' moved from the SPEC of the embedded CP to the
SPEC of the matrix CP.

Therefore, the ungrammaticality of (44) in Irish indicates that the reason adjunct wh-phrase *cén fáth* 'why' in Irish does not pattern together with
the corresponding wh-phrase *weishenme* 'why' in Chinese, and this contrast
between Chinese and Irish suggests that the behaviors of reason adverbial
wh-phrases need to be specified independently of the properties of the [+Q]
COMPs in the languages.

Thirdly, there are actually three types of wh-phrases in Irish. In the
above discussion, we saw that the manner adverbial wh-phrase *cad é an
dóigh* 'how' patterns together with argument wh-phrases, such as *cad é*
'what.' The relevant examples are repeated below.

(1) a.   Cad é a   chreideann tú   a   cheannaigh Seán t?
         what aL believe   you   aL   bought   John
         'What do you believe that John bought?'
    b.   Creideann tú   gur ceannaigh Seán cad é?
         believe   you that bought   John what
         'What do you believe that John bought?'

(13) a. *Cad é a   chonaic siad [an fear a   cheannaigh t]?
          what aL saw   they the man aL   bought
          '[Q [they saw [the man who bought what]]].'
     b. Chonaic siad [an fear a   cheannaigh cad é]?
         saw   they the man aL   bought   what
         '[Q [they saw [the man who bought what]]].'

(33) a. Cad é an dóigh a   síleann tú   gur chóirigh Seán an carr?
         what the way aN think   you that fixed   John the car
         'How do you think [that John fixed the car t]?'
     b. Síleann tú   gur chóirigh Seán an carr (ar) cad é an dóigh?
         think   you that fixed   John the car on what the way
         'How do you think [that John fixed the car t]?'

(38) a.   Cad é an   dóigh   a   bhfaca siad   [an fear   a   chóirigh an
           what   the way   aN   saw   they   the   man aL fixed   the
           carr *t*]?
           car
           '[Q [they saw [the man who fixed the car how]]].'

      b.   Chonaic siad   [an fear a   chóirigh an   carr (ar) cad é an
           saw   they   the man aL fixed   the car   on what the
           dóigh]?
           way
           '[Q [they saw [the man who fixed the car how]]].'

The *b*-examples in (1), (13), (33) and (38) show that both *cad é an dóigh* 'how' and *cad é* 'what' can be in situ, and pattern together. Since *cad é an dóigh* 'how' does not pattern with *cén fáth* 'why,' it may be concluded that there are two types of wh-phrases in Irish.

However, the patterns in A'-chains for *cad é* 'what' are not parallel to those for *cad é an dóigh* 'how,' as shown in (46) and (47).

(46) a.   Cad é a   cheannaigh Seán *t*?
           what   aL bought   John
           'What did John buy?'

      b.   Cad é ar   cheannaigh Seán é?
           what   aN bought   John it
           'What did John buy?'

(47) a.   Cad é an dóigh ar chóirigh Seán an carr?
           what   the way   aN fixed   John   the car
           'How did John fix the car?'

      b.   *Cad é an dóigh a   chóirigh Seán an carr?
           what   the way   aL fixed   John   the car
           'How did John fix the car?'

The examples in (46) indicate that there are two ways to make a wh-interrogative sentence with an argument wh-phrase in Irish, namely, by movement, as in (46a), and by resumption, as in (46b). However, as the contrast in grammaticality in (47) shows, there is one way to make a wh-interrogative sentence with the manner adverb wh-phrase *cad é an dóigh* 'how.' Therefore, although apparently the manner adverb wh-phrase *cad é an dóigh* 'how' patterns together with argument wh-phrases such as *cad é* 'what,' they are not categorized together. Thus, there are actually three types of wh-phrases in Irish, as *cad é an dóigh* 'how' does not pattern together with *cén fáth* 'why.'

5. Conclusion

This paper investigated the wh-construction in Irish that involves wh-movement and wh-in-situ. Based on the newly found data, we claimed (i) that Irish has two types of [+Q] COMPs, one with a [strong] feature, and another with a [weak] feature, (ii) that adjunct wh-phrases in Irish are categorized into two groups: the manner class and the reason class, and the manner class wh-phrases pattern together with argument wh-phrases, and (iii) that the differences in the A'-chain patterns suggest that there are actually three types of wh-phrases in Irish: argument, manner and reason wh-phrases.

It has turned out then that in terms of the wh-construction, Irish is a typologically unique language in the sense that it has two different types of [+Q] COMPs: one type of [+Q] COMP has a [strong] feature that needs to be deleted in overt syntax, which necessarily involves overt wh-movement; and another type that does not have this feature, and binds a wh-phrase in situ, so that no wh-movement takes place with this COMP.

In this paper, we did not discuss the Japanese wh-construction. There is one crucial difference between Japanese on the one hand, and Chinese and Mongolian on the other. The Japanese wh-construction exhibits a Wh-Island Condition effect, as shown in the contrast between (48) and (49).

(48)   Anata-wa [Taroo-ga   nani-o   kat-ta   to] omoi-masu ka?
        you-TOP   Taro-NOM what-ACC buy-PAST that think-polite Q
        '[Q [you think [that Taro bought what]]].'

(49)   *Anata-wa [Taroo-ga   nani-o   kat-ta   kadooka] shittei-masu
        you-TOP   Taro-NOM what-ACC buy-PAST whether   know-polite
        ka?
        Q
        '[Q [you know [whether Taro bought what]]].'

                                    (Nishigauchi (1990), Watanabe (1992b))

If Watanabe (1992b) is correct, then, Japanese [+Q] COMP has a [strong] feature, and it must be deleted in overt syntax. Then, the languages investigated in this paper are grouped together in terms of the types of COMPs and when they are put into the phrase structure, as shown in (50). Note that as it is not obvious when the COMP with a [weak] feature is inserted to the phrase structure, especially in a language without an overt COMP,

the distinction in the timing of COMP insertion is not made explicit for the
COMPs with a [weak] feature in (50).

(50)   Languages Grouped in Terms of the Two Factors: the COMP Type
        and the Timing of COMP Insertion

Type of C	Insertion Before LF	Insertion in LF
$C_{[strong]}$	English, French, Japanese, **Irish**	French
$C_{[weak]}$	Chinese, Mongolian, **Irish**	

What is special about (50) is the fact that Irish has two types of COMPs.
The fact that such a language exists in human language indicates that a
given language can pick up more than one type of COMP out of the lexicon
in principle. Of course, the question remains as to why this kind of multiple
selection is only limited to Irish, which we will leave for future research.

Chapter 8

The Cleft Construction in Irish*

Hideki Maki and Dónall P. Ó Baoill

Gifu University and *Queen's University Belfast* (Prof. Emeritus)

Keywords: *chain, cleft, English, Japanese, operator*

1. Introduction

This paper investigates properties of the cleft construction in Irish, as illustrated in (1),[1]

(1) Is   é [an carr seo]$_1$ Op$_1$ a   cheannaigh Seán t_1.
     COP.PRES it the car   this   aL bought   John
     'It is [this car]$_1$ that John bought t_1.'

and points out (i) that CPs and adjective phrases (APs) can be clefted in Irish, unlike English or Japanese, and (ii) that while NP clefting allows six chain patterns with one embedded clause, clefting of the other categories only allows two chain patterns, just like the comparative construction in Irish. Based on these findings, we claim (i) that the COMP of the clefted

---

* An earlier version of this paper was presented at the Sixth International Spring Forum by the English Linguistic Society of Japan held at the University of Tokyo on April 27, 2013. We would like to thank the audience of the conference, Jessica Dunton, Kwang-Sup Kim, Keiichiro Kobayashi, Fumikazu Niinuma and Yoshiki Ogawa for their valuable comments. Our thanks also go to the following native speakers from the eastern borders of Gweedore Parish in North West Donegal with whom the examples have been checked: Donnchadh Mac Fhionnaile, Seán Mac Giolla Chóill, Bríd Bean Mhic Íomhair, Anna Ní Bhaoill, Máire Nic Giolla Chóill, Pádraig Ó Briain, Pádraig Ó Dúgáin (Éamann), Bríd Bean Uí Ghallchóir and Méabha Bean Uí Phíopalaigh. All errors are our own. Research by the second author was supported in part by Japan Society for the Promotion of Science Grant # 25370428 to Gifu University.
[1] The abbreviations used in this paper are as follows: 2 = second person, ACC = accusative, COND = conditional, COP = copula, EX = exclamation, NOM = nominative, PRES = present tense, PAST = past tense, Q = question, RP = resumptive pronoun, SG = singular and TOP = topic.

CP does not need to be raised to V in Irish, while it must in English and Japanese, (ii) that the difference in AP clefting between Irish on the one hand, and English and Japanese on the other, lies in whether the 'stranded' copula/particle is truly stranded or not, and (iii) that the chain patterns allowed in the cleft and the comparative constructions suggest that what moves in the cleft construction that does not involve NP clefting and in the comparative construction in general is not nominal in nature.

The organization of this paper is as follows. Section 2 reviews properties of complementizers in Irish as background to subsequent sections. Section 3 provides the cleft examples in Irish. Based on the newly found data, Section 4 discusses what they might suggest for the theory of (Irish) grammar. Finally, Section 5 concludes this paper.

2.   Background

In this section, we review properties of complementizers in Irish. Irish has three types of complementizers: the [−Q] marker, the direct relative marker, and the indirect relative marker. The properties of the three COMPs are summarized in (2). See McCloskey (1979, 2002) for abundant data with complementizer alternations.

(2)   Complementizers in Irish[2]

	types of COMPs	non-past form	past form	symbol
a.	the [−Q] marker	*go*	*go/gur*	that
b.	the direct relative marker	*a*	*a*	aL
c.	the indirect relative marker	*a*	*a/ar*	aN

Let us illustrate the properties of the COMPs by relevant examples. (3) is a declarative sentence, and the embedded clause is headed by the [−Q] COMP *gur* 'that.' On the other hand, when the sentence involves wh-interrogative clause formation, as in (4), the embedded COMP must change to the direct relative marker *aL*, and at the same time, another COMP *aL* must be insert-

---

[2] The complementizer forms used with irregular verbs in the past tense in Irish, namely, the [−Q] marker and indirect relative marker *aN* do not follow the regular usage found with all other verbs. Hence, the regular complementizer forms *gur* 'that' and the indirect relative form *ar* are replaced by *go* 'that' and *a* 'aN,' respectively when used with the following irregular verbs: *bí* 'to be' >> *go/a raibh*; *déan* 'to do' >> *go/a ndearna*; *faigh* 'to get' >> *go/a bhfuair*; *tabhair* 'to give' >> *go/a dtug*; *tar* 'to come' >> *go/a dtáinig* and *téigh* 'to go' >> *go/a ndeachaigh*.

ed right after the wh-phrase.

(3)   Creideann Seán gur cheannaigh Máire an carr.
      believe   John that bought   Mary the car
      'John believes that Mary bought the car.'

(4)   [Cad é] a   chreideann tú   a   cheannaigh Seán t?
      what   aL believe   you aL bought   John
      'What$_1$ do you believe that John bought t_1?'   (movement) (aL, aL, t)

There is another way to form a wh-interrogative clause. Observe the example in (5).

(5)   [Cad é] a   gcreideann tú   gur cheannaigh Seán é/*t?
      what   aN believe   you that bought   John it
      'What$_1$ do you believe that John bought t_1?'

                                             (resumption) (aN, that, RP)

In (5), the topmost COMP of the wh-interrogative clause is an indirect relative marker aN, the COMP of the embedded clause is a [−Q] COMP, and the embedded clause contains a resumptive pronoun (RP) $é$ 'it' instead of a trace. Note that (5) becomes ungrammatical, if the resumptive pronoun is replaced by a trace, which suggests that aN must bind a resumptive pronoun.

   McCloskey (2002) shows three more cases of the wh-interrogative construction, as shown in (6)–(8), and Maki and Ó Baoill (2005) provide yet another case of the wh-interrogative construction, as shown in (9).

(6)   [Cad é] a   raibh súil agat   a   cheannófá t?
      what   aN was   hope at.you aL buy.COND
      'What$_1$ did you hope that you would buy t_1?'   (aN, aL, t)

(7)   [Cad é] a   chreideann tú   ar   cheannaigh Seán é?
      what   aL believe   you aN bought   John it
      'What$_1$ do you believe that John bought t_1?'   (aL, aN, RP)

(8)   [Cad é] a   gcreideann tú   ar   cheannaigh Seán é?
      what   aN believe   you aN bought   John it
      'What$_1$ do you believe that John bought t_1?'   (aN, aN, RP)

(9)   [Cad é] a   mheasann Seán gur cheart dúinn é a   cheannach?
      what   aL think   John that right for.us it to buy
      'What$_1$ does John think that we ought to buy t_1?'   (aL, that, RP)

McCloskey (2002) assumes that the SPEC of aL contains a null operator/

null pronoun (henceforth, null operator) as a result of movement, that in the SPEC of *aN*, there is a base-generated operator, and that in the SPEC of *go/gur*, there is no operator. If this is correct, the structure of the wh-interrogative clause construction in Irish looks like a cleft sentence, as shown in (10).

(10)   (it is) WH$_1$ [Op$_1$ aL/aN [$_{IP}$...t_1/RP$_1$...]]

In this paper, for expository purposes, we follow Chomsky's (1977) analysis of the cleft construction in English, and represent the structure of the Irish cleft construction, as in (11), where XP is a clefted phrase.

(11)   it is XP$_1$ [Op$_1$ aL/aN [$_{IP}$...t_1/RP$_1$...]]

3. Data

Having outlined the particular background, let us consider the properties of the cleft construction in Irish. We first examine examples with short distance clefting in 3.1, and then those with long distance clefting in 3.2.

3.1. Short Distance Clefting

In this subsection, we consider examples with short distance clefting in Irish. Irish allows NPs, PPs, CPs and APs to be clefted. Let us start by examining example (1), reproduced as (12), with the object NP being clefted.

NP Clefting (Object)

(12)   Is   é   [an carr seo]$_1$ Op$_1$ a   cheannaigh Seán t_1.
        COP.PRES it   the car this   aL bought   John
        'It is [this car]$_1$ that John bought t_1.'   (=(1))

In (12) the operator that corresponds to the clefted object undergoes movement from the object position of the sentence to the SPEC of *aL*. Note that *aL* signals that movement has taken place across it. However, when the clefting operation does not use the movement strategy, but uses the resumption strategy signaled by *aN*, clefting does not succeed in some cases, as shown in (13).

(13)   *Is   é   [an carr seo]$_1$ Op$_1$ ar cheannaigh Seán é$_1$.
        COP.PRES it   the car this   aN bought   John it
        'It is [this car]$_1$ that John bought t_1.'

However, when the clefted NP is heavy enough, (13) becomes grammatical, as shown in (14).

(14)　Is　　　　é　[an　carr seo　a　　ba　　　　mhaith liom　　a
　　　COP.PRES　it　the　car　this　aL　COP.PAST　good　　with.me　to
　　　dhiiol]₁ Op₁ ar　　cheannaigh Seán é₁.
　　　sell　　　　　aN bought　　John it
　　　'It is [this car which I wanted to sell]₁ that John bought t₁.'

Therefore, in the following, we assume that in principle, short distance NP clefting allows the resumption strategy, putting aside the question of why it is impossible when the clefted NP is not heavy enough.

　　　Note that in the following, we omit the operator Op and the trace t in the examples for simplicity's sake, unless these symbols make the structures of the examples clearer.

　　　Next, subject NP can be clefted by the movement strategy, as shown in (15).

NP Clefting (Subject)

(15)　(Is　　　　é)　[Seán]　a　　cheannaigh an　carr seo.
　　　(COP.PRES　it)　John　aL bought　　　the　car　this
　　　'It is John₁ that t₁ bought this car.'

However, it cannot be clefted by the resumption strategy, as shown in (16).

(16)　*(Is　　　　é)　[Seán]　ar　cheannaigh sé　an　carr seo.
　　　(COP.PRES　it)　John　aN bought　　　he　the　car　this
　　　'It is John₁ that t₁ bought this car.'

(16) is actually a case that falls under the Highest Subject Restriction (HSR). See Ó Baoill and Maki (2012) for the mechanism of the HSR.

　　　Next, let us turn to PP clefting examples. (17) shows that a place adverb can be clefted under the movement strategy, while (18) shows that it cannot be clefted under the resumption strategy.

PP Clefting (Place Adverb)

(17)　(Is　　　　é)　[i　mBéal Feirste]　a　　cheannaigh Seán an　carr
　　　(COP.PRES　it)　in　Belfast　　　　aL bought　　　John the　car
　　　seo　anuraidh.
　　　this　last.year
　　　'It is [in Belfast]₁ that John bought this car last year t₁.'

(18) *(Is   é) [i   mBéal Feirste] ar   cheannaigh Seán an carr
      (COP.PRES it) in Belfast   aN bought   John the car
      seo anuraidh.
      this last.year
      'It is [in Belfast]$_1$ that John bought this car last year t_1.'

(19) shows that a time adverb can be clefted under the movement strategy,
while (20) shows that it cannot be clefted under the resumption strategy.

PP Clefting (Time Adverb)

(19) (Is   é) [anuraidh] a   cheannaigh Seán an   carr seo i
      (COP.PRES it) last.year aL bought   John the car this in
      mBéal Feirste.
      Belfast
      'It is [last year]$_1$ that John bought this car in Belfast t_1.'

(20) *(Is   é) [anuraidh] ar cheannaigh Seán an   carr seo i
      (COP.PRES it) last.year aN bought   John the car this in
      mBéal Feirste.
      Belfast
      'It is [last year]$_1$ that John bought this car in Belfast t_1.'

Next, let us consider CP clefting examples. (21) shows that a clause
headed by the COMP *gur* 'that' can be clefted under the movement strategy,
while (22) shows that it cannot be clefted under the resumption strategy.

CP Clefting

(21) (Is   é) [gur cheannaigh Seán carr] a chreideann Máire.
      COP.PRES it that bought   John car aL believe   Mary
      '*It is [that John bought a car]$_1$ that Mary believes t_1.'

(22) *(Is   é) [gur cheannaigh Seán carr] ar chreideann Máire.
      COP.PRES it that bought   John car aN believe   Mary
      '*It is [that John bought a car]$_1$ that Mary believes t_1.'

Note here that CP clefting is impossible in English, as the gloss of the example in (21) shows.

Finally, let us consider AP clefting examples. (23) shows that an AP
can be clefted under the movement strategy, while (24) shows that it cannot
be clefted under the resumption strategy.

AP Clefting

(23)   [Róchliste] atá   Seán.
      too.clever   aL+be.PRES   John
      '*It is [too clever]$_1$ that John is t_1.'

(24) *[Róchliste] a   bhfuil   Seán.
      too.clever   aN   be.PRES   John
      '*It is [too clever]$_1$ that John is t_1.'

Note again that AP clefting is impossible in English, as the gloss of the example in (24) shows.

3.2. Long Distance Clefting

In this subsection, we examine long distance clefting in Irish. It will be shown that NP clefting allows six chain patterns with one embedded clause, just like wh-interrogative formation with one embedding shown in the examples in (4)–(9) in Section 2, reproduced as (25)–(30), while clefting of the other phrases only allows two chain patterns.

(25)   [Cad é] a   chreideann tú   a   cheannaigh Seán t?
      what   aL believe   you aL bought   John
      'What$_1$ do you believe that John bought t_1?'   (aL, aL, t) (=(4))

(26)   [Cad é] a   gcreideann tú   gur cheannaigh Seán é/*t?
      what   aN believe   you that bought   John it
      'What$_1$ do you believe that John bought t_1?'   (aN, that, RP) (=(5))

(27)   [Cad é] a   raibh súil agat   a   cheannófá t?
      what   aN was   hope at.you aL buy.COND
      'What$_1$ did you hope that you would buy t_1?'   (aN, aL, t) (=(6))

(28)   [Cad é] a   chreideann tú   ar cheannaigh Seán é?
      what   aL believe   you aN bought   John it
      'What$_1$ do you believe that John bought t_1?'   (aL, aN, RP) (=(7))

(29)   [Cad é] a   gcreideann tú   ar cheannaigh Seán é?
      what   aN believe   you aN bought   John it
      'What$_1$ do you believe that John bought t_1?'   (aN, aN, RP) (=(8))

(30)   [Cad é] a   mheasann Seán gur cheart dúinn é a   cheannach?
      what   aL think   John that right   for.us it to buy
      'What$_1$ does John think that we ought to buy t_1?'

                                                    (aL, that, RP) (=(9))

Let us start by examining NP clefting examples in (31)–(36), which are
all grammatical in Irish.

NP Clefting

(31)   Is   é [an carr seo] a chreideann tú   a   cheannaigh
        COP.PRES it the car this aL believe   you aL bought
        Seán.
        John
        'It is [this car] that you believe that John bought t_1?'   (aL, aL, t)

(32)   Is   é [an carr seo] a raibh súil   agam a
        COP.PRES it the car this aN was   hope at.me aL
        cheannófa.
        buy.COND.2.SG
        'It is this car that I hoped that you would buy.'   (aN, aL, t)

(33)   Is   é [an carr seo] a chreideann tú   ar cheannaigh
        COP.PRES it the car this aL believe   you aN bought
        Seán é.
        John it
        'It is this car that you believe that John bought.'   (aL, aN, RP)

(34)   Is   é [an carr seo] a gcreideann tú   ar cheannaigh
        COP.PRES it the car this aN believe   you aN bought
        Seán é.
        John it
        'It is this car that you believe that John bought.'   (aN, aN, RP)

(35)   Is   é [an carr seo] a gcreideann tú   gur cheannaigh
        COP.PRES it the car this aN believe   you that bought
        Seán é.
        John it
        'It is this car that you believe that John bought.'   (aN, that, RP)

(36)   Is   é [an carr seo] a mheasann Seán gur cheart
        COP.PRES it the car this aL think   John that right
        dúinn é a cheannach.
        for.us it to buy
        'It is this car that John thinks that we ought to buy.' (aL, that, RP)

These examples thus show that NP clefting with one embedded clause patterns together with wh-movement with one embedding with respect to the resulting chain patterns.

Next, let us turn to PP clefting examples in (37)–(42), which contain a place adverb. As shown directly, unlike NP clefting, PP clefting only allows two chain patterns that end with a trace.

PP Clefting (Place Adverb)

(37) (Is   é) [i   mBéal Feirste] a   chreideann Máire
      (COP.PRES it) in Belfast   aL believe   Mary
      a   cheannaigh Seán an carr seo anuraidh.
      aL bought   John the car this last.year
      'It is [in Belfast]$_1$ that Mary believes that John bought this car last
      year t_1.'   (aL, aL, t)

(38) (Is   é) [i   mBéal Feirste] a   raibh súil agam
      (COP.PRES it) in Belfast   aN was   hope at.me
      a   cheannófá   carr t_1.
      aL buy.COND car
      'It is [in Belfast]$_1$ that I hoped that you would buy a car t_1.'
                                                          (aN, aL, t)

(39) *(Is   é) [i   mBéal Feirste] a   chreideann Máire
      (COP.PRES it) in Belfast   aL believe   Mary
      ar   cheannaigh Seán an carr seo anuraidh.
      aN bought   John the car this last.year
      'It is [in Belfast]$_1$ that Mary believes that John bought this car last
      year t_1.'   (aL, aN, RP)

(40) *(Is   é) [i   mBéal Feirste] a   gcreideann Máire
      (COP.PRES it) in Belfast   aN believe   Mary
      ar   cheannaigh an carr seo anuraidh.
      aN bought   the car this last.year
      'It is [in Belfast]$_1$ that Mary believes that John bought this car last
      year t_1.'   (aN, aN, RP)

(41) *(Is   é) [i   mBéal Feirste] a   gcreideann Máire
      (COP.PRES it) in Belfast   aN believe   Mary
      gur cheannaigh Seán an carr seo anuraidh.
      that bought   John the car this last.year
      'It is [in Belfast]$_1$ that Mary believes that John bought this car last

year t_1.'   (aN, that, RP)

(42) *(Is   é) [i   mBéal Feirste] a chreideann Máire
      (COP.PRES it) in Belfast   a believe   Mary
      gur cheannaigh Seán an carr seo anuraidh.
      that bought   John the car this last.year
      'It is [in Belfast]₁ that Mary believes that John bought this car last
      year t_1.'   (aL, that, RP)

(37) and (38) are grammatical, while (39)–(42) are not.

Let us also examine PP clefting examples in (43)–(48), which contain
a time adverb. Just like PP clefting with a place adverb, PP clefting with a
time adverb also allows only two chain patterns that end with a trace.

PP Clefting (Time Adverb)

(43) (Is   é) [anuraidh] a chreideann Máire
      (COP.PRES it) last.year   aL believe   Mary
      a   cheannaigh Seán an carr seo i mBéal Feirste.
      aL bought   John the car this in Belfast
      'It is [last year]₁ that Mary believes that John bought this car in
      Belfast t_1.'   (aL, aL, t)

(44) (Is   é) anuraidh₁ a raibh súil   agam
      (COP.PRES it) last.year   aN was hope at.me
      a   cheannófá Seán an carr seo i mBéal Feirste t_1.
      aL buy.COND John the car this in Belfast
      'It is [last year]₁ that I hoped that John would buy this car in
      Belfast t_1.'   (aN, aL, t)

(45) *(Is   é) [anuraidh] a chreideann Máire
      (COP.PRES it) last.year   aL believe   Mary
      ar cheannaigh Seán an carr seo i mBéal Feirste.
      aN bought   John the car this in Belfast
      'It is [last year]₁ that Mary believes that John bought this car in
      Belfast t_1.'   (aL, aN, RP)

(46) *(Is   é) [anuraidh] a gcreideann Máire
      (COP.PRES it) last.year   aN believe   Mary
      ar cheannaigh Seán an carr seo i mBéal Feirste (é₁).
      aN bought   John the car this in Belfast   it
      'It is [last year]₁ that Mary believes that John bought this car in

Belfast t_1.'   (aN, aN, RP)

(47) *(Is   é) [anuraidh] a   gcreideann Máire
      (COP.PRES it) last.year aN believe   Mary
      gur cheannaigh Seán an carr seo i   mBéal Feirste.
      that bought   John the car this in Belfast
      'It is [last year]$_1$ that Mary believes that John bought this car in
      Belfast t_1.'   (aN, that, RP)

(48) *(Is   é) [anuraidh] a   chreideann Máire
      (COP.PRES it) last.year aL believe   Mary
      gur cheannaigh Seán an carr seo i   mBéal Feirste (é$_1$).
      that bought   John the car this in Belfast   it
      'It is [last year]$_1$ that Mary believes that John bought this car in
      Belfast t_1.'   (aL, that, RP)

Next, let us turn to CP clefting examples in (49)–(54). Just like PP
clefting, this type of clefting also only allows two chain patterns that end
with a trace.

CP Clefting

(49) Is   é [gur cheannaigh Seán carr] a chreideann Máire
      COP.PRES it that bought   John car aL believe   Mary
      a   dúirt siad.
      aL said they
      'It is [that John bought a car]$_1$ that Mary believes that they said t_1.'
                                                       (aL, aL, t)

(50) Is   é [gur cheannaigh Seán carr] a   raibh súil agam a
      COP.PRES it that bought   John car aN was hope at.me aL
      déarfá.
      say.COND.2.SG
      'It is [that John bought a car]$_1$ that I hoped that you would say t_1.'
                                                       (aN, aL, t)

(51) *Is   é [gur cheannaigh Seán carr] a   dúirt Máire ar
      COP.PRES it that bought   John car aL said Máire aN
      dhúirt siad.
      said they
      'It is [that John bought a car]$_1$ that Mary said that they said t_1.'
                                                       (aL, aN, RP)

(52) *Is   é [gur cheannaigh Seán carr] ar dhúirt Máire gur
      COP.PRES   it that bought   John car aN said   Mary that
      dhúirt siad.
      said   they
      'It is [that John bought a car]₁ that Mary said that they said t₁.'
                                                              (aN, that, RP)

(53) *Is   é [gur cheannaigh Seán carr] ar dhúirt Máire ar
      COP.PRES   it that bought   John car aN said   Mary aN
      dhúirt siad.
      said   they
      'It is [that John bought a car]₁ that Mary said that they said t₁.'
                                                               (aN, aN, RP)

(54) *Is   é [gur cheannaigh Seán carr]₁ a   dúirt Máire gur
      COP.PRES   it that bought   John car aL said   Mary that
      dhúirt siad (é₁).
      said   they it
      'It is [that John bought a car]₁ that Mary said that they said t₁.'
                                                              (aL, that, RP)

Finally, let us examine AP clefting examples in (55)–(60). Just like CP clefting, this type of clefting also only allows two chain patterns that end with a trace.

AP Clefting

(55) Is   é [róchliste] a   chreideann Máire atá   Seán.
      COP.PRES it too.clever aL believe   Mary aL+be.PRES John
      'It is [too clever]₁ that Mary believes that John is t₁.'   (aL, aL, t)

(56) Is   é [róchliste] a   raibh súil agam a   bheadh Seán.
      COP.PRES it too.clever aN was hope at.me aL be.COND John
      'It is [too clever]₁ that I hoped that John would be t₁.'   (aN, aL, t)

(57) *Is   é [róchliste] a   chreideann Máire a   bhfuil   Seán.
      COP.PRES it too.clever aL believe   Mary aN be.PRES John
      'It is [too clever]₁ that Mary believes that John is t₁.'   (aL, aN, RP)

(58) *Is   é [róchliste] a   gcreideann Máire a   bhfuil   Seán.
      COP.PRES it too.clever aN believe   Mary aN be.PRES John
      'It is [too clever]₁ that Mary believes that John is t₁.'   (aN, aN, RP)

(59) *Is   é [róchliste] a   gcreideann Máire go bhfuil   Seán.
       COP.PRES it too.clever aN believe   Mary thatbe.PRES John
       'It is [too clever]$_1$ that Mary believes that John is t_1.'   (aN, that, RP)

(60) *Is   é [róchliste] a   chreideann Máire go bhfuil   Seán.
       COP.PRES it too.clever aL believe   Mary thatbe.PRES John
       'It is [too clever]$_1$ that Mary believes that John is t_1.'

(aL, that, RP)

To summarize, two important facts were observed in this section. First, Irish allows a variety of clefting with an NP, PP, CP and AP being clefted. Second, NP clefting allows six types of chain patterns with one embedded clause, but the other types of clefting only allow two types of chain patterns with one embedded clause, which terminate with a trace.

4. Discussion

Let us now consider what the observed facts might suggest for the theory of (Irish) grammar. First, there is a difference between the categories that can be clefted between Irish on the one hand, and English and Japanese on the other. Consider the examples in (61)–(63).

(61)   Irish
   a.   Object NP
        Is   é [an   carr seo]$_1$ Op$_1$ a   cheannaigh Seán t_1.
        COP.PRES it the car this   aL bought   John
        'It is [this car]$_1$ that John bought t_1.'   (=(12))
   b.   Subject NP
        (Is   é) [Seán] a   cheannaigh an carr seo.
        (COP.PRES it) John   aL bought   the car this
        'It is John$_1$ that t_1 bought this car.'   (=(15))
   c.   Place Adverb
        (Is   é) [i   mBéal Feirste] a   cheannaigh Seán an carr
        (COP.PRES it) in Belfast   aL bought   John the car
        seo anuraidh.
        this last.year
        'It is [in Belfast]$_1$ that John bought this car last year t_1.'   (=(17))

  d. Time Adverb
     (Is   é) [anuraidh] a   cheannaigh Seán an   carr seo i
     (COP.PRES it) last.year   aL bought   John the car this in
     mBéal Feirste.
     Belfast
     'It is [last year]₁ that John bought this car in Belfast t₁.'   (=(19))

  e. CP
     (Is   é) [gur cheannaigh Seán carr] a   chreideann Máire.
     COP.PRES it   that bought   John car aL believe   Mary
     '*It is [that John bought a car]₁ that Mary believes t₁.'   (=(21))

  f. AP
     [Róchliste] atá   Seán.
     too.clever aL+be.PRES John
     '*It is [too clever]₁ that John is t₁.'   (=(23))

(62) English
  a. Object NP
     It is [this car]₁ that John bought t₁.
  b. Subject NP
     It is [John]₁ that t₁ bought this car.
  c. Place Adverb
     It is [in Belfast]₁ that John bought this car last year t₁.
  d. Time Adverb
     It was [last year]₁ that John bought this car in Belfast t₁.
  e. CP
     *It is [that John bought a car]₁ that Mary believes t₁.
  f. AP
     *It is [very clever]₁ that John is t₁.

(63) Japanese
  a. Object NP
     John-ga   katta-no-wa   kono kuruma desu.
     John-NOM bought-NO-TOP this car   be
     'It is [this car]₁ that John bought t₁.'
  b. Subject NP
     Kono kuruma-o katta-no-wa   John desu.
     this car-ACC   bought-NO-TOP John be
     'It is [John]₁ that t₁ bought this car.'

c. Place Adverb

John-ga   kyonen   kono   kuruma-o   katta-no-wa   Belfast

John-NOM   last.year   this   car-ACC   bought-NO-TOP   Belfast

de   desu.

in   be

'It is [in Belfast]$_1$ that John bought this car last year t_1.'

d. Time Adverb

John-ga   Belfast   de   kono   kuruma-o   katta-no-wa   kyonen

John-NOM   Belfast   in   this   car-ACC   bought-NO-TOP   last.year

desu.

be

'It is [last year]$_1$ that John bought this car in Belfast t_1.'

e. CP

*Mary-ga   shinjiteiru-no-wa   John-ga   kuruma-o   katta   to

Mary-NOM   believe-NO-TOP   John-NOM   car-ACC   bought   that

desu.

be

'It is [that John bought a car]$_1$ that Mary believes t_1.'

f. AP

*John-ga   no-wa   totemo   kashikoi   desu.

John-NOM   NO-TOP   very   clever   be

'It is [very clever]$_1$ that John is t_1.'

cf.

Totemo   kashikoi-no-wa   John   desu.

very   clever-NO-TOP   John   be

'It is [John]$_1$ that t_1 is very clever.'

The above examples indicate that while Irish allows clefting of NPs, PPs, CPs and APs, English and Japanese do not allow clefting of CPs and APs. In the following, we will consider what causes this difference between the languages.

We first address the question as to why CPs can be clefted in Irish, but not in English or Japanese. We will propose that this difference is attributed to the difference in word order between Irish on the one hand, and English and Japanese on the other. In English and Japanese, O (complement) is adjacent to V, while in Irish, it is not, as it is separated from V by S, as shown in (64).

(64) a.   S [V O]   (English)
     b.   S [O V]   (Japanese)
     c.   V S O   (Irish)

We take this to suggest that there is a close relationship between O and V in English and Japanese, while no such relationship holds in Irish. In English and Japanese, in terms of the relationship between V and its CP complement, (the relevant feature of) COMP will adjoin to V possibly at LF, while this operation does not take place in Irish, as shown in (65).

(65) a.   S [V CP]   (English)

     b.   S [CP V]   (Japanese)

     c.   V S CP   (Irish)

In the cleft structure under Chomsky's (1977) hypothesis, the clefted part is base-generated in the pre-CP position, as shown in (66).

(66)   it is XP_1 [$_{CP}$ Op_1 *that* [$_{IP}$...t_1...]]

Then, in English and Japanese, if CP clefting were to occur, (the relevant feature of) COMP could not adjoin to V without lowering, as shown in (67).

(67)   it is [$_{CP}$...C...]$_1$ [$_{CP}$ Op_1 *that* [$_{IP}$...V t_1...]] (order irrelevant between

V and t_1)

However, this lowering operation will cause a violation of the Proper Binding Condition (PBC). On the other hand, this movement does not take place in Irish, as there is not a close relationship between O and V in Irish, as stated above. Therefore, CP clefting in Irish does not result in a PBC violation. Thus, the contrast in CP clefting between English and Japanese on the one hand, and Irish on the other, is expected.

Let us turn to another difference, that is, AP clefting. As shown above, Irish allows AP clefting, while English and Japanese do not. It seems impossible to provide the same account as the one for the contrast in CP clefting to the contrast in AP clefting between the two groups of languages, because in English, for example, APs can be moved in some cases, but they cannot be clefted, as shown in (68).

(68) a.   How clever is John?   (Question)
   b.   How clever John is!   (Exclamation)
   c.   *It is very clever that John is.   (Clefting)

The AP *how clever* is moved by wh-question formation, as in (68a), or by exclamation formation, as in (68b), but the AP *very clever* cannot be clefted, as shown in (68c). Therefore, we cannot apply the PBC-based analysis to the impossibility of AP clefting in English.

Note that the same patterns are observed in Japanese, as shown in (69).

(69) a.   John-wa   dore   hodo   kashikoi desu ka?
         John-TOP   which   degree   clever   be   Q
         'How clever is John?'   (Question)
   b.   John-wa   nan-te   kashikoi-n(o)-desu ka!
         John-TOP   what-COMP   clever-NO-be   EX
         'How clever John is!'   (Exclamation)
   c.   *John-ga   no-wa   totemo kashikoi desu.
         John-NOM   NO-TOP   very   clever   be
         'It is very clever that John is.'   (Clefting)

These data seem to suggest that APs can in principle be clefted, but there is a condition on the copula/particle in the presupposition part of the cleft construction in English and Japanese. To see this, consider the examples in (70) in English.

(70) a.   It is John that is studying Japanese.   (Subject NP Clefting)
   b.   It is Japanese that John is studying.   (Object NP Clefting)
   c.   *It is studying Japanese that John is.   (Progressive VP Clefting)

(70a, b) are grammatical with NP being clefted. (70c) is ungrammatical with progressive VP being clefted. Note that in (70c), what is clefted is not an AP, yet the sentence is ungrammatical. What is common to the ungrammatical examples in (68c), (69c) and (70c) is the fact that the copula/particle is in a sense 'stranded' in the presupposition part of the cleft construction. In the English examples, the copula *is* is separated from the AP *very clear* within the presupposition in (68c) and it is separated from the progressive VP *studying Japanese* within the presupposition in (70c). In the Japanese example in (69c), the particle *no* 'NO' is not attached to a preceding phrase within the presupposition, and a stranded particle is not tolerated in Japanese, which leads to the ungrammaticality of (69c). It seems then that it is not what is clefted, but it is the stranded copula/particle, that is responsible for the ungrammaticality of the examples in (68)–(70) in English and Japanese.

On the other hand, in the Irish examples in (61f), reproduced as (71), and (56), reproduced as (72), the situation is a bit different from those in English and Japanese.

(71)   [Róchliste]   atá   Seán.
       too.clever   aL+be.PRES   John
       '*It is [too clever]$_1$ that John is t_1.'   (=(61f))

(72)   Is   é   [róchliste]   a   raibh súil   agam   a   bheadh   Seán.
       COP.PRES   it   too.clever   aN   was   hope   at.me   aL   be.COND   John
       'It is [too clever]$_1$ that I hoped that John would be t_1.'   (=(56))
                                                                          (aN, aL, t)

In these examples, the copula at issue is actually not stranded, because Irish has overt COMP-Predicate (verb+INFL) agreement. To see this, consider the examples in (73).

(73) a.   Síleann   Seán   *go*   *gceannófá*   carr.
          think   John   COMP   buy.COND.2.SG   car
          'John thinks that you would buy a car.'

     b.   Síleann   Seán   *gur*   *cheannaigh*   tú   carr.
          think   John   COMP.PAST   bought   you   car
          'John thinks that you bought a car.'

In (73a), the embedded predicate (verb+INFL) is of the conditional form, and the COMP is represented as *go*, while in (73b), the embedded predicate is of the past tense form, and the COMP is represented as *gur*. This indicates that there is a visible agreement relationship between COMP and the predicate (verb+INFL) in Irish. Then, in each of (71) and (72), the copula is in agreement with the COMP, so that it is not stranded, unlike in English or Japanese. Therefore, the difference in AP clefting between Irish on the one hand, and English and Japanese on the other, lies in whether the 'stranded' copula is truly stranded or not.

Next, let us turn to the second point. As shown above, NP clefting allows six chain patterns with one embedded clause, but the other XPs, namely, PPs, CPs and APs, only allow two chain patterns in the same environment. The permitted chains are terminated with a trace, not a resumptive pronoun. Maki and Ó Baoill (2011) point out that the comparative construction only allows two chain patterns, exactly like those permitted by the cleft construction that does not involve NP clefting.

Let us review the comparative construction in Irish, a typical example of which is shown in (74).

(74) Cheannaigh sí   níos mó úllaí   ná   a   cheannaigh Seán *t*.
      bought   she   more   apples than aL   bought   John
      'She bought more apples than John bought.'

In (73), *ná* is the head of the comparative clause, which is followed by the COMP *aL*. Note that when the COMP is *aN*, the sentence becomes ungrammatical, as shown in (75).

(75) *Cheannaigh sí   níos mó úllaí   ná   ar   cheannaigh Seán (iad).
      bought   she   more   apples than aN   bought   John them
      'She bought more apples than John bought.'

Let us then examine the chain patterns of the comparative clause with one embedded clause. As shown below, the comparative construction only allows two types of chains (aL, aL, *t*) and (aN, aL, *t*) in (76) and (77), and disallows all the other patterns shown in (78)–(81).

(76) Cheannaigh sí   níos mó úllaí   ná   a   chreideann tú   a
      bought   she   more   apples than aL   believe   you   aL
      cheannaigh Seán *t*.
      bought   John
      'She bought more apples than you believe that John bought.'

                                                                    (aL, aL, *t*)

(77) Cheannaigh sí   níos mó úllaí   ná   a   raibh súil   agam a
      bought   she   more   apples than aN   was   hope   at.me aL
      cheannófá   *t*.
      buy.COND.2.SG
      'She bought more apples than I hoped you would buy.'   (aN, aL, *t*)

(78) *Cheannaigh sí   níos mó úllaí   ná   a   chreideann tú   ar
      bought   she   more   apples than aL   believe   you   aN
      cheannaigh Seán (iad).
      bought   John them
      'She bought more apples than you believe that John bought.'

                                                                    (aL, aN, RP)

(79) *Cheannaigh sí   níos mó úllaí ná   a   gcreideann tú   ar
      bought   she   more   apples than aN believe   you aN
      cheannaigh Seán (iad).
      bought   John them
      'She bought more apples than you believe that John bought.'

                                                            (aN, aN, RP)

(80) *Cheannaigh sí   níos mó úllaí ná   a   gcreideann tú   gur
      bought   she   more   apples than aN believe   you that
      cheannaigh Seán (iad).
      bought   John them
      'She bought more apples than you believe that John bought.'

                                                          (aN, that, RP)

(81) *Cheannaigh sí   níos mó úllaí ná   a   chreideann tú   gur
      bought   she   more   apples than aL believe   you that
      cheannaigh Seán (iad).
      bought   John them
      'She bought more apples than you believe that John bought.'

                                                          (aL, that, RP)

To summarize, the comparative construction in Irish allows the chain patterns
in (82), but disallows those in (83).

(82) a.   (aL, aL, *t*)
     b.   (aN, aL, *t*)

(83) a.   *(aL, aN, RP)
     b.   *(aN, aN, RP)
     c.   *(aN, that, RP)
     d.   *(aL, that, RP)

The data in (76)–(81) suggest then that the generalization about chain properties of the comparative construction in Irish is (84).

(84) Generalization on the comparative construction in Irish
      In the comparative construction in Irish, the chain must end with a
      trace.

(84) is exactly parallel to the generalization on the cleft construction in Irish
that does not involve NP clefting, which is stated in (85).

(85)   Generalization on the cleft construction in Irish that does not in-
       volve NP clefting
       In the cleft construction in Irish that does not involve NP clefting,
       the chain must end with a trace.

These two generalizations indicate that the chains in the cleft construction
that does not involve NP clefting and in the comparative construction in
general must be terminated with a trace, not a resumptive pronoun, which
suggests that what moves in the cleft construction that does not involve NP
clefting and in the comparative construction in general is not nominal in nature.

5. Conclusion

This paper investigated the properties of the cleft construction in Irish,
and showed (i) that CPs and APs can be clefted in Irish, unlike English or
Japanese, and (ii) that while NP clefting allows six chain patterns with one
embedded clause, clefting of the other categories only allows two chain
patterns, just like the comparative construction in Irish. Based on these
findings, we claimed (i) that the COMP of the clefted CP does not need to
be raised to V in Irish, while it must in English and Japanese, (ii) that the
difference in AP clefting between Irish on the one hand, and English and
Japanese on the other, lies in whether the 'stranded' copula/particle is truly
stranded or not, and (iii) that the chain patterns allowed in the cleft and the
comparative constructions suggest that what moves in the cleft construction
that does not involve NP clefting and in the comparative construction in general is not nominal in nature.

Chapter 9

Embedded Topicalization in Irish[*]

Hideki Maki and Dónall P. Ó Baoill

Gifu University and *Queen's University Belfast* (Prof. Emeritus)

This paper investigates properties of Irish embedded topicalization, and argues (i) that lowering of COMP to INFL does not take place in Irish, (ii) that the Highest Subject Restriction does not apply to resumptive pronouns involved in Irish embedded topicalization, (iii) that the head positions in charge of embedded topicalization are parameterized among languages, (iv) that the difference in the head positions in charge of embedded topicalization lies in the relationship between the COMP and the INFL, and (v) that the ban against adjunction to adjuncts only disallows adjunction to adjuncts by way of internal merge.

Keywords: embedded topicalization, English, Highest Subject Restriction, Irish, Japanese

1. Introduction

Chung and McCloskey (1987) were the first researchers to examine and analyze examples of embedded topicalization in Irish. Their examples are shown in (1).[1]

---

* This is a revised version of the paper presented at the 30th Conference of the English Linguistic Society of Japan held at Keio University on November 10, 2012. We would like to thank Koji Fujita, Roger Martin, Fumikazu Niinuma, Masao Ochi and two anonymous *EL* referees for their valuable comments. Our thanks also go to the following native speakers from the eastern borders of Gweedore Parish in North West Donegal with whom the examples have been checked: Donnchadh Mac Fhionnaile, Seán Mac Giolla Chóill, Bríd Bean Mhic Íomhair, Anna Ní Bhaoill, Máire Nic Giolla Chóill, Pádraig Ó Briain, Pádraig Ó Dúgáin (Éamann), Bríd Bean Uí Ghallchóir and Méabha Bean Uí Phíopalaigh. All errors are our own. Research by the first author was supported in part by Japan Society for the Promotion of Science Grant # 25370428 to Gifu University.
[1] The abbreviations used in this paper are as follows: 2 = second person, ACC = accusative, COND = conditional, −FIN = non-finite, FUT = future, GEN = genitive, IMPS = impersonal, NOM = nominative, PROG = progressive, SG = singular and TOP = topic.

(1) a. Dúirt sé [duine ar bith a   bhí bocht] go   dtabharfadh
        said he   person any   aL was poor   that give.COND
        an   rialtas   deontas dó.
        the government a.grant to.him
        'He said that the government would give a grant to anyone who
        was poor.'

   b. Dúirt sé [duine ar bith a   bhí bocht] gan   é
       said he   person any   aL was poor   that.NEG him
       a ligean   isteach.
       let.[−FIN] in
       'He said not to let anybody in who was poor.'
       (Chung and McCloskey (1987: 221, 120a, b) with slight editing)

The examples in (1) show two remarkable properties of Irish embedded topicalization. First, the topic phrase seems to be in CP SPEC. Second, it does
not involve movement, but utilizes the resumption strategy. In this paper,
we will investigate properties of Irish topicalization in more detail, and based
on the findings, we claim (i) that lowering of COMP to INFL does not take
place in Irish, contrary to McCloskey's (1996) claim, (ii) that the Highest
Subject Restriction (HSR) does not apply to resumptive pronouns involved
in Irish embedded topicalization, (iii) that both [−Q] and [+Q] COMPs may
bear a [+TOPIC] feature in Irish, and the head positions in charge of embedded topicalization are parameterized among languages, (iv) that the difference in the head positions in charge of embedded topicalization lies in the
relationship between the COMP and the INFL, and (v) that the ban against
adjunction to adjuncts only disallows adjunction to adjuncts by way of internal merge.

The organization of this paper is as follows. Section 2 reviews properties of (i) embedded topicalization in English and Japanese and (ii) complementizers in Irish as background to subsequent sections. Section 3 provides
embedded topicalization examples in Irish, and Section 4 discusses what they
may suggest for the theory of (Irish) syntax. Section 5 addresses one remaining question. Finally, Section 6 concludes this paper.

2. Background

In this section, we first review properties of embedded topicalization in English and Japanese, and then, properties of complementizers
in Irish. First, Maki et al. (1999) report that in American English and

Japanese, embedded topicalization is permissible in complement clauses of bridge verbs, but impossible in complement clauses of factive verbs or adjunct clauses. The examples in (2) are from American English and those in (3) are from Japanese.

(2) a. John believes that this book, Mary read.
    b. John wonders whether this book, Mary read.
    c. *John regrets that this book, Mary read.
    d. *John believes the rumor that this book, Mary read.
    e. *Before this book, Mary read, John had already read it.

(3) a. John-wa   [kono hon-wa/-o   Mary-ga   yonda to]
        John-TOP   this   book-TOP/-ACC   Mary-NOM   read   COMP
        shinjiteiru.
        believe
        'John believes that this book, Mary read.'

    b. John-wa   [kono hon-wa/-o   Mary-ga   yonda kadooka]
        John-TOP   this   book-TOP/-ACC   Mary-NOM   read   whether
        shiri tai   to   omotteiru.
        know want COMP think
        'John wonders whether this book, Mary read.'

    c. John-wa   [kono hon-*wa/-o   Mary-ga   yonda
        John-TOP   this   book-TOP/-ACC   Mary-NOM   read
        no]-o   kookaishiteiru.
        COMP-ACC   regret
        'John regrets that this book, Mary read.'

    d. John-wa   [kono hon-*wa/-o   Mary-ga   yonda
        John-TOP   this   book-TOP/-ACC   Mary-NOM   read
        to]-no   uwasa-o   shinjiteiru.
        COMP-GEN   rumor-ACC believe
        'John believes the rumor that this book, Mary read.'

    e. [Kono hon-*wa/-o   Mary-ga   yomu maeni], John-wa
         this book-TOP/-ACC   Mary-NOM   read   before   John-TOP
        sudeni   yondeita.
        already had.read
        'Before this book, Mary read, John had already read it.'

Maki et al. (1999) claim that factive verb complements are not L-marked based on the previous studies by Stowell (1981a), Grimshaw (1990) and Authier (1992), among others. They state that according to Authier (1992),

Watanabe (1993), and in accordance with their own American judgments, embedded topicalization is impossible both in complement clauses of factive verbs and in noun-complement clauses, and argue that it is impossible because factive complements are not L-marked, following Authier (1992), and noun-complement clauses are adjuncts, following Stowell (1981a) and Grimshaw (1990), among others.

Then, Maki et al. (1999) claim that a topic is licensed in the projection of INFL in overt syntax, and INFL is licensed by adjoining to COMP at LF in English and Japanese. They derived restrictions on embedded topicalization in the two languages from the ban against adjunction to a projection of a non-L-marked head, following Takahashi (1994). We assume their analysis of embedded topicalization in English and Japanese in this paper.

Second, let us review the properties of complementizers in Irish. Irish has three types of complementizers: the [−Q] marker, the direct relative marker, and the indirect relative marker. The properties of the three COMPs are summarized in (4).

(4)   Complementizers in Irish[2]

	types of COMPs	non-past form	past form	symbol
a.	the [−Q] marker	*go*	*go*/*gur*	that
b.	the direct relative marker	*a*	*a*	aL
c.	the indirect relative marker	*a*	*a*/*ar*	aN

Let us illustrate the properties of the COMPs by relevant examples. (5) is a declarative sentence, and the embedded clause is headed by the [−Q] COMP *gur* 'that.' On the other hand, when the sentence involves wh-interrogative clause formation, as in (6), the embedded COMP must change to the direct relative marker *aL*, and at the same time, another COMP *aL* must be inserted right after the wh-phrase.

(5)   Creideann Seán gur cheannaigh Máire an carr.
       believe   John that bought   Mary   the car
       'John believes that Mary bought the car.'

---

[2] The complementizer forms used with irregular verbs in the past tense in Irish, namely, the [−Q] marker and indirect relative marker *aN* do not follow the regular usage found with all other verbs. Hence, the regular complementizer forms *gur* 'that' and the indirect relative form *ar* are replaced by *go* 'that' and *a* 'aN,' respectively when used with the following irregular verbs: *bí* 'to be' >> *go*/*a raibh*; *déan* 'to do' >> *go*/*a ndearna*; *faigh* 'to get' >> *go*/*a bhfuair*; *tabhair* 'to give' >> *go*/*a dtug*; *tar* 'to come' >> *go*/*a dtáinig* and *téigh* 'to go' >> *go*/*a ndeachaigh*.

(6)   Cad é   a   chreideann tú   a   cheannaigh Seán   *t*?
       what   aL believe   you   aL bought   John
       'What do you believe that John bought?'   (movement) (aL, aL, *t*)

There is another way to form a wh-interrogative clause. Observe example
(7).

(7)   Cad é   a   gcreideann tú   gur   cheannaigh Seán   é/*t?
       what   aN believe   you   that bought   John   it
       'What do you believe that John bought?'

                                                  (resumption) (aN, that, RP)

In (7), the topmost COMP of the wh-interrogative clause is an indirect relative marker *a* 'aN,' the COMP of the embedded clause is a [−Q] COMP *gur*
'that,' and the embedded clause contains a resumptive pronoun (RP) *é* 'it,'
instead of a gap. Note that (7) becomes ungrammatical, if the resumptive
pronoun is replaced by a trace, which suggests that *aN* must bind a resumptive pronoun.

    McCloskey (2002) provides an account of the distribution of the
COMPs by proposing (8).

(8) a.   C whose specifier is filled by Move is realized as *aL*.
    b.   C whose specifier is filled by Merge is realized as *aN*.
    c.   C whose specifier is not filled is realized as *go/gur*.

McCloskey assumes that the SPEC of *aL* contains a null operator/null pronoun as a result of movement, that in the SPEC of *aN*, there is a basegen-
erated operator, and that in the SPEC of *go/gur*, there is no operator, on
the basis of the properties of the mixed chains in wh-interrogative/relative
clauses, such as (9).

(9)   an   carr a   raibh súil   agam   a   cheannófá   *t*
       the car   aN was   hope   at.me aL buy.COND.2.SG
       'the car I hoped you would buy'   (aN, aL, *t*)

In (9), the head of the embedded clause is *aL*, and the head of the higher
clause is *aN*. Under the assumption that *aL* is a result of movement, and *aN*
does not involve movement, the relevant structure of (9) will look like (10).

(10)   the car [CP XP aN [IP ... [CP YP aL [IP ...*t*...]]]]

Since XP, YP and *t* are in the same (mixed) chain, one may assume that all
these have the same index, as shown in (11).

(11)   the car [$_{CP}$ XP$_1$ aN [$_{IP}$ ... [$_{CP}$ YP$_1$ aL [$_{IP}$ ...t_1...]]]]

Now, because the lower CP has *aL*, some sort of movement should be involved in the clause. Then, McCloskey assumes that some element should have moved to CP SPEC, which he calls a null operator or a null pronoun that originated from the position of t_1. In (11), then, the SPEC of *aL* has a null operator/pronoun, and McCloskey attempted to generalize this to the other cases. Then, in the higher clause in (11), the head of CP is *aN*, which indicates that no element has moved to that position. Therefore, McCloskey claims that there is a null operator in the SPEC of *aN*, and the content of the null operator is identical to that of the null operator in the SPEC of the lower CP. He then generalizes this to wh-interrogatives as well. Consider example (12).

(12)   Cad é a   cheannaigh Seán *t*?
        what aL bought   John
        'What did John buy?'

In (12), the wh-phrase is in the sentence initial position, and one may assume that it is in CP SPEC. However, McCloskey (2002) attempts to generalize the above idea to this case as well, and assumes that there is a null operator/pronoun in CP SPEC, as shown in (13).

(13)   what [$_{CP}$ XP$_1$ aL [$_{IP}$ ...t_1...]]

In this paper, following McCloskey (2002), we assume the structures in (11) and (13) for relative clauses and wh-interrogatives, respectively.

3. Irish Data

Having outlined the particular background, let us consider Irish embedded topicalization. In the following examples, the topic phrase X in the embedded topicalization construction is intended to have the connotation of 'as for X.' First, the examples in (14)–(16) show that embedded topicalization must involve resumption, not movement, and that the target is CP SPEC.

(14)   Creideann siad gur tharraing Seán [an pictiúr de Mháire].
        believe   they that drew/took John the picture of Mary
        'They believe that John drew/took the picture of Mary.'

(15)   Creideann siad [an pictiúr de Mháire]$_1$ gur tharraing Seán
        believe   they   the picture of Mary   that drew/took John
        é$_1$/*t_1.
        it
        'They believe that John drew/took the picture of Mary.'

(16)   *Creideann siad gur [an pictiúr de Mháire]$_1$ tharraing Seán é$_1$.
         believe   they that   the picture of Mary   drew/took John it
         'They believe that John drew/took the picture of Mary.'

In (16), the topic is between the COMP *gur* 'that' and the predicate *tharraing* 'drew/took,' which is not permitted.

Second, the examples in (17)–(20) show that a [+Q] COMP may host a topic.

(17)   Níl   a   fhios   agam   ar tharraing   Seán [an pictiúr
        NEG.be the knowledge with.me Q drew/took John   the picture
        de Mháire].
        of Mary
        'I don't know whether John drew/took the picture of Mary.'

(18)   Níl   a   fhios   agam   [an pictiúr de Mháire]$_1$ ar
        NEG.be the knowledge with.me   the picture of Mary   Q
        tharraing   Seán é$_1$.
        drew/took John   it
        'I don't know whether John drew/took the picture of Mary.'

(19)   Níl   a   fhios   agam   cé$_2$ a   tharraing t_2 [an
        NEG.be the knowledge with.me who aL drew/took   the
        pictiúr de Mháire].
        picture of Mary
        'I don't know who drew/took the picture of Mary.'

(20)   Níl   a   fhios   agam   [an pictiúr de Mháire]$_1$ cé$_2$
        NEG.be the knowledge with.me   the picture of Mary   who
        a   tharraing t_2 é$_1$.
        aL drew/took   it
        'I don't know who drew/took the picture of Mary.'

Third, the examples in (21) and (22) show that a resumptive pronoun is possible in the subject position in the embedded topicalization construction.

(21)   Níl   a   fhios   agam   cad é$_2$ a   cheannaigh [an fear
          NEG.be the knowledge with.me what   aL bought   the man
          a   [tharraing   an   pictiúr   de   Mháire]] t_2.
          aL   drew/took the picture of Mary
          'I don't know what the man who drew/took the picture of Mary
          bought.'

(22)   Níl   a   fhios   agam   [an fear a   [tharraing   an
          NEG.be the knowledge with.me the   man aL   drew/took the
          pictiúr de   Mháire]]$_1$ cad é$_2$ a   cheannaigh sé$_1$ t_2.
          picture of Mary   what   aL bought   he
          'I don't know what the man who drew/took the picture of Mary
          bought.'

Fourth, and finally, the examples in (23)–(28) show that embedded topicalization in Irish is permissible in non-genuine complement clauses. (23) and (24) show that embedded topicalization is possible in complement clauses of factive verbs such as *is trua le* 'regret.'

(23)   Is   trua   le   Seán   gur   tharraing   sé   [an   pictiúr   de   Mháire].
          Cop regret with John   that drew/took he   the picture of Mary
          'John regrets that he drew/took the picture of Mary.'

(24)   Is   trua   le   Seán   [an   pictiúr   de   Mháire]$_1$ gur   tharraing   sé
          Cop regret with John   the picture of Mary   that drew/took he
          é$_1$.
          it
          'John regrets that he drew/took the picture of Mary.'

(25) and (26) demonstrate that embedded topicalization is also possible in noun-complement clauses in Irish.

(25)   Creideann   siad   an   ráfla   gur   tharraing   Seán   [an   pictiúr   de
          believe   they the rumor   that drew/took John   the picture of
          Mháire].
          Mary
          'They believe the rumor that John drew/took the picture of Mary.'

(26)   Creideann   siad   an   ráfla   [an   pictiúr   de   Mháire]$_1$ gur
          believe   they the rumor the picture of Mary   that
          tharraing   Seán   é$_1$.
          drew/took John   it

'They believe the rumor that John drew/took the picture of Mary.'

(27) and (28) show that embedded topicalization is also allowed in adjunct clauses.

(27)   Sular   cheannaigh Máire [an   carr sin], cheannaigh Seán é féin
        before bought   Mary   the car that bought   John himself
        carr.
        car
        'Before Mary bought that car, John himself bought a car.'

(28)   [An carr sin]$_1$ sular   cheannaigh Máire é$_1$, cheannaigh Seán
         the car that   before   bought   Mary   it bought   John
        é féin   carr.
        himself car
        'Before Mary bought that car, John himself bought a car.'

These examples indicate that embedded topicalization in Irish is permissible in non-genuine complement clauses.

4.   Discussion

Let us now consider what the above data suggest for the theory of (Irish) syntax. First, McCloskey (1996) argues, based on the distribution of (sentential) adverbs, that Irish does not have I-to-C movement, but rather that the surface position of C is I, which is a result of C-to-I lowering, and the verb only moves up to I, not to C, in Irish. He defends these claims by adopting Chomsky's (1986b: 6) Prohibition on Adjunction defined in (29).

(29)   Adjunction to a phrase s-selected by a lexical head is ungrammati-
        cal.

Given (29), the example in (30), which is grammatical, would be incorrectly ruled out, as the adverb *an chéad Nollaig eile* 'next Christmas' seems to be adjoined to the clause s-selected by the lexical head *deiridis* 'they.used.to.say.'

(30)   Deiridís   an chéad Nollaig   eile go   dtiocfadh   sé
        they.used.to.say the first   Christmas other that would.come   he
        aníos.
        up
        'They used to say that next Christmas he would come up.'
                                    (McCloskey (1996: 59, ex. 30) with slight editing)

Therefore, he concludes that the adverb is not adjoined to the embedded clause, but the COMP is lowered to the V-I complex.

Furthermore, McCloskey (1996) presents the data in (31)–(33), which involve adjunction of adverbs to wh-interrogative clauses, to defend his claims.

(31)   *Ní   bhfuair siad amach ariamh [an bhliain sin] cé   a   bhí
         NEG found   they out   ever   that-year   who aL was
         ag goid   a gcuid móna.
         steal.PROG their   turf
         'They never found out who was stealing their turf that year.'
                              (McCloskey (1996: 65, ex. 45) with slight editing)

(32)   *Níor   thuig   mé [roimh an Nollaig] cé chomh
         NEG.PAST understand I   before Christmas   how
         gnóitheach is a   bheadh   siad
         busy   as aL be.COND they
         'I didn't realize how busy they would be before Christmas.'
                              (McCloskey (1996: 65, ex. 46) with slight editing)

(33)   *Cha   bhfuair sé amach ariamh [nuair a   moladh
         NEG found   he out   ever   when aL recommend.IMPS
         don   phost sin é] cé   a   chuir ina choinne.
         for.the job   that him who aL put   against.him
         'He never found out who opposed him when he was recommended
         for that job.'   (McCloskey (1996: 65, ex. 47) with slight editing)

According to him, (31)–(33) are ungrammatical. This is predictable under (29), because due to the existence of the wh-phrase in the wh-interrogative clause in each sentence, the adverb in each case should be adjoined to CP.

However, the fact is that at least (33) is grammatical with the interpretation in which the adverb modifies the embedded clause. Furthermore, we found that the examples in (34)–(36) are grammatical with the interpretation in which the adverbs modify the embedded clauses.

(34)   Níl   a   fhios   agam   i rith na hoíche   cé   a
         NEG.be the knowledge with.me   during the night.GEN who aL
         chuala tormán.
         heard noise
         'I don't know who heard a noise during the night.'

(35)   Níl   a   fhios   agam   i rith   na   hoíche   cén
       NEG.be   the   knowledge with.me   during   the   night.GEN   what.the
       tormán   a   chuala   mé.
       noise   aL   heard   I
       'I don't know what noise I heard during the night.'

(36)   Níl   a   fhios   agam   i rith   na   hoíche   cá
       NEG.be   the   knowledge with.me   during   the   night.GEN   what
       háit   ar   chuala   mé   tormán
       place   aN   heard   I   noise
       'I don't know where I heard a noise during the night.'

In (34)–(36), the adverbial phrase *i rith na hoíche* 'during the night' is placed before the wh-interrogative clauses, yet the sentences are grammatical with the adverb being interpreted as modifying the embedded clauses. This indicates (i) that under the assumption that the [+Q] COMPs *aL* and *aN* are in C and the wh-phrases are higher than CP SPC in Irish, the topic is also higher than CP SPEC, and (ii) that no C-to-I lowering has taken place in the examples with embedded topicalization. Furthermore, as already shown in (20), not only adjuncts, but also arguments can undergo embedded topicalization, targeting CP. Based on the examples in (34)–(36) and (20), we conclude that no C-to-I lowering takes place in Irish, contrary to McCloskey's (1996) claim.

Let us then consider the examples in (31) and (32), and examine what factor is involved in the ungrammaticality of the examples. Just like McCloskey (1996), we find (31) and (32) ungrammatical. This is actually due to the fact that the adverbs in (31) and (32) *an bhliain sin* 'that year' and *roimh an Nollaig* 'before Christmas' perfectly fit the matrix predicates *ní bhfuair* 'NEG found' and *níor thuig* 'NEG.PAST understand,' respectively, and most naturally modify them in those positions. Once this kind of close connection is established between the matrix predicate and the adverb, it is quite hard for native speakers of Irish to interpret the sentence in such a way that the adverb is actually associated with the embedded predicate. Therefore, some sort of frozen effect is involved in such a case. On the other hand, in (33), the adverb is sentential, and it is relatively easy for native speakers of Irish to associate the sentential adverb with the embedded predicate.

The following data, which use a simple adverb which is unambiguously associated with an event in the future, confirm the point at issue. In (37), the adverb *amárach* 'tomorrow' is in the embedded clause, and modifies only the predicate in the embedded clause.

(37) Níl   a   fhios   agam cé a   bheas   ag obair san
      NEG.be the knowledge at.me who aL be.FUT at work in.the
      oifig amárach
      office tomorrow
      'I wonder who will be working in the office tomorrow.'

When it undergoes embedded topicalization, as in (38), it can only modify
the embedded predicate, and the sentence is perfectly acceptable.

(38) Níl   a   fhios   agam amárach cé a   bheas   ag
      NEG.be the knowledge at.me tomorrow who aL be.FUT at
      obair san   oifig.
      work in.the office
      'I wonder who will be working in the office tomorrow.'

Therefore, as long as some sort of frozen effect is circumvented, embedded
topicalization of an adverb across a wh-interrogative clause is perfectly acceptable. Since the SPEC of *a* 'aL' is filled with the null operator of the
wh-phrase in (38) and other related examples, no matter whether lowering
of C, namely, *a* 'aL,' to the V-T complex takes place, the adverb is not
within the projection of V+T. Rather, it is in the outer SPEC of *a* 'aL.' Of
course, one cannot exclude the possibility that C-to-I lowering still takes
place. However, this kind of lowering has no syntactic effect in embedded
topicalization. If this is the case, the minimalist guidelines will prevent such
an unnecessary operation (lowering) from taking place.

     Second, the example in (22) shows that a resumptive pronoun may ap-
pear in the highest subject position. McCloskey (1979) originally claims the
Highest Subject Restriction in (39).

(39) *The Highest Subject Restriction* (HSR)
      In languages which have a fully grammaticized resumptive strategy,
      the only position from which resumptive pronouns are excluded is
      the highest subject position within the relative clause.
                              (McCloskey (2002: 201) with slight editing)

Note that Ó Baoill and Maki (2012) show that the HSR applies to subjects
of relative clauses and wh-interrogatives in a parallel fashion. The relevant
data are cited below from Ó Baoill and Maki (2012). The examples in (40)
and (41) involve relative clause formation, and those in (42) and (43) wh-
interrogative formation. The examples in (40) and (42) involve extraction

from the object position/resumption in the object position, and those in (41) and (43) involve extraction from the subject position/resumption in the subject position. The crucial data are (41b) and (43b), which have a resumptive pronoun in the highest subject position, and are ungrammatical.

(40) a. an leabhar$_1$ a   léigh Seán t_1
         the book   aL   read John
         'the book that John read'   (movement)

   b. an leabhar$_1$ ar   léigh Seán é$_1$
         the book   aN   read John it
         'the book that John read'   (resumption)

(41) a. an fear$_1$ a   bhí t_1 breoite
         the man   aL   was   ill
         'the man who was ill'   (movement)

   b. *an fear$_1$ a   raibh sé$_1$ breoite
         the man   aN   was   he   ill
         'the man who was ill'   (resumption)

(42) a. Cad é$_1$ a   léigh Seán t_1?
         what   aL   read John
         'What did John read?'   (movement)

   b. Cad é$_1$ ar   léigh Seán é$_1$?
         what   aN   read John it
         'What did John read?'   (resumption)

(43) a. Cé$_1$ a   léigh t_1 an leabhar seo?
         who   aL   read   the book   this
         'Who read this book?'   (movement)

   b. *Cé$_1$ ar   léigh sé$_1$ an leabhar seo?
         who   aN   read he   the book   this
         'Who read this book?'   (resumption)

Then, the example in (22) indicates that the HSR is cancelled by a phrase in the topic position, and the generalization on the HSR in (39) does not always hold.

   Let us now consider what factor is actually behind the cancellation of the HSR. In the following discussion, we will follow the possible account provided by Ó Baoill and Maki (2012). Ó Baoill and Maki (2012) first provide examples in (44) and (45), and claim that the HSR is cancelled by an additional phrase, such as an adverb.

(44) *Cé₁ ar   imigh sé₁?
      who aN   left   he
      'Who left?'

(45) Cé₁ ar   imigh sé₁ trí   lá   ó shin?
      who aN   left   he   three days ago
      'Who left three days ago?'

They then provide the examples in (46) and (47), which show that the HSR is cancelled not only by an adverb, but also by a coordinate clause.

(46) *Cé₁ a   raibh sé₁ breoite?
      who   aN   was   he   ill
      'Who was ill?'

(47) Cé₁ a   raibh sé₁ breoite agus ag   fáil   bháis?
      who aN   was   he   ill   and   at   getting death
      'Who was ill and dying?'

Based on these data, they propose (48).

(48)   The highest subject is saved by an adverb or a coordinate structure.

At first sight, (48) does not seem to be a true generalization, and the question arises as to what properties an adverb and a coordinate structure share. Ó Baoill and Maki (2012) revise (48), following Higginbotham's (1985) idea that adjuncts involve coordination. Following Davidsonian event semantics, Higginbotham (1985) claims that the example in (49) is given the semantic representation in (50).

(49)   John walks slowly.

(50) $\exists e$ [Walk (John, e) & Slow (e)]

(50) indicates that there is an event such that it is a walking by John and it is slow (for a walk). If this is true, the structure with an adverb in (45) has a coordinate structure in its semantic representation, just like the structure with a coordinate clause in (47). Then, (48) is further generalized to (51), and one may say that the HSR is cancelled by the addition of a coordinate clause to the HSR structure.

(51)   The highest subject is saved by a coordinate structure.

This makes sense, because when a resumptive pronoun in the subject position is in a conjunct of a coordinate structure, it is within a larger constituent, and thus, does not count as the highest resumptive pronoun in the subject position.

In this paper, we essentially adopt this view for the cancellation of the HSR for examples with embedded topicalization. In examples such as (22), reproduced as (52), the resumptive pronoun *sé* 'he' is in the highest subject position, yet the sentence is perfectly grammatical.

(52)   Níl   a   fhios   agam   [an fear a   [tharraing   an
        NEG.be the   knowledge with.me   the man aL drew/took   the
        pictiúr de Mháire]]$_1$ cad é$_2$ a   cheannaigh sé$_1$ t$_2$.
        picture of Mary   what aL bought   he
        'I don't know what the man who drew/took the picture of Mary
        bought.'

(52) involves embedded topicalization, and the subject *[an fear a [tharraing an pictiúr de Mháire]]* 'the man aL drew/took the picture of Mary' functions as the topic of the embedded clause. Then, in a sense, the embedded clause consists of two parts, namely, a topic and its comment, as in (53).

(53) a.   a topic X, and
     b.   a comment on X

If this is true, the embedded structure with a topic in (52) has a coordinate structure in its semantic representation, so that the resumptive pronoun in the subject position in (52) is in a conjunct of a coordinate structure, and thus, does not count as the highest resumptive pronoun in the subject position.

Third, all the examples shown above indicate that [−Q] COMPs, whether they are selected by the higher verbs or not (complements or non-complements of the verbs), and [+Q] COMPs, may bear a [+TOPIC] feature in Irish. On the other hand, in English, for example, C cannot bear a [+TOPIC] feature, as shown in (54).

(54) a.   *John believes this book that Mary read.
     b.   *John wonders this book whether Mary read.
     c.   *John regrets this book that Mary read.
     d.   *John believes the rumor this book that Mary read.
     e.   *This book before Mary read, John had already read it.

The contrast between Irish and English thus suggests that the relevant head for embedded topicalization is COMP in Irish, and it is INFL in English. Note that the parallel behavior in English and Japanese embedded topicalization suggests that the relevant head for embedded topicalization is also INFL in Japanese. This indicates that the head positions in charge of embedded topicalization are parameterized among languages. If this is true, no independent head for a topic phrase need be assumed unless it is independently needed in the language.

Fourth, the difference in the head positions in charge of embedded topicalization lies in the relationship between the COMP and the INFL in the given languages. Irish has overt COMP-Predicate (verb+INFL) agreement, as shown in (55).

(55) a. Síleann Seán go gceannófá carr.
       think John COMP buy.COND.2.SG car
       'John thinks that you would buy a car.'

    b. Síleann Seán gur cheannaigh tú carr.
       think John COMP.PAST bought you car
       'John thinks that you bought a car.'

In (55a), the embedded predicate (verb+INFL) is in the conditional form, and the COMP is represented as *go*, while in (55b), the embedded predicate is in the past tense form, and the COMP is represented as *gur*. The same agreement patterns appear with embedded topicalization as well, as shown in (56).

(56) a. Síleann Seán [an carr mór sin]$_1$ go gceannófá é$_1$.
       think John the car big that COMP buy.COND.2.SG it
       'John thinks that you would buy that big car.'

    b. Síleann Seán [an carr mór sin]$_1$ gur cheannaigh
       think John the car big that COMP.PAST bought
       tú é$_1$.
       you it
       'John thinks that you bought that big car.'

This indicates that there is a visible agreement relationship between the COMP and the predicate (verb+INFL) in Irish. Then, once the head in charge of embedded topicalization is placed between COMP and INFL, this morphological agreement relationship cannot hold, so that no embedded topicalization is allowed.

On the other hand, if COMP can do the work for embedded topicalization, the agreement is successfully established. In English and Japanese, being non-verb initial languages, however, there is no such visible agreement between COMP and INFL which would be blocked when INFL is in charge of embedded topicalization.

5. One Remaining Question

Before closing, we will address one remaining question arising from a comparative study of embedded topicalization in Irish, English and Japanese. Maki et al. (1999) claim, based on the parallel behavior of embedded topicalization in English and Japanese, that the phenomenon in these two languages receives a uniform account, and propose that INFL licenses an embedded topic in its SPEC, and INFL itself needs to be licensed by COMP by adjoining to it at LF. Therefore, the contrast between (2a) and (2e) in English, reproduced as (57a) and (57b), and the contrast between (3a) and (3e) in Japanese, reproduced as (58a) and (58b), are explained in the following way.

(57) a.   John believes that this book, Mary read.
    b.   *Before this book, Mary read, John had already read it.

(=(2a) and (2e))

(58) a.   John-wa   [kono hon-wa/-o   Mary-ga   yonda to]
        John-TOP this book-TOP/-ACC Mary-NOM read   COMP
        shinjiteiru.
        believe
        'John believes that this book, Mary read.'
    b.   [Kono hon-*wa/-o   Mary-ga   yomu maeni], John-wa
        this book-TOP/-ACC Mary-NOM read before   John-TOP
        sudeni   yondeita.
        already had.read
        'Before this book, Mary read, John had already read it.'

(=(3a) and (3e))

First, in all of these examples, the topics are licensed in IP SPEC, and then, INFL moves to COMP at LF. However, the *b*-examples in (57) and (58) involve adjunction of INFL to the head of adjunct clauses, which is prohibited by Takahashi's (1994) ban against adjunction to non-L-marked phrases, namely, adjuncts and derived subjects.

In Irish, embedded topicalization is possible in complement clauses and adjunct clauses, as shown in (15) and (28), reproduced as (59) and (60), respectively.

(59)   Creideann siad [an   pictiúr de Mháire]$_1$ gur tharraing   Seán
       believe   they   the picture of Mary   that drew/took John
       é$_1$/*t_1.
       it
       'They believe that John drew/took the picture of Mary.'   (=(15))

(60)   [An   carr sin]$_1$ sular   cheannaigh Máire é$_1$, cheannaigh Seán
       the car that before bought   Mary it   bought   John
       é féin   carr.
       himself car
       'Before Mary bought that car, John himself bought a car.'   (=(28))

In (59) and (60), the topic is in CP SPEC in each case, and these examples
are grammatical. The question that immediately arises is why (60) is perfectly grammatical, in spite of the fact that the topic is in the SPEC of the
clause which is an adjunct, which indicates that the merge operation necessarily involves adjunction to an adjunct.

However, there is a clear difference between embedded topicalization
in Irish and embedded topicalization in English, for example. Lasnik and
Saito (1992) point out that English embedded topicalization does not allow
the resumptive pronoun strategy, as shown in the contrast between (61a) and
(61b).

(61) a.   I believe that this book, you should read *t*.

                        (Lasnik and Saito (1992: 76, ex. 37a))

      b.   *I believe that this book, you should read it.

                        (Lasnik and Saito (1992: 77, ex. 42))

On the other hand, embedded topicalization in Irish must leave a resumptive pronoun. Therefore, a topic in an embedded clause in Irish is merged/
adjoined to C'/CP by external merge, while a topic in an embedded clause
in English is merged/adjoined to IP by internal merge. Furthermore, licensing of INFL in the embedded topicalization construction in English involves
movement/adjunction to COMP, again, by internal merge. On the other
hand, in embedded topicalization in Irish, COMP itself does not move further in order to be licensed, as it can license the topic phrase in its SPEC if
it has to.

Thus, the above facts seem to suggest that the ban against adjunction
to adjuncts distinguishes internal merge from external merge, and it only
disallows adjunction to adjuncts by way of internal merge. If this is correct,
then it follows that embedded topicalization in Irish is allowed within non-L-

marked phrases, and the contrast between Irish on the one hand, and English and Japanese on the other, is correctly captured. Therefore, the question we addressed in this section turned out to suggest that the ban against adjunction to adjuncts only disallows adjunction to adjuncts by way of internal merge.

Furthermore, as one of the referees correctly points out, our analysis, in which the topicalized phrase in Irish embedded topicalization occupies the (outer) SPEC of C, and is introduced there by means of Merge, seems to contradict McCloskey's generalization of the distribution of Cs in (8), because the form of C should be *aN*, rather than *gur*. If McCloskey is correct, what moves/is inserted in wh-interrogatives and relative clauses is a null pronoun or a null operator. On the other hand, in embedded topicalization, what is actually inserted is not a null pronoun or a null operator, but a phrase with phonetic content in McCloskey's analysis and our analysis. We thus claim that this difference is reflected in the form of COMP. Therefore, the contradiction between our analysis and McCloskey's COMP system has turned out to suggest a new property of COMP in Irish, where merger of a phrase with phonetic content does not change the form of COMP in Irish.

6. Conclusion

In this paper, we investigated the properties of Irish embedded topicalization in detail, and based on the findings, we argued (i) that lowering of COMP to INFL does not take place in Irish, contrary to McCloskey's (1996) claim, (ii) that the Highest Subject Restriction (HSR) does not apply to resumptive pronouns involved in Irish embedded topicalization, (iii) that both [−Q] and [+Q] COMPs may bear a [+TOPIC] feature in Irish, and the head positions in charge of embedded topicalization are parameterized among languages, (iv) that the difference in the head positions in charge of embedded topicalization lies in the relationship between the COMP and the INFL, and (v) that the ban against adjunction to adjuncts only disallows adjunction to adjuncts by way of internal merge.

Chapter 10

Clausal Arguments in Irish[*]

Hideki Maki and Dónall P. Ó Baoill

Gifu University and *Queen's University Belfast* (Prof. Emeritus)

This paper investigates various phenomena related to clausal arguments in Irish, and based on the findings, we claim (i) that Irish grammar should contain a language-particular condition on A'-resumption chains, (ii) that the subject position is not a properly governed position in Irish, (iii) that human language allows a bare IP to function as a subject, and (iv) that the chain pattern (aL, that, RP) turns out to be real in movement constructions with one embedded clause in Irish.

Keywords: *chain, clausal argument, extraction, Irish, subject*

1. Introduction

This paper investigates various phenomena related to clausal arguments in modern Ulster Irish (abbreviated as Irish, hereafter, only for space reasons), and points out (i) that a bare IP can be a subject, and clefted, (ii) that extraction out of a sentential object (complement) is permissible, but extraction out of a sentential subject is not, (iii) that the resumption strategy cannot save a resumptive pronoun in certain configurations headed by the COMP *go/gur* 'that,' and (iv) that the chain pattern (aL, that, RP) turns out to be well-formed in examples with extraction from a sentential

* This is a revised version of the paper presented at the 146th Meeting of the Linguistic Society of Japan held at Ibaraki University on June 15, 2013. We would like to thank the audience of the meeting, Jessica Dunton, Megumi Hasebe, Fumikazu Niinuma, Satoshi Oku, Naoto Sato and three anonymous *EL* referees for their valuable comments. Our thanks also go to the following native speakers from the eastern borders of Gweedore Parish in North West Donegal with whom the examples have been checked: Donnchadh Mac Fhionnaile, Seán Mac Giolla Chóill, Bríd Bean Mhic Íomhair, Anna Ní Bhaoill, Máire Nic Giolla Chóill, Pádraig Ó Briain, Pádraig Ó Dúgáin (Éamann), Bríd Bean Uí Ghallchóir and Méabha Bean Uí Phíopalaigh. All errors are our own. Research by the first author was supported in part by JSPS KAKENHI Grant Number 25370428 to Gifu University.

subject. Based on these findings, we claim (i) that Irish grammar should contain a condition such as the Condition on A′-Resumption Chains which states that the base-generated operator in the SPEC of the COMP *aN* which constitutes the head of the chain, cannot bind its corresponding resumptive pronoun when there is a COMP *go/gur* 'that' whose maximal projection is not complement to a verb in the structure that c-commands the resumptive pronoun, (ii) that the subject position is not a properly governed position in Irish, providing further support for Maki and Ó Baoill's (2011) claim, (iii) that human language allows a bare IP to function as a subject, and there seems to be a COMP-Predicate (verb+INFL) agreement in human language, and (iv) that the chain pattern (aL, that, RP), which has not been reported in the literature except Maki and Ó Baoill (2011), turns out to be real in movement constructions with one embedded clause in Irish.

The organization of this paper is as follows. Section 2 reviews properties of the wh-interrogative construction in Irish as background to subsequent sections. Section 3 provides relevant examples with clausal arguments in Irish. Based on the properties of clausal arguments in Irish, Section 4 discusses what they might suggest for the theory of (Irish) syntax. Finally, Section 5 concludes this paper.

2. Background

Let us start by briefly summarizing properties of the wh-interrogative construction in Irish. See McCloskey (1979, 1990) and Maki and Ó Baoill (2011), among others, for discussion of operator constructions in Irish. Irish has three types of complementizers: the [−Q] marker, the direct relative marker, and the indirect relative marker. The properties of the three COMPs are summarized in (1).

(1) Complementizers in Irish

	types of COMPs	non-past form	past form	symbol
a.	the [−Q] marker	*go*	*go/gur*	that
b.	the direct relative marker	*a*	*a*	aL
c.	the indirect relative marker	*a*	*a/ar*	aN

Let us illustrate the properties of the COMPs by relevant examples. (2) is a declarative sentence, and the embedded clause is headed by the [−Q] COMP *gur* 'that.' On the other hand, when the sentence involves wh-interrogative clause formation, as in (3), the embedded COMP must change to the direct relative marker *aL*, and at the same time, another COMP *aL* must be inserted right after the wh-phrase.[1]

(2) Creideann Seán gur cheannaigh Máire an   carr.
    believe   John   that bought   Mary   the car
    'John believes that Mary bought the car.'

(3) Cad é a   chreideann tú a   cheannaigh Seán *t*?
    what aL believe   you aL bought   John
    'What do you believe that John bought?'   (movement) (aL, aL, *t*)

There is another way to form a wh-interrogative clause in Irish. Observe the example in (4).

(4) Cad é a   gcreideann tú   gur cheannaigh Seán é/*/*t*?
    what aN believe   you that bought   John   it
    'What do you believe that John bought?'   (resumption) (aN, that, RP)

In (4), the topmost COMP of the wh-interrogative clause is an indirect relative marker *aN*, the COMP of the embedded clause is a [−Q] COMP, and the embedded clause contains a resumptive pronoun (RP) *é* 'it' instead of a gap. Note that (4) becomes ungrammatical, if the resumptive pronoun is replaced by a trace, which suggests that *aN* must bind a resumptive pronoun.

    McCloskey (2002) provides an account of the distribution of the COMPs by proposing (5).

(5) a.   C whose specifier is filled by Move is realized as *aL*.
    b.   C whose specifier is filled by Merge is realized as *aN*.
    c.   C whose specifier is not filled is realized as *go/gur*.

McCloskey assumes that the SPEC of *aL* contains a null operator/null pronoun (henceforth, null operator) as a result of movement, that in the SPEC of *aN*, there is a base-generated operator, and that in the SPEC of *go/gur*, there is no operator. In this paper, for expository purposes only, we represent the structure of a wh-interrogative clause by putting a wh-phrase, not its operator, in the SPEC of *aL/aN*, as shown in (6).

(6) $[_{CP}$ WH$_1$ aL/aN $[_{IP}...t_1/RP_1...]]$

---

[1] The abbreviations used in this paper are as follows: 1 = first person, 2 = second person, COND = conditional, COP = copula, NEG = negation, PAST = past tense, PRES = present tense, PROG = progressive, RP = resumptive pronoun and SG = singular.

3. Data

Let us observe the phenomena related to clausal arguments in Irish. First, IP can be a subject. In Irish, some verbs take both finite and infinitival complement clauses, as shown in (7) and (8).

(7) Is   cuimhin le   Liam [gur cheannaigh Seán carr].
     COP.PRES memory with Bill   that bought   John car
     'Bill remembers that John bought a car.'

(8) Is   cuimhin le   Liam [Seán carr a   cheannach].
     COP.PRES memory with Bill   John car   to buy
     'Bill remembers that John bought a car.'

In (7) and (8), the finite and infinitival complement clauses are in the object position. The examples in (9) and (10) show that finite and infinitival clauses may appear in the subject position as well.

(9) Chuir [go gceannódh Seán carr] iontas ar Mháire.
     put   that would.buy John car   surprise on Mary
     'That John would buy a car surprised Mary.'

(10) Chuir [Seán carr a   cheannach] iontas ar Mháire.
     put   John car   to buy   surprise on Mary
     'That John bought a car surprised Mary.'

Second, IP and CP can be clefted in Irish, as shown in (11)–(14). (11) and (12) show that infinitival subject IPs may be clefted, and (13) and (14) show that subject CPs may be clefted.

(11) Is   é [Seán carr a   cheannach]₁ a   chuir *t*₁ iontas   ar
     COP.PRES it   John car   to buy   aL put   surprise on
     Mháire.
     Mary
     '*It is [that John bought a car] that surprised Mary.'

(12) Is   é [Seán carr a   cheannach]₁ a   chreideann Liam
     COP.PRES it   John car   to buy   aL believe   Bill
     a   chuir *t*₁ iontas   ar Mháire.
     aL put   surprise on Mary
     '*It is [that John bought a car] that Bill believes that surprised Mary.'

(13)   Is   é [gur cheannaigh Seán carr]₁ a   chuir *t*₁ iontas
       COP.PRES it that bought   John   car   aL put   surprise
       ar   Mháire.
       on   Mary
       '*It is [that John bought a car] that surprised Mary.'

(14)   Is   é [gur cheannaigh Seán carr]₁ a   chreideann Liam
       COP.PRES it that bought   John   car   aL   believe   Bill
       a   chuir *t*₁ iontas   ar   Mháire.
       aL   put   surprise on   Mary
       '*It is [that John bought a car] that Bill believes that surprised
       Mary.'

Note here that IP/CP clefting is impossible in English, as the translations of
the examples in (11)–(14) show.

    Third, (15)–(23) clearly indicate a subject/object asymmetry in wh-
movement in Irish. (15) and (16) involve extraction out of a complement
clause, and the examples are grammatical.

(15)   Cad é₁ atá   súil   ag Liam [a   cheannódh   Seán *t*₁]?
       what   aL+is hope   at Bill   aL   would.buy   John
       'What does Bill hope that John would buy?'

(16)   Cad é₁ atá   súil   ag Liam [Seán *t*₁ a   cheannach]?
       what   aL+is hope   at Bill   John   to buy
       'What does Bill hope that John would buy?'

On the other hand, (17)–(23) involve extraction out of a clause in the subject
position, and the examples are all ungrammatical.

(17)   *Cad é₁ a   chuir [Seán *t*₁ a   cheannach] iontas   ar   Mháire?
        what   aL   put   John   to buy   surprise   on   Mary
        'What₁ did [that John bought *t*₁] surprise Mary?'

(18)   *Cad é₁ a   chuir [go   gceannódh Seán *t*₁] iontas   ar   Mháire?
        what   aL   put   that would.buy   John   surprise   on   Mary
        'What₁ did [that John would buy *t*₁] surprise Mary?'

(19)   *Cad é₁ a   chuir [a   cheannódh   Seán *t*₁] iontas   ar   Mháire?
        what   aL   put   aL   would.buy   John   surprise   on   Mary
        'What₁ did [that John would buy *t*₁] surprise Mary?'

(20) *Cad é₁ a   chreideann Liam a   chuir [Seán t₁ a   cheannach]
      what   aL   believe   Bill aL   put   John   to   buy
      iontas   ar   Mháire?
      surprise on   Mary
      'What₁ does Bill believe that [that John bought t₁] surprised Mary?'

(21) *Cad é₁ a   gcreideann Liam a   chuir [Seán t₁ a   cheannach]
      what   aN   believe   Bill aL   put   John   to   buy
      iontas   ar   Mháire?
      surprise on   Mary
      'What₁ does Bill believe that [that John bought t₁] surprised Mary?'

(22) *Cad é₁ a   chreideann Liam a   chuir [go   gceannódh Seán t₁]
      what   aL   believe   Bill aL   put   that would.buy John
      iontas   ar   Mháire?
      surprise on   Mary
      'What₁ does Bill believe that [that John would buy t₁] surprised
      Mary?'

(23) *Cad é₁ a   chreideann Liam a   chuir [a   cheannódh Seán t₁]
      what   aL   believe   Bill aL   put   aL would.buy John
      iontas   ar   Mháire?
      surprise on   Mary
      'What₁ does Bill believe that [that John would buy t₁] surprised
      Mary?'

Fourth, the resumption strategy allows the chain patterns in (24)–(28), which are all disallowed under the movement strategy.

(24) Cad é₁ ar   chuir [Seán é₁/*t₁ a   cheannach] iontas   ar   Mháire?
      what   aN   put   John it   to   buy   surprise on   Mary
      'What₁ did [that John bought it₁] surprise Mary?'

(25) Cad é₁ a   gcreideann Liam gur   chuir [Seán é₁/*t₁ a
      what   aN   believe   Bill that put   John it   to
      cheannach] iontas   ar   Mháire?
      buy   surprise on   Mary
      'What₁ does Bill believe that [that John bought it₁] surprised Mary?'

(26) Cad é₁ a   gcreideann Liam ar   chuir [Seán é₁/*t₁ a
      what   aN   believe   Bill aN   put   John it   to
      cheannach] iontas   ar   Mháire?
      buy   surprise on   Mary
      'What₁ does Bill believe that [that John bought it₁] surprised Mary?'

(27) Cad é₁ a   chreideann Liam ar   chuir [Seán é₁/*t₁ a
      what   aL   believe   Bill aN   put   John it   to
      cheannach] iontas   ar   Mháire?
      buy   surprise on   Mary
      'What₁ does Bill believe that [that John bought it₁] surprised Mary?'

(28) Cad é₁ a   chreideann Liam gur   chuir [Seán é₁/*t₁ a
      what   aL   believe   Bill that put   John it   to
      cheannach] iontas   ar   Mháire?
      buy   surprise on   Mary
      'What₁ does Bill believe that [that John bought it₁] surprised Mary?'

Fifth, the resumption strategy, however, cannot save a resumptive pronoun in the *that*-clause in the subject position, as shown in (29)–(31).

(29) *Cad é₁ ar   chuir [go gceannódh Seán é₁] iontas   ar   Mháire?
       what   aN put   that would.buy John it   surprise on   Mary
       'What₁ did [that John would buy t₁] surprise Mary?'

(30) *Cad é₁ a   gcreideann Liam gur   chuir [go gceannódh Seán é₁]
       what   aN believe   Bill that put   that would.buy John it
       iontas   ar   Mháire?
       surprise on   Mary
       'What₁ does Bill believe that [that John would buy t₁] surprised
       Mary?'

(31) *Cad é₁ a   gcreideann Liam ar   chuir [go gceannódh Seán é₁]
       what   aN believe   Bill aN   put   that would.buy John it
       iontas   ar   Mháire?
       surprise on   Mary
       'What₁ does Bill believe that [that John would buy t₁] surprised
       Mary?'

4. Discussion

First, the data in (24)–(31) seem to suggest that Irish grammar contains a condition such as the Tensed-Subject Condition formalized in (32), because in these examples, the resumptive pronoun can be bound by the COMP *aN* only when it is contained in a sentential subject without tense.

(32) *Tensed Subject Condition*
      No rule can involve X, Y in the structure ...X...[$_\alpha$...Y...]...
      where α is a tensed subject.

It is well-known that the resumption strategy in Irish prevents island violations. Therefore, the Wh-Island Condition violation in (33) and the Complex NP Constraint violation in (35) are prevented by the resumption strategy. The data are from Basri and Maki (2012).

(33) *Cé   atá   fhios   agat   cén cineál mná   a
       who   aL+is   knowledge   with.you   what sort of a woman aL
       phósfadh   *t*?
       would.marry
       'Who do you know what woman would marry?'

(34) Cé   a   bhfuil fhios   agat   cén cineál mná   a
       who   aN   is   knowledge   with.you   what sort of a woman aL
       phósfadh   *é*?
       would.marry him
       'Who do you know what woman would marry?'

(35) *Cén   teanga   a   bheadh   meas   agat   ar   dhuine ar bith
       which   language aL   would.be respect at.you on   person any
       atá   ábalta *t* a   labhairt?
       aL+is   able   to speak
       'Which language would you respect anyone who could speak?'

(36) Cén   teanga   a   mbeadh   meas   agat   ar   dhuine ar bith
       which   language aN   would.be respect at.you on   person any
       atá   ábalta *í* a   labhairt?
       aL+is   able   it to speak
       'Which language would you respect anyone who could speak?'

In (34) and (36), *aN* can bind a resumptive pronoun across a syntactic island, and the examples are grammatical. However, in (29)–(31), *aN* does not seem able to bind the resumptive pronoun in a tensed subject, in spite of the fact that it c-commands it. The ungrammaticality of these examples thus suggests that Irish grammar should contain a condition such as (32).

However, the fact that (32) is not sufficient is shown by the examples in (37)–(40).

(37)   Chuir [an ráfla   gur cheannaigh Seán carr] iontas   ar Mháire.
       put   the rumor that bought   John car   surprise on Mary
       'The rumor that John bought a car surprised Mary.'

(38)   *Cad é$_1$ ar chuir [an ráfla   gur cheannaigh Seán é$_1$] iontas
       what   aN put   the rumor that bought   John it   surprise
       ar Mháire?
       on Mary
       'What$_1$ did the rumor that [that John bought t_1] surprise Mary?'

(39)   Chreideann Máire an ráfla   gur cheannaigh Seán carr.
       believe   Mary the rumor that bought   John car
       'Mary believes the rumor that John bought a car.'

(40)   *Cad é$_1$ a   gcreideann Máire an ráfla   gur cheannaigh Seán é$_1$?
       what   aN believe   Mary the rumor that bought   John it
       'What$_1$ does Mary believe the rumor that John bought t_1'

In (38), the subject is an NP, which contains a complement clause to the head noun, which in turn contains a resumptive pronoun. The complement clause, which is tensed, is not a subject by itself, so that the ungrammaticality of (38) does not fall under (32). Furthermore, the ungrammaticality of (40) shows that even when the same NP is in the object position, the sentence does not improve, which indicates that (32) is not relevant to the ungrammaticality of (40).

(40) is also surprising, given the fact that the resumption strategy saves island violations in Irish. All these data then seem to suggest that the complementizer *go*/*gur* 'that' blocks association between the COMP *aN* and the resumptive pronoun. Given the fact that (4), reproduced as (41), is perfectly grammatical, Irish grammar should contain a condition such as the one in (42).[2]

---

[2] One of the referees points out the following. "If the condition in (42) applies at LF/ the CI-interface, how does a child acquire such a language-particular interface condition? It seems impossible for a child to acquire such a language-particular interface condition "from scratch." Would the author claim that there is some "universal" interface condition which is potentially present in the initial state of every child's grammar, and the condition is "activated" by some trigger present in Irish (and not in other languages)? If so, what might be the trigger that activates the universal condition and turns it into a language-particular condition in Irish?"

(41)   Cad é a   gcreideann tú   gur cheannaigh Seán é/*í?
       what aN believe   you that bought   John it
       'What do you believe that John bought?'

                                              (resumption) (aN, that, RP)

(42)   *Condition on A'-Resumption Chains*
       The base-generated operator in the SPEC of the COMP *aN* which
       constitutes the head of the chain, cannot bind its corresponding
       resumptive pronoun when there is a COMP *go/gur* 'that' whose
       maximal projection is not complement to a verb in the structure
       that c-commands the resumptive pronoun.

(42) suggests that in an A'-resumption chain, the head of the chain *aN* sees

---

This is a very important question. The following we speculate is a possible answer to
the question. In Irish, a wh-phrase directly followed by the indirect relative marker *a/ar*
'aN' must bind a resumptive pronoun rather than a trace, as shown in (41). Apparently,
examples such as (41) indicate that the wh-phrase directly followed by the indirect relative marker *a/ar* 'aN' binds a resumptive pronoun, and the intermediate COMP(s) with *gur*
'that' seem(s) irrelevant to the resumptive A'-chains. By hypothesis, there is no operator
or any element in the SPEC of *gur* 'that' in Irish. Therefore, it must be assumed that *gur*
'that' does not enter into the chain formation headed by the wh-phrase followed by *aN*.
   However, in this paper, we found that example (40) is ungrammatical. Since *gur* 'that'
does not enter into the chain formation headed by the wh-phrase followed by *aN*, the A'-
chain headed by the wh-phrase followed by *aN* in (40) should be allowed. However, this
is not the case.
   The crucial difference between (41) and (40) is the fact that the syntactic status of *gur*
'that' in (40) is different from the syntactic status of *gur* 'that' in (41). It is required by
the verb in (41), while it is required by the noun in (40). This difference and the difference in the grammaticality between (41) and (40) seem to indicate (i) that A'-chain formation with resumptive pronouns by native speakers of Irish not only involves operator-
resumptive pronoun relations, but also the intermediate [−Q] COMP(s) with *gur* 'that,' and
(ii) that there is an algorithm that automatically incorporates the COMP *gur* 'that' into an
A'-chain headed by *aN* in Irish. This indicates that A'-chains with resumptive pronouns
might consist of two parts shown in (i). (We will not go into the issue of whether (ia)
could be integrated into (ib) in this paper.)

   (i) a.   Operator-resumptive pronoun chains (Op, RP).
       b.   COMP-resumptive pronoun chains (aN, (gur, ...), RP)

In grammatical A'-chains with resumptive pronouns with more than one embedding, if
the embedded clause has a [−Q] COMP, its maximal projection CP is always required by
the higher verb. Therefore, the CP is a complement. On the other hand, in the ungrammatical A'-chain with a resumptive pronoun in (40), the maximal projection of the [−Q]
COMP is not required by the verb. Rather, it is a complement to the noun. Note that the
complement to a noun constitutes a barrier for movement, as shown by the ungrammaticality of example (ii).

every intermediate COMP on the way to the tail of the chain, that is, the resumptive pronoun, and when it finds a COMP that is not selected by a verb,
the association does not hold between the head and the tail of the chain. If
this is true, examples such as (38) and (40) suggest that the chain tail search
by the chain head is a kind of agreement, and involves the phase that has
already been passed. This constitutes evidence for Bošković (2007), who
argues, contra Chomsky (2000, 2001), that the locality of Move and Agree is
radically different in the sense that Agree is free from mechanisms constrain-
ing Move, such as the Phase-Impenetrability Condition (PIC) in (43).

(43)   *Phase-Impenetrability Condition (PIC)*
        In phase α with head H, the domain of H is not accessible to op-
        erations outside α, only H and its edge are accessible to such op-
        erations.   (Chomsky (2000: 108))

(ii) *Cad é₁ a   cheideann tú   gur chreid   Máire an ráfla   gur cheannaigh Seán t_1?
      what aL believe   you that believed Mary the rumor that bought   John
      'What do you believe that Mary believed the rumor that John bought?'

Suppose here that *gur* 'that' itself has a certain feature that needs to be checked when
it enters into an A'-chain, and that it moves to the higher COMP to be checked. Then,
the contrast between the grammatical example in (41) and the ungrammatical example
in (40) is expected in terms of a version of the locality condition on chain links, such as
Chomsky and Lasnik's (1993) Minimize Chain Links (MCL). This is because in (40),
not (41), the position of the intermediate COMP *gur* 'that' is separated from the position
of the topmost COMP *aN* by a barrier (a complex NP), and if *gur* 'that' moves to *aN* at
LF, the trace will cause an anomaly, such as a violation of the Empty Category Principle
(ECP) in the pre-Minimalist framework.
  This hypothesis automatically accounts for the ungrammaticality of (29), where the
clause headed by *go* 'that' (the non-PAST form of *gur* 'that') is in the subject position, which is not a complement position in Irish, which is to be shown directly in the
text. Under the hypothesis, in (29), the algorithm that incorporates the COMP *gur* 'that'
into an A'-chain headed by *aN* forms a chain (aN, *go*, RP), and the intermediate COMP
go 'that' moves to *aN* across a barrier (a non-complement clause) in violation of the
MCL. Therefore, example (29) is predicted to be ruled out.
  Under this hypothesis, what must be acquired by native speakers of Irish is the connection between the COMPs in an A'-chain in (ib), and what need not be acquired is a
condition on such a connection or movement like the MCL, as it is assumed to be part of
universal grammar. Let us now consider whether native speakers of Irish can acquire the
relevant connection between the COMPs in an A'-chain. Irish makes frequent use of resumptive pronouns, and allows A'-chains with resumptive pronouns, as in examples such as
(41). Therefore, native speakers of Irish are exposed to the A'-chains with *gur* 'that' in the
intermediate COMP(s). Thus, based on this positive evidence, it is plausible to assume that
native speakers of Irish posit a sort of connection between *aN* and *gur* 'that.' It seems then
possible to derive the Condition on A'-Resumption Chains in (42) from a universal condition
such as the MCL and a language-particular property related to *aN* and *gur* 'that.'

The PIC in (43) will block the relation between C_1 and RP_1 in (44), when C_1 agrees with RP_1.

(44) $[_{CP1}\ C_1\ [...\ [_{vP}\ v\ [...\ [_{CP2}\ ...RP_1...$

Therefore, the fact that (38) and (40) are ungrammatical, while (41) is grammatical, suggests that the chain tail search by the chain head is a kind of agreement, and supports Bošković's (2007) view that the locality of Move and Agree is different.

Second, the clausal argument data in Irish provide further evidence for the claim that the subject position in Irish is not a properly governed position. Chung and McCloskey (1987) claim, under the theory with the Empty Category Principle (ECP), that the subject and the object positions are properly governed by the verb-INFL complex and (the trace of) the verb, respectively. They argue for this, based on the examples in (45). (45a) involves object extraction, and (45b) involves subject extraction.

(45) a. ?? rud   nach   bhfuil   mé ag súil   go bhfeicfinn   *t*
        a.thing that.NEG be.PRES I   expect.PROG that see.COND.1.SG
        'something that I do not expect that I would see'

    b. ?? rud   nach   dócha   go mbeadh   *t* air
        a.thing that.NEG+COP probable that be.COND on.him
        'something that probably would not be on him'
        (lit. 'something that it is not probable would be on him')

                               (Chung and McCloskey (1987: 224))

According to them, both (45a) and (45b) are equally marginal in grammaticality. Note that the intermediate COMP in both examples has not undergone COMP alternation, and remains *go* 'that.' This indicates that the SPEC of the intermediate COMP was not used as an escape hatch. Therefore, provided that only X^0 categories can be proper governors (for both antecedent and lexical government), as argued in Stowell (1981a), Rizzi (1986) and Lasnik and Saito (1992), the intermediate COMP cannot be an antecedent governor for the subject trace, because the COMP would not have the same index as the subject trace, and thus, the former does not bind the latter. Hence, the subject trace is not saved by antecedent-government in (45b). This leads Chung and McCloskey (1987) to propose that in (45b), the subject trace is lexically governed by the verb-INFL complex, just as the object trace in (45a) is lexically governed by (the trace of) the verb, hence the subject and the object positions are properly governed positions in Irish.

Maki and Ó Baoill (2011) then found a subject/object asymmetry in wh-fronting shown in (46).

(46) a. De cé   a   tharraing Seán [pictiúr *t*]?
         of whom aL take   John picture
         'Of whom did John take a picture?'
     b. *De cé   a   fuair [pictiúr *t*] duais?[3]
         of whom aL got   picture   prize
         'Of whom did a picture get a prize?'

Following Chung and McCloskey (1987), they assume that both subject and object positions are properly governed positions in Irish, and attribute the ungrammaticality of (46b), a case of extraction from a subject, to the prohibition against adjunction to agreeing specifiers and adjuncts (see Takahashi (1994) and Maki and Ó Baoill (2011) for relevant discussion), not to Huang's (1982) Condition on Extraction Domain (CED)[4]), as the CED would incorrectly predict that (46b) is grammatical under the assumption that the subject position is properly governed in Irish.

The clausal argument data in Irish provide supporting evidence for Maki and Ó Baoill's (2011) argument. Consider the examples in (15)–(18). If the

---

[3] Note that Irish shows Kuno's (1973) Internal Constituent Effect (ICE): extraction out of "internal constituents" is prohibited in general. Therefore, (ii) is worse than (i) in Irish, just like the English counterparts shown in (iii) and (iv).

  (i)   De cé   a   tharraing Seán [pictiúr *t*]?
        of whom aL took   John picture
        'Who did John take a picture of?'

 (ii) *De cé   a   thug   Seán [pictiúr *t*] do Liam?
        of whom aL gave John picture   to Bill
        'Who did John give a picture of to Bill?'

(iii)   Who did John take [a picture of *t*]?

(iv) ??Who did John give [a picture of *t*] to Bill?
                                   (Lasnik and Saito (1992: 91) slightly edited)

However, (46b), a case of extraction from a subject, is worse than extraction out of internal constituents in (ii) in Irish, just as (v) is worse than (iv) in English.

  (v) ?*Who did [pictures of *t*] please you?   (Lasnik and Saito (1992: 89))

This indicates that the ungrammaticality of (46b) is not solely due to the ICE, thus, involves some other factor independent of the ICE.

[4] The Condition on Extraction Domain (CED) is defined in (i).

  (i)   *Condition on Extraction Domain (CED)*
        A phrase A may be extracted out of a domain B only if B is properly governed.
                                                                    (Huang (1982))

subject position is a properly governed position, the CED will predict that extraction out of the subject is possible in (17) and (18), which is not correct. The contrast between (15) and (16), and (17) and (18) thus indicates that the subject position is not properly governed in Irish.

This is related to the issue of Chung and McCloskey's (1987) claim that both subject and object positions are properly governed positions in Irish. Note, however, that their claim needs careful examination, because the examples in (45a, b) do not constitute a minimal pair, thus do not provide a fair comparison between object extraction and subject extraction. Examples such as (47a, b) constitute a minimal pair, and both are grammatical.

(47) a. Cad é a chreideann tú a cheannaigh Seán *t*?
          what aL believe   you aL bought   John
          'What do you believe that John bought?'
     b.   Cé   a chreideann tú a cheannaigh *t* carr?
          who aL believe   you aL bought   car
          'Who do you believe bought a car?'

When the intermediate COMP does not change to *a* 'aL,' and remains *gur* 'that' in (47a, b), the resulting sentences are both ungrammatical, as shown in (48a, b). However, more importantly, (48b) is worse than (48a) in grammaticality.

(48) a. *Cad é a chreideann tú   gur cheannaigh Seán *t*?
          what aL believe   you that bought   John
          'What do you believe that John bought?'
     b.**Cé   a chreideann tú   gur cheannaigh *t* carr?
          who aL believe   you that bought   car
          'Who do you believe bought a car?'

This indicates that the subject position in (48b) should not be properly (lexically) governed. This fact is then consistent with the data in (15)–(18), supporting the claim that the subject position is not a properly governed position in Irish.

If this is the case, the ungrammaticality of (46b), for example, can be attributed to either the prohibition against adjunction to agreeing specifiers and adjuncts (Takahashi (1994) and Maki and Ó Baoill (2011)) or Huang's (1982) CED, which then raises the question of which should be necessary in grammar. Note here that 'proper government' in the definition of the CED can be restated as 'selection by a (lexical) head,' so that the definition of the CED does not contain the devices unfavorable within Chomsky's (1995)

Minimalist Program, such as 'government,' and the function of the prohibition against adjunction to agreeing specifiers and adjuncts is fundamentally identical to the function of the CED. In this paper, we leave this question open for future research.

Third, human language allows the option that a bare IP can be a subject. As shown in (10), for example, reproduced as (49), IP can be a subject in Irish.

(49)   Chuir [Seán carr a cheannach] iontas   ar Mháire.
        put   John car to buy   surprise on Mary
        'That John bought a car surprised Mary.'

Note that IP cannot be a subject in English, which in one analysis (Stowell (1981b)) is due to an ECP violation by the empty category in C, as shown in (50b).

(50) a.   [$_{CP}$ That [$_{IP}$ John bought a car]] surprised Mary.
     b.   *[$_{CP}$ e [$_{IP}$ John bought a car]] surprised Mary.
     c.   Mary said [$_{CP}$ that [$_{IP}$ John bought a car]].
     d.   Mary said [$_{CP}$ e [$_{IP}$ John bought a car]].

If the infinitival subject is headed by an empty C in Irish, as in (51), (49) would be incorrectly predicted to be ungrammatical.

(51)   Chuir [$_{CP}$ e [$_{IP}$ Seán carr a cheannach]] iontas   ar Mháire.
        put   John car to buy   surprise on Mary
        'That John bought a car surprised Mary.'

The fact that (49) is perfectly grammatical in Irish thus suggests that human language in principle allows a bare IP to be a subject. This conclusion, however, raises the question as to why (50b) is ungrammatical under the assumption that the subject can be a bare IP in English as well. The answer to this question seems to lie in the fact that even in Irish, a tensed clause cannot be a bare IP, as shown in (52) and (53).

(52) a.   Síleann Seán go   gceannófá   carr.
           think   John COMP buy.COND.2.SG car
           'John thinks that you would buy a car.'
     b.   Síleann Seán gur   cheannaigh tú   carr.
           think   John COMP.PAST bought   you car
           'John thinks that you bought a car.'

(53) *Síleann Seán [_{CP} *e* [_{IP} cheannaigh tú   carr]].
      think   John   bought   you car
      'John thinks that you bought a car.'

(52) shows that Irish has overt COMP-Predicate (verb+INFL) agreement. In (52a), the embedded predicate (verb+INFL) is in the conditional form, and the COMP is represented as *go*, while in (52b), the embedded predicate is in the past tense form, and the COMP is represented as *gur*. This indicates that there is a visible agreement relationship between COMP and the predicate (verb+INFL) in Irish. (53) shows that without an overt COMP, (52b), for example, becomes ungrammatical. This indicates that there seems to be a COMP-Predicate (verb+INFL) agreement in human language, and this agreement must be overt in Irish, and can be covert in English. If English has covert COMP-Predicate (verb+INFL) agreement, the empty C must be present, whether or not the CP is in the object position. Then, in (50b), the empty COMP must be present, which will run afoul of the principle that has the effect of the ECP.

This parametric variation between Irish and English in terms of overt/covert COMP-Predicate (verb+INFL) agreement is further linked to another parametric variation between both languages. Maki and Ó Baoill (2014b) examine embedded topicalization in Irish and English, and point out that COMP can bear a [+TOPIC] feature in Irish, not in English, so that Irish, not English, allows a topic phrase to be in CP SPEC. They claim that the contrast between Irish and English suggests that the relevant head for embedded topicalization is COMP in Irish, and it is INFL in English.

They go on to suggest that the difference in the head positions in charge of embedded topicalization lie in the relationship between the COMP and the predicate (verb+INFL) in the given languages. It was shown in this paper that there is a visible agreement relationship between the COMP and the predicate (verb+INFL) in Irish. Then, once the head in charge of embedded topicalization is placed between COMP and INFL, this morphological agreement relationship cannot hold, so that no embedded topicalization is allowed. However, if COMP can do the work for embedded topicalization, the agreement is successfully established. On the other hand, in English, being a non-verb initial language, there is no such visible agreement between COMP and INFL which would be blocked when INFL is in charge of embedded topicalization.

Fourth, and finally, (28), reproduced as (54), clearly indicates that the chain pattern (aL, that, RP) is essentially possible in movement constructions with one embedded clause in Irish.

(54)   Cad é₁ a   chreideann Liam gur chuir [Seán é₁ a cheannach]
        what aL believe   Bill that put   John it to buy
        iontas   ar Mháire?
        surprise on Mary
        'What does Bill believe that [that John bought it] surprised Mary?'

Maki and Ó Baoill (2011) were the first researchers who found the sixth pattern of COMP alternation in Irish, when there are two COMP positions in a
relative clause. The pattern is (aL, that, RP), as shown in (55).

(55)   Sin an carr a   mheasann Seán gur cheart dúinn é a cheannach.
        that the car aL think   John that right for.us it to buy
        'That's the car that John thinks that we ought to buy it.'

                                                              (aL, that, RP)

Under McCloskey's (2002) system, the chains in (54) and (55) should be illicit, as *aL* appears without an obvious movement operation, that is, the element locally bound by the relevant *aL* is not a trace. Therefore, the fact that
the chains in (54) and (55) are fundamentally licit is an interesting problem
for the theory of chain formation in general, and forces us to reconsider the
mechanism of A'-chain formation in Irish on the whole. In this paper, we
follow Maki and Ó Baoill (2011), who argue that given McCloskey's claim
that COMP whose specifier is not filled are realized as *go/gur* 'that,' *go/gur*
'that' may optionally have a feature that would reside in the operator base-
generated in the SPEC of *aN*, and only when it agrees with *aL* in a local relation, does this feature force *go/gur* 'that' to function as *aN*. See Maki and
Ó Baoill (2011) for the precise argument for this claim.

5. Conclusion

This paper investigated the properties of clausal arguments and chain
patterns that arise from extraction from these in Irish. Based on the newly
found facts, we argued (i) that Irish grammar should contain a condition
such as the Condition on A'-Resumption Chains, (ii) that the subject position is not a properly governed position in Irish, (iii) that there seems to be
a COMP-Predicate (verb+INFL) agreement in human language, and (iv) that
the chain pattern (aL, that, RP) is real in movement constructions with one
embedded clause in Irish.

Chapter 11

Puzzles with the Subject Position in Irish[*]

Dónall P. Ó Baoill and Hideki Maki

Queen's University Belfast (Prof. Emeritus) and *Gifu University*

Keywords: *English, Exceptional Case Marking, Heavy NP Shift, Irish, subject*

1. Introduction

This paper points out two puzzles that arise from the syntactic phenomena involving the subject position in Irish. First, as shown in (1b), a wh-phrase in the subject position may co-occur with an adjunct wh-phrase in CP SPEC. This is a puzzle, as the corresponding English sentence is totally ungrammatical, as shown in (2b).

(1) a. Cén fáth   ar cheannaigh Seán cad é?
      what reason aN bought   John what
      'Why did John buy what?'
   b. Cén fáth   ar cheannaigh cé   an leabhar?
      what reason aN bought   who the book
      'Why did who buy the book?'

* This is a revised version of the paper presented at the 148th Meeting of the Linguistic Society of Japan held at Hosei University on June 7, 2014. We would like to thank the audience of the meeting, Jessica Dunton, Megumi Hasebe, Michael LoPresti, Yoichi Miyamoto, Takashi Munakata, Fumikazu Niinuma, Yoshitaka Nishikawa, Michael Sevier, Shigeko Sugiura, Hisao Tokizaki and two anonymous *EL* referees for their valuable comments. Our thanks also go to the following native speakers from the eastern borders of Gweedore Parish in North West Donegal with whom the examples have been checked: Donnchadh Mac Fhionnaile, Seán Mac Giolla Chóill, Bríd Bean Mhic Íomhair, Anna Ní Bhaoill, Máire Nic Giolla Chóill, Pádraig Ó Briain, Pádraig Ó Dúgáin (Éamann), Bríd Bean Uí Ghallchóir and Méabha Bean Uí Phíopalaigh. All errors are our own. Research by the second author was supported in part by Japan Society for the Promotion of Science Grant # 25370428 to Gifu University.

(2) a.   Why did John buy what?
  b. *Why did who buy the book?

Second, a phrase in the subject position cannot undergo Heavy NP Shift (HNPS) in Irish, as shown in (4), which is derived from (3), in spite of the fact that the position seems head-governed by the verb, which does not seem inert in the sense of Rizzi (1990).

(3)   Cheannaigh [an fear a bhí ag staidéar teangeolaíochta] carr.
  bought   the man aL was at studying linguistics   car
  'The man who was studying linguistics bought a car.'

(4)   *Cheannaigh t_1 carr [an fear a bhí ag staidéar teangeolaíochta]$_1$.
  bought   car   the man aL was at studying linguistics
  'The man who was studying linguistics bought a car.'

In this paper, we will argue that these puzzles suggest (i) that Irish allows argument wh-phrases to stay in the base-generated positions throughout the derivation, (ii) that HNPS is triggered by agreement with *v*, not T, in Irish and English, and (iii) that Irish is an ECM-less language.

The organization of this paper is as follows. Section 2 reviews properties of the wh-interrogative construction in Irish as background to subsequent sections. Section 3 provides more data related to the two puzzles, and examines what factors lie behind them. Finally, Section 4 concludes this paper.

2.   Background

This section reviews (i) Irish complementizer system and (ii) properties of the wh-construction in Irish. Irish has three types of complementizers: the [−Q] marker, the direct relative marker, and the indirect relative marker. The properties of the three COMPs are summarized in (5).

(5)   Complementizers in Irish

	types of COMPs	non-past form	past form	symbol
a.	the [−Q] marker	*go*	*go/gur*	that
b.	the direct relative marker	*a*	*a*	aL
c.	the indirect relative marker	*a*	*a/ar*	aN

Below, the properties of the COMPs are illustrated by relevant examples. (6) is a declarative sentence, and the embedded clause is headed by the [−Q]

COMP *gur* 'that.' When the sentence involves wh-interrogative clause formation, as in (7), the embedded COMP must change to the direct relative marker *aL*, and at the same time, another COMP *aL* must be inserted right after the wh-phrase. In this paper, for expository purposes only, we represent A'-chains using the symbols *aL/aN* rather than the wh-phrase itself, as in (aL, aL, *t*).

> (6)   Creideann Seán gur cheannaigh Máire an   carr.
>   believe   John that bought   Mary the car
>   'John believes that Mary bought the car.'

> (7)   Cad é a   chreideann tú   a   cheannaigh Seán *t*?
>   what aL believe   you aL bought   John
>   'What do you believe that John bought?'   (movement) (aL, aL, *t*)

There is another way to form a wh-interrogative clause in Irish, as shown in (8).

> (8)   Cad é a   gcreideann tú   gur cheannaigh Seán é/*t*?
>   what aN believe   you that bought   John it
>   'What do you believe that John bought?'
>
>   (resumption) (aN, that, RP)

In (8), the topmost COMP of the wh-interrogative clause is an indirect relative marker *a*, the COMP of the embedded clause is a [−Q] COMP, and the embedded clause contains a resumptive pronoun *é* 'it' instead of a gap. Note that (8) is ungrammatical, if the resumptive pronoun is replaced by a trace.

Next, let us review the properties of the wh-construction in Irish. Ó Baoill and Maki (2014a) originally point out that Irish has a [+Q] COMP that may or may not attract a wh-phrase in overt syntax. Therefore, Irish allows both (9a) and (9b).

> (9) a.   Cad é a   cheannaigh Seán *t*?
>   what aL bought   John
>   'What did John buy *t*?'   (movement)
>   b.   Cheannaigh Seán cad é?
>   bought   John what
>   '[Q [John bought what]].'   (in-situ)

A wh-phrase may also be in situ in the embedded clause, as shown in (10b).

(10) a. Cad é a chreideann tú a cheannaigh Seán *t*?
   what aL believe you aL bought John
   'What do you believe that John bought?'
   b. Creideann tú gur ceannaigh Seán cad é?
   believe you that bought John what
   'What do you believe that John bought?'

Furthermore, wh-in-situ is possible within a complex NP island, while wh-movement out of a complex NP island is not, as shown in (11).

(11) a. *Cad é a chonaic siad [an fear a cheannaigh *t*]?
   what aL saw they the man aL bought
   'What did they see [the man who bought *t*]?'
   b. Chonaic siad [an fear a cheannaigh cad é]?
   saw they the man aL bought what
   '[Q [they saw [the man who bought what]]].'

3. Data and Discussion

Having established the particular background, we now consider the two puzzles. Let us first address the subject wh-phrase puzzle. Huang (1982) and Lasnik and Saito (1992), among others, point out that in English, a wh-phrase in the subject position cannot co-occur with an adjunct wh-phrase in CP SPEC, as shown in (2b), and attribute the ungrammaticality to the Empty Category Principle (ECP) that applies to the LF trace of the subject wh-phrase.

Suppose that the wh-phrase in the subject position in (1b) moves to CP SPEC at LF in Irish, just like English. Then, the subject trace is not antecedent-governed by the COMP, and (1b) would be incorrectly ruled out. One might argue, however, that the subject position in Irish is a lexically governed position, hence a properly governed position, so that the LF trace will not cause an ECP violation. However, Maki and Ó Baoill (2011) show, on the basis of extraction data in Irish, that the subject position is not a lexically governed position. Therefore, as shown in the contrast between (12a) and (12b), extraction out of the subject position leads to ungrammaticality.

(12) a. De cé a tharraing Seán [pictiúr *t*]?
   of whom aL took John picture
   'Who did John take a picture of *t*?'

b. *De cé   atá   [pictiúr *t*] ar   an   bhalla?
   of   whom   aL+is   picture   on   the   wall
   'Of whom is a picture *t* on the wall?'

Thus, the hypothesis that the subject wh-phrase undergoes LF movement will incorrectly predict that (1b) is ungrammatical in Irish.

However, there is a crucial difference between Irish and English. As shown in Section 2, in Irish, argument wh-phrases may appear in their base-generated positions, unlike English, as shown in (10b) and (11b). Based on this fact, we claim that in Irish, the subject wh-phrase in situ in (1b) is licensed by being bound by the [+Q] COMP, and because of this, it does not move to CP SPEC at LF. Note that the adjunct wh-phrase *cén fáth* 'why' is merged to CP SPEC. If an adjunct wh-phrase base-generated in CP SPEC can take scope at that position, no trace will be created that would cause an ECP violation. As long as this is correct, the subject wh-phrase puzzle suggests that an argument wh-phrase in situ in Irish may not move to CP SPEC throughout the derivation.

Let us then turn to the HNPS puzzle. Rizzi (1990) provides a set of HNPS data in English, as shown in (13)–(19).

(13)   [All the students who can solve this problem] are intelligent.

(14)   *[t_1 are intelligent] [all the students who can solve this problem]$_1$.

(15)   *Are$_2$ [t_1 t_2 intelligent] [all the students who can solve this problem]$_1$?

(16)   I would like to introduce [all the students who can solve this problem] to Mary.

(17)   I would like to introduce t_1 to Mary [all the students who can solve this problem]$_1$.

(18)   I believe [all the students who can solve this problem] to be intelligent.

(19)   I believe t_1 to be intelligent [all the students who can solve this problem]$_1$.

Rizzi (1990) states that (14) and (15) are ungrammatical, and argues that in (14), the subject trace is not head-governed, causing an ECP violation, because there is no head that m-commands the trace of the HNPS subject, and in (15), the subject trace is not head-governed, either, as the element in

COMP *are* is inert. Note that Rizzi (1990: 32) defines the ECP in such a way that a non-pronominal empty category must be (i) properly head-governed (Formal Licensing), and (ii) antecedent governed or Theta-governed (Identification). Therefore, in order for a trace to be legitimate, it must be properly head-governed in any case.

Let us then examine the Irish HNPS data in (20)–(23), along with (3) and (4).

(20) Thug Seán [an leabhar a   scríobh Máire] do Shiubhán.
      gave John the book   aL wrote   Mary   to Susan
      'John gave the book which Mary wrote to Susan.'

(21) Thug Seán t_1 do Shiubhán [an leabhar a   scríobh Máire]$_1$.
      gave John   to Susan   the book   aL wrote   Mary
      'John gave to Susan the book which Mary wrote.'

(22) Creideann Máire [an fear a bhí ag staidéar teangeolaíochta]
      believe   Mary   the man aL was at studying linguistics
      a   bheith cliste.
      to be.VN smart
      'Mary believes [the man who used to be studying linguistics] to be smart.'

(23) *Creideann Máire t_1 a bheith cliste [an fear a bhí ag staidéar
      believe   Mary   to be.VN smart   the man aL was at studying
      teangeolaíochta]$_1$.
      linguistics
      'Mary believes [the man who used to be studying linguistics] to be smart.'

(4) shows that HNPS is not possible from the subject of a finite clause in Irish. (23) shows that HNPS is not possible from the subject of an infinitival clause in Irish, either.

Let us first consider the ungrammaticality of (4). Let us assume with Maki and Ó Baoill (2011) that the verb is in T, and the subject is within *v*P, as shown in (24).

(24) $[_{T'}$ V$_1$ $[_{vP}$ SBJ $[_{VP}$ t_1 OBJ]]]

Let us also assume that *v*P is L-marked by T, and thus, it is not a barrier, extending Lasnik and Saito's (1992: 106) original idea that VP can be L-marked by INFL, and thus, it is not a barrier. Then, in (4), the subject position is head-governed by the verb in T in Irish. Furthermore, in (4), the verb should not be inert, since it has a full semantic content. Therefore, the head-government requirement is satisfied in (4).

On the other hand, (21) is grammatical with the direct object undergoing HNPS. Maki and Ó Baoill (2011) argue that rightward movement of the direct object across the indirect object targets vP SEPC, essentially following Nishikawa's (1990) analysis of HNPS in English. Then, the relevant structure of (21) should be (25).

(25) $[_{T'}$ V $[_{vP}$ SBJ $[_{VP}$ t_1 IOBJ] DOBJ$_1$]]

This movement should be allowed, as the trace of the direct object is head-governed by V. Then, what is wrong with (4)? The relevant structure should be either (26) or (27).

(26) $[_{T'}$ V $[_{vP}$ t_1 $[_{VP}$ OBJ] SBJ$_1$]]

(27) $[_{TP}$ $[_{T'}$ V $[_{vP}$ t_1 $[_{VP}$ OBJ]]] SBJ$_1$]

In (26), the subject in vP SPEC moves to vP SPEC in the right side of the head, which means that it virtually does not move at all. In (27), the subject in vP SPEC moves to TP SPEC on the right side of the head. In (26), the movement involved takes place within the same maximal projection vP, and does not move out of it, so that the movement has virtually no distance. We argue that this operation is prohibited, as it has a sort of superfluous step of movement, which should be prohibited by economy conditions on derivation.[1] In (27), the movement involved seems legitimate, yet the resulting sentence is not grammatical. This is apparently a problem. However, if we return to the English example in (15), it may provide an indication as to why (4) is ungrammatical.

Rizzi (1990) argues that *are* in C in (15) is inert, so that it cannot head-govern the subject trace, which leads to an ECP violation. However, (28) is grammatical in English.

---

[1] The first referee points out that (26) is structurally identical to its non-moved counterpart in (i).

(i) $[_{T'}$ V $[_{vP}$ $[_{VP}$ OBJ SBJ]]]

In this paper, we hypothesize that syntactic structure is created from the bottom up, as in (26). Phillips (1996, 2003), however, proposes that it is built from left to right, as in (i). Note here that whichever structure building is correct, both (26) and (i) are ill-formed, and demand an explanation. Therefore, we will leave open the issue of the manner of structure building.

(28)   Are$_1$ you t_1 Irish?

Since (28) is grammatical, *are$_1$* should be able to antecedent-govern and head-govern its own trace t_1. If it is inert, or if it becomes inert in the domain of C′, it should not be able to antecedent-govern or head-govern its own trace t_1, so that (28) would be incorrectly ruled out. The fact that (28) is grammatical thus indicates that *are* in C is not inert, and can function as a head-governor for any trace that needs to be formally licensed, namely, head-governed. Therefore, contrary to Rizzi's (1990) claim that *are* in C in (15) is inert, so that it cannot head-govern the subject trace, which leads to an ECP violation, it must be assumed that the head-government requirement is actually met in (15), and the ungrammaticality of the sentence must follow from some other factor. Now, what is common to (15) and (27) is the fact that the element that undergoes HNPS adjoins to TP or moves to TP SPEC. This seems to indicate that HNPS cannot target T′/TP in either English or Irish, which in turn suggests that T does not have a relevant feature that triggers HNPS.[2] Then, this idea correctly accounts for the ungrammaticality of (14) and (15) in English, along with the ungrammaticality of

---

[2] As this is a strong claim, it will be necessary to carefully examine the traditional data and arguments of HNPS analysis. Ross (1967/1986) found a rule he called Complex NP Shift, which we now call Heavy NP Shift, and claimed (i).

(i)   Any rule whose structural index is of the form ... A Y, and whose structural change specifies that A is to be adjoined to the right of Y, is upward bounded.
                                        (Ross (1986: 179))

He states that he knows of no exceptions to this generalization.

The data that fall under this generalization are shown below. First, an object can undergo rightward movement within the sentence, as shown in (ii).

(ii)   I gave e_1 to the officer in charge [the blackjack which I had found in the cookie jar]$_1$.   (Ross (1986: 140) slightly edited)

Second, as (14) shows, subject NPs in tensed clauses cannot undergo rightward movement. Third, as Postal (1974) points out, an NP cannot move out of a tensed clause, as (iii) shows.

(iii)   *I have expected [that I would find e_1] since 1939 [the treasure said to have been buried on that island]$_1$.   (Postal (1974: 93) slightly edited)

It seems that the generalization in (i) has not been challenged since Ross (1967). Shiobara (2010) also claims (iv).

(iv)   Heavy NP Shift in English
        When an NP is prosodically heavier than the neighboring element, it may appear in the VP-internal position.   (Shiobara (2010: 9) slightly edited)

Therefore, it seems correct to assume that HNPS cannot target T′/TP in English.

(4) in Irish, where the subject NP moves to TP SPEC. We thus conclude, based on the HNPS data in English and Irish, (i) that superfluous steps of movement are prohibited, and (ii) that T does not have a feature that motivates HNPS.

Let us now consider the Irish example in (23), which involves HNPS of the subject of the Exceptional Case Marking (ECM) complement. As shown above, the English counterpart in (19) is grammatical. If (23) is an instance of ECM structure, the question remains as to why HNPS of the subject of the ECM complement is allowed in English, while it is not in Irish. To address this question, it is worth examining whether Irish really has the same ECM construction as English. There are two pieces of evidence that the Irish ECM is different from the English ECM. First, the ECM subject cannot be separated from the matrix predicate by an adverb in English, but it can in Irish, as shown by the contrast between (29a, b) and (30).

(29) a. *John believes sincerely [Bill to be the best man].

(Chomsky and Lasnik (1977: 478))

    b. *Mary believes firmly [[the man who used to be studying linguistics] to be smart].

(30)   Creideann Máire go daingean [[an fear a bhí ag staidéar
    believe Mary firmly   the man aL was at studying
    teangeolaíochta] a bheith cliste].
    linguistics   to be.VN smart
    (*)'Mary believes firmly [the man who used to be studying linguistics] to be smart.'

Second, when the ECM subject is wh-extracted in Irish, the chain can terminate with a trace, as in (31), or as a resumptive pronoun, as in (32).

(31)   Cé a chreideann Máire go daingean [t a bheith cliste]?
    who aL believe Mary firmly   to be.VN smart
    'Who does Mary firmly believe to be smart?'   (aL, t)

At the same time, HNPS cannot target T'/TP in Irish, either. First, (21) shows that an object can undergo rightward movement within the sentence in Irish. Second, as (4) shows, subject NPs in tensed clauses cannot undergo rightward movement. Third, an NP cannot move out of a tensed clause, as the Irish counterpart of (iii) is ungrammatical. Therefore, it seems correct to assume that HNPS cannot target T'/TP in Irish, either.

(32)   Cé   a   gcreideann Máire go daingean [é   a   bheith cliste]?
       who aN believe   Mary firmly   him to be.VN smart
       'Who does Mary firmly believe to be smart?'   (aN, RP)

If the Irish ECM is the same as the English ECM, the question immediately arises as to how the ECM subjects in (30) and (32) can get accusative Case.

Note here that in Irish, accusative Case is a default Case, as shown by (33).

(33)   Bhuail mé leis   agus [é   ar   an   bhealach 'na bhaile].
       struck I   with.him and   him on   the   way   home
       'I met him as he was on the way home.'

                    (Chung and McCloskey (1987: 175), with brackets added)

In (33), the small clause is positioned after *agus* 'and,' which does not assign/check any Case. Therefore, it is plausible to assume that accusative Case is default in Irish, and one may say that an NP bears accusative Case as an inherent Case in Irish when no Case is structurally assigned to it. If this is true, the accusative Case on the ECM subjects in (30) and (32) is inherent, and is not structurally assigned to them, which in turn accounts for the contrast between (29a, b) and (30) in English and Irish.

Let us now consider what is wrong with HNPS of the 'ECM' subject in Irish, as shown in (23), under the assumption that the 'ECM' subject bears inherent Case in Irish. If T does not have a relevant feature that triggers HNPS, as argued above, v is the only head that may attract the 'ECM' subject in (23). Let us first consider cases in which v has accusative Case. In such cases, since the 'ECM' subject has inherent Case, which is different from structural accusative Case, the inherent Case on the subject and the accusative Case on the head are not compatible. Therefore, the accusative Case on v is not properly checked/licensed due to the feature mismatch, and thus, (23) will be correctly ruled out.

Next, let us consider cases in which v does not have any Case, which should be possible, since the verb *creideann* 'believe' in Irish can take either an infinitival complement, as shown in (22), or a finite complement, as shown in (34), where the complement clause does not seem to bear accusative Case.

(34)   Creideann Máire go   bhfuil   an   fear a   bhí ag staidéar
       believe   Mary that be.PRES the man aL was at studying
       teangeolaíochta cliste.
       linguistics   smart

'Mary believes that the man who used to be studying linguistics is smart.'

In such cases, too, there seems to arise a feature mismatch, because the head v, which does not have any Case, attracts the 'ECM' subject that bears inherent Case to its SPEC, so that the head which does not need any Case by hypothesis and an NP with inherent Case will be in the same local domain, or the checking domain of the head in Chomsky's (1995) terms, where features on the head and the NP should be compatible in terms of Case. Therefore, in any event, HNPS of the 'ECM' subject in Irish causes a Case-related problem. Hence, (23) is ungrammatical in Irish.[3]

Let us then examine why (19), the English counterpart of (23), is grammatical. The ECM subject in English bears accusative Case, as shown in (35).

(35)   I believe him to be intelligent.

Following the essential insight of Nishikawa (1990), we assume that the ECM subject undergoes rightward movement into the SPEC of the matrix v, when it is subject to HNPS. In this case, the head v has accusative Case, and the ECM subject also has accusative Case, so that there is no Case mismatch in the derived structure. Hence, (19) is correctly predicted to be grammatical in English.

If the above argument is correct, HNPS is possible in English and Irish only when the head v and the NP that is to undergo HNPS have structural

---

[3] Woolford (2006) claims that Icelandic datives are inherent Cases, because the regular dative on DP goals remains dative when the sentence passivizes, as shown in (ib).

(i) a.   Þeir skiluðu Maríu   bókinni.
         they returned Mary-*DAT* book-the-*DAT*
         'They returned the book to Mary.'   (Jónsson (1996: 137) with slight editing)
    b.   Maríu   var skilað   þessari bók.
         Mary-*DAT* was returned this   book-*DAT*
                                           (Jónsson (1996: 139) with slight editing)

Since the subject of the sentence has nominative Case in (ia), there seems to be a Case mismatch between the Case assigner (T) and the dative NP in (ib), yet the passive sentence is grammatical. If the claim in our paper is generalized to these cases, they would be incorrectly ruled out. However, there is one crucial difference between these cases and the Irish case. That is, the head that tolerates inherent Case is T in Icelandic, while it is not in Irish. Several languages have been reported to allow non-nominative subjects, which seems to suggest that T is more tolerant than the other Case-licensing heads in allowing Cases other than nominative. Of course, a careful examination is in order to prove that this line of analysis is correct, which we will leave for future research.

accusative Case. Therefore, one may say that the feature that triggers HNPS is parasitic to accusative Case on a head, and HNPS is a feature-driven movement operation.

4. Conclusion

This paper addressed two puzzles arising from syntactic phenomena involving the subject position in Irish, and argued (i) that Irish allows argument wh-phrases to stay in the base-generated positions throughout the derivation, (ii) that HNPS is triggered by agreement with v, not T, in Irish and English, and (iii) that the Irish ECM is different from the English ECM, and in this sense, Irish is an ECM-less language.

Chapter 12

Extraction from the Complement Clause of the Factive Predicate *Is Trua Le* 'To Regret' in Irish[*]

Dónall P. Ó Baoill and Hideki Maki

Queen's University Belfast (Prof. Emeritus) and *Gifu University*

Keywords: *barrier, complementizer, extraction, factive, resumptive pronoun*

1. Introduction

This paper examines wh-extraction from the complement clause of the factive predicate *is trua le* 'to regret' in Irish, and based on newly elicited data, we will argue (i) that the complementizer *go/gur* 'that' in Irish optionally has an operator, contrary to McCloskey's (2002) claim, (ii) that Irish allows an invisible COMP, which can host an operator, (iii) that the invisible COMP subcategorized by the factive predicate *is trua le* 'to regret' is a nominalizer, and makes the infinitival complement a barrier for movement, and (iv) that Irish has two types of [+Q] COMPs, one that attracts a wh-phrase in overt syntax, and another that does not.

The organization of this paper is as follows. Section 2 reviews properties of the wh-interrogative construction in Irish as background to subsequent sections. Section 3 provides data with extraction from the complement clause of the factive predicate *is trua le* 'to regret' in Irish. Based on the newly found data, Section 4 discusses what they might suggest for the the-

---

 * This is a revised version of the paper presented at the 149th Meeting of the Linguistic Society of Japan held at Ehime University on November 15, 2014. We are indebted to Jessica Dunton, Masatoshi Koizumi, Kazumi Matsuoka, Fumikazu Niinuma and Satoshi Oku for their helpful comments on an earlier version of this paper. Our thanks also go to the following native speakers from the eastern borders of Gweedore Parish in North West Donegal with whom the examples have been checked: Donnchadh Mac Fhionnaile, Seán Mac Giolla Chóill, Bríd Bean Mhic Íomhair, Anna Ní Bhaoill, Máire Nic Giolla Chóill, Pádraig Ó Briain, Pádraig Ó Dúgáin (Éamann), Bríd Bean Uí Ghallchóir and Méabha Bean Uí Phíopalaigh. All errors are our own. Research by the second author was supported in part by JSPS KAKENHI Grant Number 25370428 to Gifu University.

ory of (Irish) syntax. Section 5 addresses one remaining question. Finally, Section 6 concludes this paper. An appendix is provided to show a difference between English and Irish with respect to the extractability from tensed factive complements.

2. Background

Let us start by briefly summarizing properties of the wh-interrogative construction in Irish. (See McCloskey (1979, 1990) and Maki and Ó Baoill (2011), among others, for details of the construction.) Irish has three types of complementizers: the [−Q] marker, the direct relative marker, and the indirect relative marker. The properties of the three COMPs are summarized in (1).

(1)   Complementizers in Irish[1]

	types of COMPs	non-past form	past form	symbol
a.	the [−Q] marker	*go*	*go/gur*	that
b.	the direct relative marker	*a*	*a*	aL
c.	the indirect relative marker	*a*	*a/ar*	aN

Let us illustrate the properties of the COMPs by relevant examples. (2) is a declarative sentence, and the embedded clause is headed by the [−Q] COMP *gur* 'that.'

(2)   Creideann Seán gur cheannaigh Máire an carr.
       believe John that bought   Mary the car
       'John believes that Mary bought the car.'

When the sentence involves wh-interrogative clause formation, as in (3), the embedded COMP must change to the direct relative marker *aL*, and at the same time, another COMP *aL* must be inserted right after the wh-phrase. In this paper, for expository purposes only, we represent A′-chains using the symbols *aL/aN* rather than the wh-phrase itself, as in (aL, *t*) or (aN, RP),

---

[1] The complementizer forms used with irregular verbs in the past tense in Irish, namely, the [−Q] marker and indirect relative marker *aN* do not follow the regular usage found with all other verbs. Hence, the regular complementizer forms *gur* 'that' and the indirect relative form *ar* are replaced by *go* 'that' and *a* 'aN,' respectively when used with the following irregular verbs: *bí* 'to be' >> *go/a raibh*; *déan* 'to do' >> *go/a ndearna*; *faigh* 'to get' >> *go/a bhfuair*; *tabhair* 'to give' >> *go/a dtug*; *tar* 'to come' >> *go/a dtáinig* and *téigh* 'to go' >> *go/a ndeachaigh*.

where *RP* stands for a resumptive pronoun.

(3) Cad é a   chreideann tú   a   cheannaigh Seán *t*?
     what aL believe   you aL bought   John
     'What do you believe that John bought?'   (movement) (aL, aL, *t*)

There is another way to form a wh-interrogative clause in Irish, as shown in (4).

(4) Cad é a   gcreideann tú   gur cheannaigh Seán é/*t*?
     what aN believe   you that bought   John it
     'What do you believe that John bought?'

                                            (resumption) (aN, that, RP)

In (4), the topmost COMP of the wh-interrogative clause is an indirect relative marker *a*, the COMP of the embedded clause is a [−Q] COMP, and the embedded clause contains a resumptive pronoun *é* 'it' instead of a gap. Note that (4) is ungrammatical, if the resumptive pronoun is replaced by a trace, which suggests that *aN* must bind a resumptive pronoun.

McCloskey (2002) provides an account of the distribution of the COMPs by proposing (5).

(5) a.   C whose specifier is filled by Move is realized as *aL*.
    b.   C whose specifier is filled by Merge is realized as *aN*.
    c.   C whose specifier is not filled is realized as *go/gur*.

McCloskey assumes that the SPEC of *aL* contains a null operator/null pronoun (henceforth, null operator) as a result of movement, that in the SPEC of *aN*, there is a base-generated operator, and that in the SPEC of *go/gur*, there is no operator. If this is correct, the structure of the wh-interrogative clause construction in Irish looks like a cleft sentence, as shown in (6).

(6) (it is) WH_1 [**Op**$_1$ aL/aN [$_{IP}$...t_1/RP$_1$...]] (where *RP* stands for resumptive pronoun)

In this paper, following McCloskey (2002), we represent the structure of a wh-interrogative clause by putting a null operator that corresponds to the wh-phrase, not the wh-phrase itself, in the SPEC of *aL/aN*.

3. Data

Having established the particular background, let us now examine examples that involve extraction from factive complements in Irish. Firstly, the factive predicate *is trua le* 'to regret' takes either a tensed complement clause or an infinitival complement clause, as shown in (7) and (8), respectively.

(7)   Is   trua   le   Seán [gur léigh Máire an   leabhar seo].
       COP regret with John that read Mary the book   this
       'John regrets that Mary read this book.'   (tensed)

(8)   Is   trua   le   Seán [Máire an   leabhar seo a   léamh].
       COP regret with John Mary the book   this to read.VN
       'John regrets that Mary read this book.'   (infinitival)

Secondly, while the examples in (9)–(12) indicate that extraction out of a tensed factive complement is allowed, the examples in (13)–(16) show that extraction out of an infinitival factive complement is not.

(9)   Cén   leabhar is   trua   le   Seán [a   léigh Máire *t*]?
       which book   aL+COP regret with John aL read Mary
       'Which book does John regret [that Mary read *t*]?'   (aL, aL, *t*)

(10)   Cén   teanga   is   trua   le   Seán [a   labhair Máire *t*]?
       which language aL+COP regret with John aL spoke Mary
       'Which language does John regret [that Mary spoke *t*]?' (aL, aL, *t*)

(11)   Cén   fear   is   trua   le   Seán [a   léigh *t* an   leabhar
       which man   aL+COP regret with John aL read   the book
       seo]?
       this
       'Which man does John regret [that *t* read this book]?'   (aL, aL, *t*)

(12)   Cén   fear   is   trua   le   Seán [a   labhair *t* an
       which man   aL+COP regret with John aL spoke   the
       teanga   seo]?
       language this
       'Which man does John regret [that *t* spoke this language]?'
                                                               (aL, aL, *t*)

(13)   *Cén   leabhar is   trua   le   Seán [Máire *t* a   léamh]?
       which book   aL+COP regret with John Mary   to read.VN
       'Which book does John regret [Mary to have read *t*]?'   (aL, *t*)

(14) *Cén   teanga   is   trua   le   Seán [Máire *t* a labhairt]?
      which language aL+COP regret with John Mary   to speak.VN
      'Which language does John regret [Mary to have spoken *t*]?' (aL, *t*)

(15) *Cén   fear   is   trua   le   Seán [*t* an leabhar seo a
      which man aL+COP regret with John   the book   this to
      léamh]?
      read.VN
      'Which man does John regret [*t* to have read this book]?'   (aL, *t*)

(16) *Cén   fear   is   trua   le   Seán [*t* an teanga   seo a
      which man aL+COP regret with John   the language this to
      labhairt]?
      speak.VN
      'Which man does John regret [*t* to have spoken this language]?'
      (aL, *t*)

Thirdly, the resumption strategy is available to the wh-construction with the factive predicate *is trua le* 'to regret,' so that the chain can be terminated with a resumptive pronoun, as shown in (17)–(20).

(17) Cén   leabhar ar   trua   le   Seán [gur léigh Máire **é**]?
      which book   aN+COP regret with John that read Mary it
      'Which book does John regret [that Mary read *t*]?'
      (aN, that, RP) (tensed)

(18) Cén   leabhar is   trua   le   Seán [gur léigh Máire **é**]?
      which book   aL+COP regret with John that read Mary it
      'Which book does John regret [that Mary read *t*]?'
      (aL, that, RP) (tensed)

(19) Cén   fear   ar   trua   le   Seán [gur léigh **sé** an leabhar
      which man aN+COP regret with John that read he the book
      seo]?
      this
      'Which man does John regret [that *t* read this book]?'
      (aN, that, RP) (tensed)

(20) Cén   fear   is   trua   le   Seán [gur léigh **sé** an leabhar
      which man aL+COP regret with John that read he the book
      seo]?
      this

'Which man does John regret [that *t* read this book]?'

(aL, that, RP) (tensed)

Fourthly, the wh-chain that has not been observed in the Irish literature (aL, RP) turns out to be possible, as shown in (21) and (22).

(21)   Cén   leabhar is   trua   le   Seán [Máire **é** a   léamh]?
       which book   aL+COP regret with John Mary   it to read.VN
       'Which book does John regret [Mary to have read *t*]?'

(aL, RP) (infinitival)

(22)   Cén   fear is   trua   le   Seán [**é**   an   leabhar seo a
       which man aL+COP regret with John him the book   this to
       léamh]?
       read.VN
       'Which man does John regret [to have read this book]?'

(aL, RP) (infinitival)

Fifthly, a wh-phrase may be in situ in the complement clause of *is trua le* 'to regret,' as shown in (23)–(26), although overt movement of the wh-phrase results in ungrammaticality, as shown in (13)–(16). Note that (23)–(26) are well-formed as non-echo wh-questions.

(23)   Is   trua   le   Seán [gur léigh Máire **cén**   leabhar]?
       COP regret with John that read Mary which book
       'Which book does John regret [that Mary read *t*]?'   (tensed)

(24)   Is   trua   le   Seán [Máire **cén**   leabhar a   léamh]?
       COP regret with John Mary which book   to read.VN
       'Which book does John regret [that Mary read *t*]?'   (infinitival)

(25)   Is   trua   le   Seán [gur léigh **cén**   fear an   leabhar seo]?
       COP regret with John that read which man the book   this
       'Which man does John regret [that *t* read this book]?'   (tensed)

(26)   Is   trua   le   Seán [**cén**   fear an   leabhar seo a   léamh]?
       COP regret with John which man the book   this to read.VN
       'Which man does John regret [that *t* read this book]?'   (infinitival)

4.   Discussion

Let us now consider what the observed facts might suggest for the theory of (Irish) syntax. Firstly, (18) and (20) show that the head of the chain is *aL*, and the tail of the chain is a resumptive pronoun.

(18)   Cén   leabhar   is   trua   le   Seán   [gur   léigh   Máire   é]?
       which book   aL+COP   regret with John   that   read   Mary   it
       'Which book does John regret [that Mary read *t*]?'

                                                        (aL, that, RP) (tensed)

(20)   Cén   fear   is   trua   le   Seán   [gur   léigh   **sé**   an
       which man   aL+COP   regret with John   that   read   he   the
       leabhar   seo]?
       book   this
       'Which man does John regret [that *t* read this book]?'

                                                        (aL, that, RP) (tensed)

This type of chain is not possible under McCloskey's (2002) hypothesis, in which there is no element in the SPEC of *go/gur* 'that.' McCloskey's (2002) system allows five possible A'-chain patterns headed by an argument wh-phrase, when they contain two COMP positions, as shown in (27)–(31).

(27)   Cad é   a   chreideann   tú   a   cheannaigh   Seán   *t*?
       what   aL   believe   you   aL   bought   John
       'What do you believe that John bought?'   (aL, aL, *t*)

(28)   Cad é   a   gcreideann   tú   gur   cheannaigh   Seán   é?
       what   aN   believe   you   that bought   John   it
       'What do you believe that John bought?'   (aN, that, RP)

(29)   Cad é   a   gcreideann   tú   ar   cheannaigh   Seán   é?
       what   aN   believe   you   aN   bought   John   it
       'What do you believe [that John bought *t*]?'   (aN, aN, RP)

(30)   Cad é   a   chreideann   tú   ar   cheannaigh   Seán   é?
       what   aL   believe   you   aN   bought   John   it
       'What do you believe [that John bought *t*]?'   (aL, aN, RP)

(31)   Cad é   a   raibh   súil   agat   a   cheannófá   *t*?
       what   aN   was   hope   at.you   aL   buy.COND
       'What did you hope [that you would buy *t*]?'   (aN, aL, *t*)

The chain pattern (aL, that, RP) found in (18) and (20) is not possible, because the intermediate COMP *gur* 'that' does not have a null operator in its SPEC, so that the topmost COMP cannot be *aL*, as it must reflect some sort of movement. Since this kind of chain is possible in Irish, we take it to suggest that the [−Q] COMP *gur* 'that' can optionally host a base-generated null operator in its SPEC, which in turn moves to the SPEC of the higher COMP. Then, the chain pattern (aL, that, RP) in (18) and (20) is correctly expected.

Note here that Maki and Ó Baoill (2011) first found the sixth pattern of COMP alternation in Irish, when there are two COMP positions in a relative clause. Their examples are shown in (32) and (33).

(32) Sin an carr a   mheasann Seán gur   cheart dúinn é   a
      that the car   aL   think   John that right   for.us it to
      cheannach.
      buy
      'That's the car that John thinks that we ought to buy it.'

                                                          (aL, that, RP)

(33) Sin an carr a   mheasann tú   gurbh fhiú   dúinn é   a
      that the car   aL   think   you   that   worth for.us it to
      cheannach.
      buy
      'That's the car that you think that it would be worth our while to
      buy it.'   (aL, that, RP)

They propose that *gur* 'that' may optionally have a feature that would reside in the operator base-generated in the SPEC of *aN*, and only when it agrees with *aL* in a local relation, does this feature force *that* to function as *aN*. In this paper, we slightly revise the original claim, and propose that *gur* 'that' can optionally host a base-generated null operator in its SPEC, which in turn moves to the SPEC of the higher COMP, just as in the case of *aN*. This revision is plausible, as it makes the hypothesis consistent with the idea that *aL* is a reflex of operator movement.

Secondly, the chain pattern (aL, RP) is not allowed in general, as shown by the contrast between (34) and (35), but it is allowed in (21) and (22).

(34) *Cad é a   cheannaigh Seán é?
       what aL   bought   John it
      'What did John buy?'   (aL, RP)

(35) Cad é a   cheannaigh Seán *t*?
      what aL   bought   John
      'What did John buy?'   (aL, *t*)

(21) Cén   leabhar is   trua le   Seán [Máire é a léamh]?
      which book   aL+COP regret with John Mary   it to read.VN
      'Which book does John regret [Mary to have read *t*]?'

                                            (aL, RP) (infinitival)

(22) Cén   fear   is   trua le   Seán [é   an leabhar seo a
      which man   aL+COP regret with John him the book   this to
      léamh]?
      read.VN
      'Which man does John regret [to have read this book]?'

                                            (aL, RP) (infinitival)

The ungrammaticality of (34) indicates that *aL* cannot bind a resumptive
pronoun in the chain pattern (aL, RP), and the grammaticality of (21) shows
that it can bind a resumptive pronoun in the chain pattern (aL, RP), a contradiction.

    There is a clear difference between (34) on one hand, and (21) and (22)
on the other. That is, (21) and (22) contain an embedded clause, while (34)
does not. Therefore, the fact that the chain pattern (aL, RP) is allowed in
(21) and (22), and not in (34), seems to suggest that the infinitival factive
complement should be headed by a null COMP, which can host an operator
in its SPEC, which then moves to the matrix CP SPEC, as shown in (36).

(36) $[_{CP}$ Op$_1$ aL...$[_{CP}$ t_1 C$_\emptyset$ $[_{IP}$...RP$_1$...]]]

In (36), the matrix COMP *aL* does not locally bind the resumptive pronoun
due to the intervening COMP, which is invisible, and the grammaticality of
(21) and (22) is expected, as the relevant chain pattern involved in the examples is a three-membered chain, as shown in (37), which is fundamentally
identical to the chain pattern in (38), as found in grammatical examples such
as (18).

(37) (aL, ø$_{COMP}$, RP)

(38) (aL, that, RP)

(18) Cén   leabhar is   trua le   Seán [gur léigh Máire é]?
      which book   aL+COP regret with John that read Mary   it
      'Which book does John regret [that Mary read *t*]?'

    Thirdly, the contrast between extraction out of a tensed factive comple-
ment and extraction out of an infinitival factive complement, as shown in (9)
and (13), for example, suggests that an infinitival factive complement, not a

tensed factive complement, becomes a barrier for movement. See Chomsky
(1986b) for the original definition of barrier for movement.

(9)   Cén   leabhar is   trua le   Seán [a   léigh Máire *t*]?
      which book   aL+COP regret with John aL read Mary
      'Which book does John regret [that Mary read *t*]?'   (aL, aL, *t*)

(13) *Cén   leabhar is   trua le   Seán [Máire *t* a   léamh]?
      which book   aL+COP regret with John Mary   to read.VN
      'Which book does John regret [Mary to have read *t*]?'   (aL, *t*)

Let us consider how the complement functions as a barrier for movement. In the above discussion, it was argued that an infinitival factive
complement is headed by a null COMP. Then, the relevant structure of (13)
is (39).

(39) *Cén   leabhar is   trua le   Seán [$_{CP}$ *t'* [$_{C'}$ ø$_{COMP}$
      which book   aL+COP regret with John
      [$_{IP}$ Máire *t* a   léamh]]]?
            Mary   to read.VN
      'Which book does John regret [Mary to have read *t*]?'

                                                        (aL, ø$_{COMP}$, *t*)

On the other hand, the relevant structure of (9) is (40).

(40) Cén   leabhar is   trua le   Seán [$_{CP}$ *t'* [$_{C'}$ a   [$_{IP}$ léigh
      which book   aL+COP regret with John   aL read
      Máire *t*]]]?
      Mary
      'Which book does John regret [that Mary read *t*]?'   (aL, aL, *t*)

The crucial difference between (39) and (40) is the intermediate COMP. In
(40), the intermediate COMP is realized as *aL*, which indicates that the
sentence-initial wh-phrase has once moved into its SPEC position. The same
kind of movement takes place in (39) as well. The sentence-initial wh-
phrase moves into the SPEC of the invisible COMP before reaching the final
landing site. It seems then that the ungrammaticality of (39) stems from the
fact that the invisible COMP hosts a wh-phrase in the course of the derivation.

    However, it must be noted that this account needs a refinement, given
the fact that examples such as (41) are grammatical in Irish.

(41)   Cén   leabhar atá   súil   ag Seán Máire *t* a   léamh?
       which book   aL+is hope   at John Mary   to read.VN
       'Which book does John expect [Mary to read]?'   (aL, *t*)

(41) contains a non-factive predicate *bí súil ag* 'to hope' in the matrix clause, and the relevant structure is (42).

(42)   Cén   leabhar atá   súil   ag Seán [CP *t′* [C′ øCOMP [IP Máire *t* a
       which book   aL+is hope   at John   Mary   to
       léamh]]]?
       read.VN
       'Which book does John expect [Mary to read]?'   (aL, øCOMP, *t*)

(39) and (42) are fundamentally identical, yet only (39) is excluded.

What is then the difference between (39) and (42)? The crucial difference is that in (39), the matrix predicate is factive, and in (42), it is non-factive. Interestingly enough, in languages like Japanese, factive complements are nominalized, while non-factive complements are not, as shown in (43) and (44), respectively. Note that *koto* 'fact' in (43) is a nominalizer.

(43)   Kimi-wa [Mary-ga   dono hon-o   yonda koto]-o
       you-TOP Mary-NOM which book-ACC read   fact-ACC
       kookaishiteiru no?
       regret   Q
       'Which book do you regret [that Mary read]?'

(44)   Kimi-wa [Mary-ni dono   hon-o   yonde hoshii to]
       you-TOP Mary-to which book-ACC read   want   that
       omotteiru no?
       hope   Q
       'Which book do you hope [that Mary will read]?'

We hypothesize that this kind of difference is reflected in Irish as well, and propose that infinitival factive complements are nominalized, while infinitival non-factive complements are not in Irish. Then, in (39), the intermediate invisible COMP corresponds to the nominalizer *koto* 'fact' in Japanese, and makes the infinitival complement IP nominalized, so that it becomes a barrier for movement.

(39) *Cén   leabhar is   trua le   Seán [$_{CP}$ t' [$_{C'}$ ⌀$_{COMP}$ [$_{IP}$ Máire t
      which book   aL+COP regret with John   Mary
      a léamh]]]?
      to read.VN
      'Which book does John regret [Mary to have read t]?'   (aL, ⌀$_{COMP}$, t)

Therefore, (39) is predicted to be ungrammatical.

On the other hand, in (42), the intermediate invisible COMP does not correspond to the nominalizer *koto* 'fact' in Japanese. Therefore, it does not make the infinitival complement a barrier for movement.

(42) Cén   leabhar atá   súil   ag Seán [$_{CP}$ t' [$_{C'}$ ⌀$_{COMP}$ [$_{IP}$ Máire t
      which book   aL+is hope   at John   Mary
      a léamh]]]?
      to read.VN
      'Which book does John expect [Mary to read]?'   (aL, ⌀$_{COMP}$, t)

Therefore, (42) is predicted to be grammatical.

Fourthly, the fact that (23) and (9) are grammatical, indicates that Irish has two types of [+Q] COMPs, namely, a strong [+Q] COMP and a non-strong [+Q] COMP, and only the former attracts a wh-phrase in overt syntax.

(23) Is   trua   le   Seán [gur léigh Máire **cén**   leabhar]?
      COP regret with John that read Mary which book
      'Which book does John regret [that Mary read t]?'   (in-situ)

(9) Cén   leabhar is   trua le   Seán [a   léigh Máire t]?
      which book   aL+COP regret with John aL read Mary
      'Which book does John regret [that Mary read t]?'   (movement)

Ó Baoill and Maki (2014a) originally pointed out that Irish has a strong [+Q] COMP and a non-strong [+Q] COMP on the basis of the examples in (43)–(46).

(43) a. Cad é a   cheannaigh Seán t?
         what aL bought   John
         'What did John buy t?'   (movement)
     b. Cheannaigh Seán cad é?
         bought   John what
         '[Q [John bought what]].'   (in-situ)

(44) a. Cad é a   chreideann tú   a   cheannaigh Seán *t*?
         what aL believe   you aL bought   John
         'What do you believe that John bought *t*?'   (movement)

   b. Creideann tú   gur ceannaigh Seán cad é?
       believe   you that bought   John what
       '[Q [you believe that John bought what]].'   (in-situ)

(45) a. *Cad é a   chreideann siad [an   ráfla gur cheannaigh Seán *t*]?
         what   aL believe   they the rumor that bought   John
         'What do they believe [the rumor that John bought *t*]?'
                                                                        (movement)

   b. Creideann siad [an   ráfla gur cheannaigh Seán cad é]?
       believe   they the rumor that bought   John what
       '[Q [they believe [the rumor that John bought what]]].'   (in-situ)

(46) a. *Cad é a   chonaic siad [an fear a   cheannaigh *t*]?
         what   aL saw   they the man   aL bought
         'What did they see [the man who bought *t*]?'   (movement)

   b. Chonaic siad [an   fear a   cheannaigh cad é]?
       saw   they the man   aL bought   what
       '[Q [they saw [the man who bought what]]].'   (in-situ)

(43b) and (44b) show that wh-in-situ is possible in matrix clauses and embedded complement clauses, respectively. (45b) and (46b) show that wh-
in-situ is also possible within a complex NP island. The examples with
the factive predicate *is trua le* 'to regret' in (23) and (9) completely pattern together with the examples provided by Ó Baoill and Maki (2014a).
Therefore, it is plausible to hypothesize that Irish has two types of [+Q]
COMPs, namely, a strong [+Q] COMP and a weak [+Q] COMP, and only
the former attracts a wh-phrase in overt syntax.

5.   A Remaining Question

Before closing this paper, let us address one remaining question. We
saw above that (21) and (22) are grammatical in Irish.

(21) Cén   leabhar is   trua le   Seán [Máire é a   léamh]?
      which book   aL+COP regret with John Mary it to read.VN
      'Which book does John regret [Mary to have read *t*]?'

                                                   (aL, RP) (infinitival)

(22) Cén   fear   is   trua   le   Seán [é   an leabhar seo a
      which man   aL+COP regret with John him the book   this to
      léamh]?
      read.VN
      'Which man does John regret [to have read this book]?'

                                              (aL, RP) (infinitival)

Interestingly enough, deletion of the resumptive pronoun leads to a grammatical sentence in (21), as shown in (47), and an ungrammatical sentence in (22), as shown in (48).

(47)(*)Cén   leabhar is   trua   le   Seán [Máire *t* a   léamh]?
       which book   aL+COP regret with John Mary   to read.VN
       'Which book does John regret [Mary to have read *t*]?'

                                              (aL, *t*) (infinitival)

(48) *Cén   fear   is   trua   le   Seán [*t* an   leabhar seo a
      which man   aL+COP regret with John   the book   this to
      léamh]?
      read.VN
      'Which man does John regret [to have read this book]?'

                                              (aL, *t*) (infinitival)

Since extraction takes place from within the factive complement in each case, the prediction is that the two sentences are both ungrammatical. However, (47) is perfect in one of the dialects in Irish, namely, Ulster Irish. To see what factor is actually involved in (47), let us consider the case that is saved by a resumptive pronoun shown in (49), which is cited from McCloskey (1979) with slight editing.

(49) Sin   teanga   a   mbeadh   meas   agam   ar dhuine ar bith
      that a.language aN   would.be respect at.me on person any
      atá   ábalta í   a   labhairt.
      aL+is able   it to speak.VN
      '??That's a language that I would respect anyone who could speak it.'

In (49), the resumptive pronoun *í* 'it' that refers to *teanga* 'a language' is in a complex NP, and the sentence is perfect. However, deletion of the resumptive pronoun also results in grammaticality of the example, as shown in (50).

(50)   Sin   teanga   a   mbeadh   meas   agam   ar   dhuine   ar   bith
      that   a.language   aN   would.be   respect   at.me   on   person   any
      atá   ábalta   a   labhairt.
      aL+is   able   to   speak.VN
      '??That's a language that I would respect anyone who could speak it.'

The question is why (50) does not cause a complex NP island violation. The answer seems to lie in the fact that in Ulster Irish, the infinitival maker *a* 'to' before the verbal noun optionally contains a possessive resumptive pronoun that refers to the relative head. Then, it is expected that the infinitival maker *a* 'to' before the verbal noun in (47) also contains a possessive resumptive pronoun, which saves the island violation in the example. On the other hand, in (48), since the embedded subject is extracted, no such saving effect is expected. Therefore, the question about the contrast between (47) and (48) has turned out to be reduced to the nature of the infinitival marker in Ulster Irish.[2]

6.   Conclusion

In this paper, based on the newly found data with the factive predicate *is trua le* 'to regret' in Irish, we argued (i) that the complementizer *go/gur* 'that' in Irish optionally has an operator, contrary to McCloskey's (2002) claim, (ii) that Irish allows an invisible COMP, which can host an operator, (iii) that the invisible COMP subcategorized by the factive predicate *is trua le* 'to regret' is a nominalizer, and makes the infinitival complement a barrier for movement, and (iv) that Irish has two types of [+Q] COMPs, one that at-

---

[2] The ambiguity arising from the infinitival marker *a* 'to/to+resumptive pronoun' in Ulster Irish is clearly disambiguated by the plural form of the wh-phrase to be moved. Consider the examples in (i) and (ii).

    (i)   Cé   na   leabharthaí   atá   súil   ag   Seán   Máire   **a**   cheannacht?
        which   the.PL   book.PL   aL+is   hope   at   John   Mary   to   read.VN
        'Which books does Seán expect Máire to read?'

    (ii)   Cé   na   leabharthaí   atá   súil   ag   Sean   Máire   **a**   gceanancht?
        which   the.PL   book.PL   aL+is   hope   at   John   Mary   to.them   read.VN
        'Which books does Seán expect Máire to read them?'

The infinitival marker *a* has the reading 'to' in (i), and the reading 'to+resumptive pronoun' in (ii). Notice that the plain infinitival marker *a* 'to' induces Lenition on a following consonant, as in *a cheannacht* 'to read.VN' in (i), but the infinitival marker containing a resumptive pronoun *a* 'to+resumptive pronoun' induces Eclipsis/Nasalization on a following consonant, as in *a gceanancht* 'to.them read.VN' in (ii).

tracts a wh-phrase in overt syntax, and another that does not.

Appendix: A Difference Between English and Irish

This appendix points out a difference between English and Irish with respect to the extractability from tensed factive complements. Postal (1998) provides the examples in (51), which involve extraction from factive complements.

(51) a.   the person who$_1$ I regret (that) Carla tickled t_1
      b. *the person who$_1$ I regret t_1 tickled Melissa
                              (Postal (1998: 62), Exs. (31a, b))

Postal (1998: 61) states that in general, NP objects extract from selective islands such as complement clauses of factive verbs, but nothing else can, hence, not finite subjects, adverbials or predicational phrases. Postal (1998: 65) further states that extraction from a selective island is possible only when a resupmptive pronoun (RP) is present in the extraction site. Therefore, he hypothesizes that (51a) contains an invisible resumptive pronoun in the object position of the verb, but (51b) does not contain an invisible resumptive pronoun in the subject position.

However, we have seen that Irish allows extraction of NP objects and NP subjects out of tensed factive complements, as shown in (9) and (11).

(9)   Cén   leabhar is   trua le   Seán [a   léigh Máire *t*]?
      which book   aL+COP regret with John aL read Mary
      'Which book does John regret [that Mary read *t*]?'   (aL, aL, *t*)

(11) Cén   fear   is   trua le   Seán [a   léigh *t* an leabhar
      which man   aL+COP regret with John aL read   the book
      seo]?
      this
      'Which man does John regret [that *t* read this book]?'   (aL, aL, *t*)

Therefore, there is a difference between English and Irish with respect to the extractability of subjects out of tensed factive complements. Note here that Postal's (1998) hypothesis that extraction from a selective island is possible only when a resumptive pronoun is present in the extraction site, does not directly apply to the Irish examples in (9) and (11), because in these examples, the extraction sites should not contain invisible resumptive pronouns, as the intermediate COMP is realized as *a* 'aL,' a sign of overt movement, in each example.

We will leave the issue related to the difference between English and Irish open for future research.

Bibliography

2006 Census (Census 2006 Principal Demographic Results) http://www.cso.ie/census/documents/Final%20Principal%20Demographic%20Results%202006.pdf (Retrieved on March 25, 2016).

2011 Census (Census 2011—This is Ireland) http://www.cso.ie/en/media/csoie/census/documents/census2011pdr/Pdf,8,Tables.pdf (Retrieved on March 25, 2016).

Authier, Marc (1992) "Iterated CPs and Embedded Topicalization," *Linguistic Inquiry* 23, 329–336.

Baker, C. L. (1995) "Contrast, Discourse Prominence, and Intensification, with Special Reference to Locally Free Reflexives in British English," *Language* 71, 63–101.

Basri, Hasan and Hideki Maki (2012) "On the Nature of Resumptive Pronouns in Selayarese," paper presented at the 14th Japanese Society for Language Sciences.

Borer, Hagit (1984) "Restrictive Relatives in Modern Hebrew," *Natural Language and Linguistic Theory* 2, 219–260.

Bošković, Željko (1997) *The Syntax of Nonfinite Complementation: An Economy Approach*, MIT Press, Cambridge, MA.

Bošković, Željko (2000) "Sometimes in SpecCP, Sometimes In-Situ," *Step by Step: Essays on Minimalism in Honor of Howard Lasnik*, ed. by Roger Martin, David Michaels and Juan Uriagereka, 53–87, MIT Press, Cambridge, MA.

Bošković, Željko (2007) "On the Locality and Motivation of Move and Agree: An Even More Minimal Theory," *Linguistic Inquiry* 38, 589–644.

Chomsky, Noam (1964) *Current Issues in Linguistic Theory*, Mouton, The Hague.

Chomsky, Noam (1970) "Deep Structure, Surface Structure, and Semantic Interpretation," *Studies in General and Oriental Linguistics*, ed. by Roman Jakobson and Shigeo Kawamoto, 52–91, TEC Company, Tokyo.

Chomsky, Noam (1973) "Conditions on Transformations," *A Festschrift for Morris Halle*, ed. by Stephen R. Anderson and Paul Kiparsky, 287–307, Holt, Rinehart and Winston, New York.

Chomsky, Noam (1977) "On Wh-Movement," *Formal Syntax*, ed. by Peter Culicover, Thomas Wasow and Adrian Akmajian, 71–132, Academic Press, New York.

Chomsky, Noam (1981) *Lectures on Government and Binding: The Pisa Lectures*, Dordrecht, Foris.

Chomsky, Noam (1986a) *Knowledge of Language: Its Nature, Origin, and Use*, Praeger, New York.

Chomsky, Noam (1986b) *Barriers*, MIT Press, Cambridge, MA.

Chomsky, Noam (1991) "Some Notes on Economy of Derivation and Representation," *Principles and Parameters in Comparative Grammar*, ed. by Robert Freidin, 417–454, MIT Press, Cambridge, MA.

Chomsky, Noam (1995) *The Minimalist Program*, MIT Press, Cambridge, MA.

Chomsky, Noam (2000) "Minimalist Inquiries: The Framework," *Step by Step: Essays on Minimalist Syntax in Honor of Howard Lasnik*, ed. by Roger Martin, Juan Uriagereka and David Michaels, 89–151, MIT Press, Cambridge, MA.

Chomsky, Noam (2001) "Derivation by Phase," *Ken Hale: A Life in Language*, ed. by Michael Kenstowicz, 1–50, MIT Press, Cambridge, MA.

Chomsky, Noam and Howard Lasnik (1977) "Filters and Control," *Linguistic Inquiry* 8, 425–504.

Chomsky, Noam and Howard Lasnik (1993) "Principles and Parameters Theory," *Syntax: An International Handbook of Contemporary Research*, ed. by Joachin Jacobs, Armin van Stechow, Wolfgang Sternefeld and Theo Venneman, 506–569, Walter de Gruyter, Berlin.

Chung, Sandra and James McCloskey (1987) "Government, Barriers, and Small Clauses in Modern Irish," *Linguistic Inquiry* 18, 173–237.

Cinque, Guglielmo (1990) *Types of A′-Dependencies*, MIT Press, Cambridge, MA.

Cinque, Guglielmo (1999) *Adverbs and Functional Heads: A Cross-Linguistic Perspective*, Oxford University Press, Oxford.

Endo, Yoshio (2007) *Locality and Information Structure*, John Benjamins, Amsterdam/Philadelphia.

Ferro, Lisa (1993) "On 'Self' as a Focus Marker," *Proceedings of the Ninth Eastern States Conference on Linguistics*, ed. by Michael Bernsten, 68–79, Cornell University Department of Modern Languages and Linguistics, Ithaca, New York.

Giorgi, Alessandra and Giuseppe Longobardi (1991) *The Syntax of Noun Phrases: Configuration, Parameters and Empty Categories*, Cambridge University Press, Cambridge.

Grimshaw, Jane (1990) *Argument Structures*, MIT Press, Cambridge, MA.

Hayon, Yehiel (1973) *Relativization in Hebrew*, Mouton, The Hague.

Higginbotham, James (1985) "On Semantics," *Linguistic Inquiry* 16, 547–594.

Hoji, Hajime (1985) *Logical Form Constraints and Configurational Structures in Japanese*, Doctoral dissertation, University of Washington, Seattle.

Huang, C.-T. James (1982) *Logical Relations in Chinese and the Theory of Grammar*, Doctoral dissertation, MIT.

Jónsson, Jóhannes Gísli (1996) *Clausal Architecture and Case in Icelandic*, Doctoral dissertation, University of Massachusetts, Amherst.

Katada, Fusa (1991) "The LF Representations of Anaphors," *Linguistic Inquiry* 22, 287–313.

Katz, Jerrold and Paul Postal (1964) *An Integrated Theory of Linguistic Description*, MIT Press, Cambridge, MA.

Kayne, Richard (1984) *Connectedness and Binary Branching*, Foris, Dordrecht.

Keenan, Edward (1988) "Complex Anaphors and Bind α," *CLS* 24, 216–232.

Ko, Heejeong (2005) "Syntax of *Why*-In-Situ: Merge into [Spec,CP] in the Overt Syntax," *Natural Language and Linguistic Theory* 23, 867–916.

Kuno, Susumu (1973) "Constraints on Internal Clauses and Sentential Subjects," *Linguistic Inquiry* 4, 363–385.

Kuroda, Shige-Yuki (1968) "English Relativization and Certain Related Problems," *Language* 44, 244–268.

Lasnik, Howard and Mamoru Saito (1984) "On the Nature of Proper Government," *Linguistic Inquiry* 15, 235–289.

Lasnik, Howard and Mamoru Saito (1992) *Move-α: Conditions on Its Application and Output*, MIT Press, Cambridge, MA.

Lin, Jo Wang (1992) "The Syntax of *Zenmeyang* 'How' and *Weishenme* 'Why' in Mandarin Chinese," *Journal of East Asian Linguistics* 1, 293–331.

Longobardi, Giuseppe (1987) "Extraction from NP and the Proper Treatment of Head Government," ms., Scuola Normale Superiore di Pisa.

Maki, Hideki (1995) *The Syntax of Particles*, Doctoral dissertation, University of Connecticut.

Maki, Hideki and Masao Ochi (1998) "Scrambling of Wh-Phrases and the Move-F Hypothesis," *Japanese/Korean Linguistics 8*, ed. by David Silva, 487–500, CSLI Publications, Stanford, CA.

Maki, Hideki, Lizanne Kaiser and Masao Ochi (1999) "Embedded Topicalization in English and Japanese," *Lingua* 109, 1–14.

Maki, Hideki and Dónall P. Ó Baoill (2005) "The Sixth Pattern of COMP Alternation in Modern Irish," *Handbook of the 130th Meeting of the Linguistic Society of Japan*, 212–217.

Maki, Hideki and Dónall P. Ó Baoill (2011) *Essays on Irish Syntax*, Kaitakusha, Tokyo.

Maki, Hideki and Dónall P. Ó Baoill (2012a) "A Mystery with the *Ceart* 'Correct' Construction in Modern Ulster Irish," *Handbook of the 144th Meeting of the Linguistic Society of Japan*, 50–55.

Maki, Hideki and Dónall P. Ó Baoill (2012b) "The Genitive Case in Modern Ulster Irish," *Handbook of the 145th Meeting of the Linguistic Society of Japan*, 262–267.

Maki, Hideki and Dónall P. Ó Baoill (2013) "Scope Ambiguity in WH/Quantifier Interactions in Modern Irish," *Ambiguity: Multifaceted Structures in Syntax, Morphology and Phonology*, ed. by Anna Bondaruk and Anna Malicka-Kleparska, 215–237, Wydawnictwo KUL, Lublin, Poland.

Maki, Hideki and Dónall P. Ó Baoill (2014a) "The Cleft Construction in Irish," *JELS* 31, 338–344.

Maki, Hideki and Dónall P. Ó Baoill (2014b) "Embedded Topicalization in Irish," *English Linguistics* 31, 130–148.

Maki, Hideki and Dónall P. Ó Baoill (2014c) "Clausal Arguments in Irish," *English Linguistics* 31, 545–562.

May, Robert (1985) *Logical Form: Its Structure and Derivation*, MIT Press, Cambridge, MA.

McCloskey, James (1979) *Transformational Syntax and Model Theoretic Semantics: A Case Study in Modern Irish*, Reidel, Dordrecht.

McCloskey, James (1985) "The Modern Irish Double Relative and Syntactic Binding," *Ériu* 36, 45–84.

McCloskey, James (1990) "Resumptive Pronouns, A′-Binding and Levels of Representations in Irish," *Syntax of the Modern Celtic Languages, Syntax and Semantics* 23, ed. by Randall Hendrick, 199–248, Academic Press, New York.

McCloskey, James (1996) "On the Scope of Verb Movement in Irish," *Natural Language and Linguistic Theory* 14, 47–104.

McCloskey, James (2002) "Resumption, Successive Cyclicity, and the Locality of Operations," *Derivation and Explanation in the Minimalist Program*, ed. by Samuel Epstein and Daniel Seely, 184–226, Blackwell, Cambridge, MA.

McCloskey, James and Peter Sells (1988) "Control and A-Chains in Modern Irish," *Natural Language and Linguistic Theory* 6, 143–189.

Murasugi, Keiko and Mamoru Saito (1993) "Quasi-Adjuncts as Sentential Arguments," *WECOL* 5, 251–264.

Nishigauchi, Taisuke (1986) *Quantification in Syntax*, Doctoral dissertation, University of Massachusetts, Amherst.

Nishigauchi, Taisuke (1990) *Quantification in the Theory of Grammar*, Reidel, Dordrecht.

Nishikawa, Yoshitaka (1990) "Evidence for the Existence of AGRP: English Heavy NP Shift," *English Linguistics* 7, 14–31.

Ó Baoill, Dónall P. (1995) "The Modern Irish Reflexive Form *Fein* as a Three-In-One Anaphor," paper read at *the First Celtic Linguistics Conference* held at University College Dublin on June 23, 1995.

Ó Baoill, Dónall P. and Hideki Maki (2012) "On the Highest Subject Restriction in Modern Irish," *English Linguistics* 29, 357–368.

Ó Baoill, Dónall P. and Hideki Maki (2013) "*Cad é an Dóigh* 'How' in Irish," *Handbook of the 147th Meeting of the Linguistic Society of Japan*, 524–529.

Ó Baoill, Dónall P. and Hideki Maki (2014a) "Irish [+Q] COMPs," *JELS* 31, 123–129.

Ó Baoill, Dónall P. and Hideki Maki (2014b) "Extraction from the Complement Clause of the Factive Predicate *Is Trua Le* 'To Regret' in Irish," *Handbook of the 149th Meeting of the Linguistic Society of Japan*, 290–295.

Ó Baoill, Dónall P. and Hideki Maki (2015) "Puzzles with the Subject Position in Irish," *English Linguistics* 32, 102–113.

Pesetsky, David (1987) "*Wh*-in-Situ: Movement and Unselective Binding," *The Representation of (In)definiteness*, ed. by Eric. J. Reuland and Alice. G. B. ter Meulen, 98–129, MIT Press, Cambridge, MA.

Phillips, Colin (1996) *Order and Structure*, Doctoral dissertation, MIT.

Phillips, Colin (2003) "Linear Order and Constituency," *Linguistic Inquiry* 34, 37–90.

Postal, Paul (1974) *On Raising: One Rule for English Grammar and Its Theoretical Implications*, MIT Press, Cambridge, MA.

Postal, Paul (1998) *Three Investigations of Extraction*, MIT Press, Cambridge, MA.

Reinhart, Tanya and Eric Reuland (1991) "Anaphors and Logophors: An Argument Structure Perspective," *Long-Distance Anaphora*, ed. by Jan Koster and Eric Reuland, 283–321, Cambridge University Press, Cambridge.

Reinhart, Tanya and Eric Reuland (1993) "Reflexivity," *Linguistic Inquiry* 24, 657–

720.

Rizzi, Luigi (1986) "Null Objects in Italian and the Theory of *pro*," *Linguistic Inquiry* 17, 501–557.

Rizzi, Luigi (1990) *Relativized Minimality*, MIT Press, Cambridge, MA.

Ross, John Robert (1967) *Constraints on Variables in Syntax*, Doctoral dissertation, MIT.

Ross, John Robert (1970) "Declarative Sentences," *Readings in English Transformational Grammar*, ed. by Roderick A. Jacobs and Peter S. Rosenbaum, 222–272, Ginn, Waltham, MA.

Ross, John Robert (1986) *Infinite Syntax!*, ABLEX, Norwood, NJ.

Saito, Mamoru (1994) "Scrambling and the Functional Interpretation of Wh-Phrases," *Explorations in Generative Grammar: A Festschrift for Dong-Whee Yang*, ed. by Young-Sun Kim, Byung-Choon Lee, Kyoung-Jae Lee, Hyun-Kwon Yang and Jong-Yurl Yoon, 571–588, Hankuk Publishing Company, Seoul.

Saito, Mamoru (1999) "Wh-Quantifier Interaction and the Interpretation of Wh-Phrases," *In Search of the Human Mind: A Festschrift for Kazuko Inoue*, ed. by Masatake Muraki and Enoch Iwamoto, 588–621, Kaitakusha, Tokyo.

Shiobara, Kayono (2010) *Derivational Linearization at the Syntax-Prosody Interface*, Hituzi Syobo, Tokyo.

Shlonsky, Ur (1992) "Resumptive Pronouns as Last Resort," *Linguistic Inquiry* 23, 443–468.

Shlonsky, Ur and Gabriela Soare (2011) "Where's 'Why'?" *Linguistic Inquiry* 42, 651–669.

Sloan, Kelly (1991) "Quantifier-Wh Interaction," *MIT Working Papers in Linguistics 15: More Papers on Wh-Movement*, ed. by Lisa Cheng and Hamida Demirdache, 219–227, Cambridge, MA.

Soh, Hooi Ling (2001) "On the Intervention Effect: Some Notes from Chinese," ms, University of Minnesota, Twin Cities.

Stowell, Tim (1981a) *Origins of Phrase Structure*, Doctoral dissertation, MIT.

Stowell, Tim (1981b) "Complementizers and the Empty Category Principle," *NELS* 11, 345–363.

Takahashi, Daiko (1993) "Movement of Wh-Phrases in Japanese," *Natural Language and Linguistic Theory* 11, 655–678.

Takahashi, Daiko (1994) *Minimality of Movement*, Doctoral dissertation, University of Connecticut.

Ura, Hiroyuki (1993) "On Feature-Checking for Wh-Traces," *MIT Working Papers in Linguistics 18: Papers on Case and Agreement I*, ed. by Jonathan D. Bobaljik and Colin Phillips, 243–280, Cambridge, MA.

Watanabe, Akira (1992a) *MIT Occasional Papers in Linguistics 2: Wh-in-Situ, Subjacency, and Chain Formation*, Cambridge, MA.

Watanabe, Akira (1992b) "Subjacency and S-structure Movement of Wh-in-Situ," *Journal of East Asian Linguistics* 1, 255–291.

Watanabe, Akira (1993) "Larsonian CP Recursion, Factive Complements, and Selection," *NELS* 23, 523–537.

Woolford, Ellen (2006) "Lexical Case, Inherent Case, and Argument Structure," *Linguistic Inquiry* 37, 111–130.

Yoshida, Keiko and Tomoyuki Yoshida (1996) "Question Marker Drop in Japanese," *ICU Language Research Bulletin* 11, 37–54.

Zribi-Hertz, Anne (1989) "Anaphor Binding and Narrative Point of View: English Reflexive Pronouns in Sentence and Discourse," *Language* 65, 695–727.

Index

Essays on Irish Syntax II

著作者　　牧　秀樹・ドナル P. オボイル

発行者　　武村哲司

2017 年 10 月 28 日　第 1 版第 1 刷発行©

発行所　　株式会社　開 拓 社

〒113-0023　東京都文京区向丘 1-5-2
電話　（03）5842-8900　（代表）
振替　00160-8-39587
http://www.kaitakusha.co.jp

印刷　株式会社 あるむ　　　　　ISBN978-4-7589-2250-0　C3080